55

4∩'

This book may be kept

FOURTEEN DAYS

A fine will be charged for each day the book is kept overtime.

JAN 3 0/ 79			
GAYLORD 142			PRINTED IN U.S.A.

The Meaning
of the City

JACQUES ELLUL

Professor of the History and Sociology of Institutions
The Faculty of Law and Economic Sciences
The University of Bordeaux

Introduction by John Wilkinson
Senior Fellow at the
Center for the Study of Democratic Institutions
Santa Barbara, California

Translated by Dennis Pardee

WILLIAM B. EERDMANS PUBLISHING COMPANY
GRAND RAPIDS, MICHIGAN

Copyright © 1970 by William B. Eerdmans Publishing Company
All rights reserved
Library of Congress Catalog Card Number: 70-103446
ISBN 0-8028-1555-3
Printed in the United States of America
First printing, July 1970
Second printing, August 1973

Translated from the French Sans Feu ni Lieu

40,565

In memory
of my son Simon
who passed away
as this book was being born

INTRODUCTION

> We believe that the Word contained in these books has proceeded from God, and receives its authority from him alone, and not from men. And inasmuch as it is the rule of all truth, containing all that is necessary for the service of God and for our salvation, it is not lawful for men, nor even for angels, to add to it, to take away from it or to change it. Whence it follows that no authority, whether of antiquity, or custom, or numbers, or human wisdom, or judgments, or proclamations, or edicts, or decrees, or councils, or visions, or miracles, should be opposed to these Holy Scriptures, but, on the contrary, all things should be examined, regulated and reformed according to them.
>
> — FRENCH REFORMED CONFESSION OF 1559

In a time when preachers are as loath to preach as teachers to teach, both preferring to devote themselves to setting up or tearing down institutional or cultish arrangements of some sort or other, Jacques Ellul is still concerned with the traditional problem of the Reformation: How shall all things be examined, regulated and reformed according to the Scriptures? The authority of these Scriptures remains untouched in the bibliocentric theology of Ellul, as in the theology of Karl Barth; but a vast number of new problems of interpretation have arisen since the sixteenth century, and the demand of the Reformers that the text be "understood of the people" seems naive to us. Ellul, for example, does not factually know, and apparently does not care, whether Jesus had x or 2x genes. What is important theologically is that the Word somehow became flesh. Here we encounter problems of different "levels of discourse," which arise in biblical criticism as starkly as in physics. "The Word became flesh" is a statement not only more interesting but of a different (though related) logical and semiotic order than a statement about the nature of the water supply of the city of Jerusalem. Each of these statements has a different relational conception of, for example, *time*. The naive, anecdotal level is naively historical, ordered according to clock-time or something resembling it. The theological order is dialectic and timeless. If the two are confused, the result is an endless debate, like the one about whether the Kingdom of God is *in* us or *upon* us.

* * *

The Meaning of the City is the theological "counterpoint" to Ellul's *Technological Society,* a work that analyzed the phenomenon of the autonomous and totally manipulative post-industrial world. Ellul systematically applies the principle of examining the biblically based theological significance of *every* social and political problem that he has studied. Thus, his work *Politics of Man, Politics of God* is the theological pendant to the book *The Political Illusion.* This distinction between theological and social or political significance has not so much to do with the order of thought as with the order of the expression of that thought, to echo an Aristotelian dichotomy. For Ellul the Bible is to be understood as ceaselessly putting questions to us; and we, of course, are ceaselessly putting questions to it. The ceaseless "feedback"-interaction established in this way is an integral part of the Ellulian dialectic.

Ellul, as against Rudolf Bultmann, regards "myth" as the "addition of theological significance" to some fact that as such does not obviously have any. Dialectically speaking, "myth" as the addition of significance (rather than the subtraction of it until nothing is left) reaches out to the concrete-universal of revelation that bears up and is borne by the biblical texts.[1] Ellul says that he hesitates to use the term "myth" because of the different meanings that have been given to it in the course of centuries. Despite his hesitancy, however, he employs it in the way that Plato and the Greek mysteries did. *Fact* and *theologized fact* correspond to

---

[1] Edmund Leach ("The Legitimacy of Solomon," *European Journal of Sociology,* VII, 1966) writes: "My subject matter here is also the subject matter of theology, but whereas a theologian can find in the Old Testament text a mystical message which has hermeneutic import for the whole of humanity, my own analysis reveals only a patterning of arguments about endogamy and exogamy, legitimacy and illegitimacy, as operative in the thought processes of Palestinian Jews of the third century B.C." Somewhat disingenuously Leach adds that he has a "deficiency of understanding" and that his conclusions might have been "less thin" if he could only understand Levi-Strauss' *esprit,* Hegel's *Geist,* and even the basic idea of God himself as the mediator between what the Bible says and the interpretation of it. In this essay Leach is maintaining a view of myth as subtraction.

the well-known Barthian distinction between *Historie* — a kind of chronicle — and *Geschichte* — the meaning of *Historie*. I take it that the so-called "quest for the historical Jesus" is an example of *Historie*. On the whole, this quest has not been successful and has been, if not abandoned, at least pushed into a subsidiary position, like most of the other unstable "results" of liberal theology, since everything that is said about the historicity of Jesus by one authority is contradicted by another. The French scholar Guignebert wrote in the 1930's after a lifelong study that nothing, in effect, was known of Jesus except that he was born, lived, and died. On the other hand, David Flusser of the Hebrew University of Jerusalem has recently written that there are very few historical figures of whom more is known. Yet the only important evidence available to Flusser that was not available to Guignebert is the Dead Sea Scrolls, which allow Flusser to identify Jesus, and even more convincingly, John the Baptist, as having existed "on the periphery" of the community at Qumran. This is not unimportant for exegesis, but it scarcely says much about the historical Jesus. But it is Christ, as the *Geschichte* of Jesus, as he appeared to the Greco-Roman-Occidental world, who is a subject of the intensive addition of theological significance that lies at the very heart of Ellulian Christianity.

The uncertainties regarding Jesus do not make uninteresting the intensive historical research that has been carried out for more than a century to discover the essential features of the man. Nearly everything that a theological interpretation of the Christ of the Scriptures affirms is affected by the *beliefs* about Jesus that every theologian possesses, even though these beliefs may fall anywhere within the whole spectrum from complete skepticism to complete certainty. The same range of belief and unbelief can be found in what scholars have written about almost all the persons and events of the Old Testament, too. In part, the problem is a false one insofar as it naively presupposes that the *history* of men and events has only one meaning. But it is a commonplace today that historical entities have an essential ambivalence that creates an almost unbearable tension very welcome to a dialectical theology but fatal to a "linear" one. The ambivalence of historicity might be compared to the sociological notion of the multiplicity of "roles" that individuals and societies play.

Regardless of this ambivalence, the Christ-event as portrayed by John or Paul is relatively unambivalent. In the same way Ellul's conception of the "City," which becomes for him the locus not only of the results of the rebellious sin of Cain in inventing

a technologized and manipulative society, but also of the independence and the creativity of man is coherent and, in this sense,
free of ambiguity. I think most readers will be astonished at the
virtuosity of Ellul's synthesis. (Whether they believe this account
— or any other, for that matter — because of its consistency is
quite another question.)

In its early years, the Christian Church spent a great deal of
time elaborating just such unambivalent theologies. People today
sometimes express wonder at the controversy, for example, that
raged between the Homoousians and the Homoiousians. These
two positions (between which for us there is only a single *iota* of
difference) represented very different views of the specifically
Christian life, both politically and socially. But more than that,
there was always the danger that Christianity would collapse
either into one of the Mediterranean mystery religions or into one
of the philosophico-religious schools of thought. In the face of
this, the elaboration of theological orthodoxy was a pressing need.
It is often thought that this process of rendering Christian belief
orthodox by the establishment of scriptural canon and dogma was
completed by the fourth century. Indeed, Barth and Ellul have
often been reproached for accepting as final the canon of Scripture
and dogma at a period very close to the point in time at which
Christianity became the official religion of the Roman Empire.
Considering Ellul's novel theologizing about the City, I do not
believe the reproach justified, for such theologizing itself *becomes
a part of the canon.*

The reign of terror of Throne and Altar that began with the
Constantinian era might best be taken as having introduced into
canon and dogma a vast number of theological deformations that
ought to be rejected. But both Ellul and Barth pose in different
ways the question to the Scriptures: What of the *post*-Constan-
tinian era? Drastic reinterpretation of the canon is unavoidable in
a radically altered society. I am holding here that such revision
belongs organically to Revelation itself. One would not wish to
push too far this concept of "progressive revelation," for, like
liberal monopoly-capitalism and its wrecking of nature, the term
has come to mean very many things that no one could undertake
to admire, much less to believe in. Why is Genesis 1:26 preferable
to Isaiah 15:3 (that would make "the desert bloom like Eden and
the waste land like the Garden of the Lord"); or to Romans 8:22
(in which "the whole creation groans and travails in pain together
until now")? To bring even the smallest coherence into the clash-
ing texts of Scripture has nearly always implied a radical trans-

formation of man's condition along with the understanding of the Bible itself. The Bible cannot have posed questions relating to the technological society before that society supervened.

The position of some Structuralists that Freud's analysis of the Oedipus complex becomes an essential part of the Oedipus myth is useful here *as a paradigm*. Neither Barth nor Ellul, in their theologizing, can be thought *not* to have changed, at least insofar as understanding is concerned, the canon of the Scriptures. Unless one holds to the low-level doctrine of "verbal inspiration," one must conclude that textual criticism, hermeneutics, and exegesis contribute mightily to the expansion of the Bible; and Barth and Ellul are passionate exegetes. It is, in any case, philosophically always implausible to maintain that radically new understandings of texts do not themselves become integral parts of the text. What we possess of the Old and New Testaments was not *verbally* fixed prior to the latter part of the second century. Even so textual criticism cannot yet render these texts to us verbatim. Are we not to suppose that the understanding of these texts in a highly technologized society represents in a very important way an alteration in the texts themselves, not so much on the naive level of temporally retailed anecdotes, as on the level of theological structure? To suppose otherwise would be to fall back again into the largely discarded doctrine of verbal inspiration. And, further, it would imply that disputes among Christians of the second century were somehow more perspicacious or useful than those of Christians today. I take it, then, that Ellul's theology of the technological society represents a radical change in biblical matter to match the demands of a radically different society.

The Word that proceeds changelessly from God alone is, in the "dialectic" order of things, "fallible," insofar as it is expressed in human language. T. S. Eliot often remarked that he was "astounded" at the number of things that graduate students found in his works that he had not known were there. He said that he "had done as much for Shakespeare," and allowed himself to be persuaded that at least some of these new interpretations had been unconsciously and only implicitly present in works that he had written many years before. It is, I think, a mark of greatness that the texts of great works allow this sort of expansion. "Shakespeare," said Eliot, "would doubtless have been astounded to learn how much Freud had been anticipated by *Hamlet*."

It is admittedly dangerous, considering the difficulty of the definitions of "implicit" and "explicit," to build too much of an edifice on foundations that will be unable to bear it. The distinction in question here must be used with great distrust. My own notion is that by finding a coherent theological account in the Bible of the City, as the theater of the technological society, Ellul has taken an important step forward giving to "urbanism" (to take just one example) its proper "theological" focus. Indeed, it is the constant complaint by all or nearly all city planners I have ever met that there is "no meaning to city planning anywhere" and that the whole enterprise as it presently exists is the greatest of hoaxes. Independently of Ellul, even nonbelieving city planners have, probably under the influence of scholars like Mircea Eliade, taken to speaking of the "desacralization of the city." Moreover, I do not think that the present account of the meaning of the technological society as the City is just another one of those profuse "cheap solutions," which arise in response to city problems, and which Barth and Ellul so much abhor. For example, Schillebeeckx' mere assertion, unsupported as far as I can see by any convincing analysis, that "the concrete world is by definition an implicit Christianity" is no great addition to our understanding either of the secular and profane city, or of the *eschaton* represented by the New Jerusalem. Of course, the reader of this volume must make up his own mind whether Ellul's arguments are sound, and this will depend, in part, on the conventions he has adopted or inherited, more or less accidentally, from his ambient culture.

The conventions of the technological society in themselves are a kind of rhetoric that force men to believe only in technological answers to *any* sort of problem.

* * *

The major problem in writing an introduction to any work of Ellul is not to recapitulate the argument but to persuade sensible people not to throw it down before they have negotiated even the first ten pages. The Bible as revelation is increasingly an unacceptable convention to a world that has "radically refused transcendence." For many years institutional Christianity has often been rightly regarded as "the enemy of the human race." So there are many who feel no more need to study the Old and New Testaments than to read *Mein Kampf* sympathetically. Even among those who will seem to accept Ellul's account of the meaning of the City many will accept it in the way they accept Tolstoy's *The Kingdom of God is Within You,* in which a radical criticism of the vicious Czarist establishment is accompanied by devotion to the no less radical Sermon on the Mount. Ellul, who seems to have become required reading for a large number of "radical" persons in the United States, may find that his theology, like Tolstoy's, is tolerated unconsciously only because his readers value his critique of the evils of the wholly technologized and manipulative society. Those who tolerate in Ellul what they would normally reject make Ellul's theology of the City a mere epiphenomenon.

Any conventional acceptance of theological groundings of the evils of modern society, however ingenious it might be, is likely to raise the question: What is *specifically* Christian about any of this? The only completely acceptable answer to any Christian would be that such sociological analyses are *truly* based on Christian revelation. There is no question here of a "proof" in the mathematical or scientific sense. Nothing can be demonstrated by tautologies or empirical observations, even though it be granted that Ellul has added a dimension of meaningfulness to sociology.

There are very few convincingly religious analyses of the sociological phenomena of the present day. As far as I am concerned, the only successful rival to Ellul is Van Leeuwen, and possibly Ernst Bloch, who is not a Christian at all but a Marxist philosopher. Although Barth was able to translate his theology into *political* terms, he always seemed to me to be nonplused by any reference to technology, unless it could be politicized. One of his students has written that, in this area, Barth always "reacted angrily, sarcastically or melancholically," a good enough gloss on what I have called "nonplused." Barth's theology got stuck at the stage represented by Social Democracy, an ideology that contains little of the sociological. His accomplishments in the realm of politics were of great importance, since he was able to furnish spiritual substance to the Confessing Church, the only body of German Christians that opposed the Nazis. In an analogous way, Ellul's biblically based sociology is today furnishing the matter for a large and growing group of social protestants, particularly in the United States. If a purely "pragmatic" test of meaningfulness be demanded, Barth and Ellul are able to meet the test, for with them Christianity *does* make a specific difference. But meaningfulness and coherence do not necessarily imply truth. The objection might be raised: "I see what you mean and it all hangs together, but I don't believe it." How, then, may one go further?

Here the problem of belief involving the transcendent reference of Christianity is at issue. I have argued at length elsewhere that, although consistency alone is the sufficient reason for the acceptance of the truth of *mathematical* propositions, it cannot be adduced in discourse except as a *sine qua non;* and, further, that a new and improved version of the so-called "ontologic argument" is necessary to secure the reference of the Christian religion to God. Most modern theologians have nothing transcendent to point to that might serve as an ostensive definition of their objects. "Christian atheism" and Zen Buddhism reinterpretation point to enlightenment or salvation in the purely here and now, for it is recognized by their modern proponents that both these religions in their pristine state incorporated indispensable moral and philosophic truth, which either historic piety or genuine attachment makes unbearable to discard.

Nearly every religion has its secularizers, for no matter how much reference-beyond-ourselves is implied in the overcoming of the I-Thou (and its corresponding sense of "community"), it is yet a far cry from God. I can only point out here that the traditional solipsism implied in the denial of "the other" may have its counterpart in today's denial of God's existence. "Solipsism," after all, was never refuted; it was merely abandoned as a philosophical doctrine. The time may well come again when the existential transparence of the relation of God to man will once more assert itself, as it did during long ages before "science" in some unexplained way was supposed to have made it obsolete. I cannot find that Ellul or Barth have overmuch concerned themselves with proofs for the existence of their ostensible referents. But "faith" considered as "rhetorical persuasion" cannot avoid the issue when it confronts those whom it would persuade.

It ought to be remembered that physics, too, considered in the most analytic way, tends to lose its transcendent reference. James Clerk Maxwell's equations of electromagnetism are still canonical among physicists even though the luminiferous ether, which was their vehicle, has disappeared from any possible experience (in somewhat the same way that God to many moderns has become a "gaseous vertebrate" of infinite extension and zero density). If one asks a physicist what the electron is, he will point to a blackboard full of equations representing a "cloud of probability," and not to an entity like a billiard ball localized in time and space. It takes as much faith to be a physicist today as to be a theologian.

My point here is that it is easy to assert catechetically some doctrine, like the French confession of faith of 1559, but that the paradoxes encountered by a theologian in sorting out the levels of discourse and their dynamic interaction are exceedingly difficult. Sooner or later one must break out of the solipsistic circle and assert the transcendent reference of his symbols. This is what

Ellul is always up to, particularly in his theological writings, in the present case, with respect to the City. He begins with Cain, who founded the first city according to the Bible, and carries on to the Heavenly Jerusalem.

All the justifications I have thought up for Ellul's dialectical procedure, as well as his own present account in this book, do seem to represent closed logical circles. But so does every other discourse. The important thing is to make the circle universal, so that nothing is left out. I think Ellul does this successfully. There is even in this universality of account a theological principle, namely, that in the covenant of God all our actions and values will find a safe and secure resting place, even those that contain, in the framework of the City, perhaps more of evil than of good.

There is in Ellul's interpretation of the biblical city no mindless "return to the country" or to a long past Golden Age. The heavenly City that recapitulates and saves the whole of creation is not a Happy Hunting Ground or an Elysian field. It is the City transfigured.

"Covenant" is the key term of the Old Testament and the New. It is not usual to speak of Cain's covenant with God; but he had one. Although God might condemn him for his disobedience, he nevertheless protected him, since he foreshadows "progress" in this world. Cain, driven from his fields, makes a city: the first murderer becomes the first city builder. Jewish scholasticism, much later, interpreted the murder of Abel by Cain in a vaguely sympathetic way by making the whole affair revolve, as it doubtless did on the most concrete historical level, about an unavoidable dispute concerning property rights. The tendency to vindicate Cain was so strong in some Christian quarters that it had to be declared a heresy in the early Church. There was good warrant for this sympathy to Cain, for in a theologically meaningful interpretation, God's rigor towards sinners is *never* the complete story.

E. C. Blackman is correct in saying that, in all these covenants, God's actions towards man are "judgment and mercy, mercy and judgment, neither to be understood apart from reference to the other, and both combined in the untranslatable *tsedaqah,* which means essentially an activity of God by which he 'justifies the ungodly,' and which is, in Biblical witness, the characteristic activity of God." Perhaps we ought not be too surprised at this paradox of meaning in the idea of "covenant," since we conceive of something very similar in our notion of "contract," in which "sanction" (originally something sacred, as the word implies) both authorizes the contract and at the same time implies the detriment to which a violator is exposed. It is Ellul's great merit to have discerned clearly the way in which the whole process of the City works out, in the train of events to which Abel's murder led. The translation of Judaic metaphors into Indo-European metaphors is a task that can only be undertaken by a relentless dialectic. And that, carried out in a masterful fashion, is what the *Meaning of the City* succeeds in doing.

—JOHN WILKINSON

Center for the Study of Democratic Institutions
Santa Barbara, California

PREFACE

This book may seem to belong to an outmoded tradition of biblical study, in that it throughout takes the biblical text as it is found today, in its entirety. This is the result, of a deliberate decision. I am aware of classical exegesis, of form criticism, of the extensive research into literary and cultural history, of the new hermeneutics, and even of the more recent studies of structuralism. And I believe that it is certainly useful to be acquainted with this information and its analyses, for they enable one to avoid gross misunderstandings and to discern the main problems. But there remains a major difficulty: These critical studies reduce to separate parts a text that has been elaborated and at one time received as a whole. It is a good thing to know the strata of tradition in a text and its literary form, but is one sure that all has then been said, or even the essential? Does taking a text back to its date, its primitive identity, give it its real meaning, or the meaning it was at least meant to have when it was made a part of the whole? Is each text not destined (and voluntarily so) to throw light on the others and vice versa? And is this mutual illumination not destroyed if the text is fragmented and dispersed according to time and place? Through the diversity of sources and origins, which diversity is never dissimulated anyway, is it not the whole which contains the truth of the message, is it not the text handed down in its last construction that is meaningful?

In other words, we wear ourselves out finding the original wording and form of each fragment, but is not the composer, the compiler, just as important as the first author? Is the truth included in every cultural remnant not snuffed out if it is separated from the others? And by pressing the individual text too hard, do we not run the risk of obliterating that meaning discerned only by the reflection of one fragment in the mirror of another? If it is true that the God of Israel and of Jesus Christ is a God who reveals himself *in history,* are we taking this revelation seriously if we fix a given word of this revelation to one moment in history, like a butterfly tacked to the wall, so that, completely framed by cultural data, it can no longer be moved from there to mean something else? Is there not a contradiction between that hermeneutic attitude and the very truth of the incarnate God? Is the important point not that these texts — the bearers of the Word — *have* moved, that they have come together, that they have adapted to each other in order to bear a wider and deeper meaning? This is why an inclusive reading of the text appears indispensable to me. When one discovers from the first text of today's Bible to the last, from the text dated as the oldest to the most recent, an identical, continuous, and coherent revelation, would one not be losing the essential if he insisted on considering only each solitary fragment instead of the movement carrying it along? Of such a nature is the scriptural revelation about the city. It concerns men's essential work — *the* culture of man in history and eternity.

— J. E.

CONTENTS

Chapter One

THE BUILDERS

I. CAIN

The First Builder of a City Was Cain. The Circumstances were these:

After he had murdered his brother, Cain was summoned by God and cursed: "When you till the ground, it shall no longer yield to you its strength; you shall be a fugitive and a wanderer on the earth."

But Cain is afraid that he himself will surely be killed in revenge: "My punishment is greater than I can bear. Behold thou hast driven me this day from the ground; and from thy face I shall be hidden; and I shall be a fugitive and a wanderer on the earth, and whoever finds me will slay me."

The Lord, however, says to him, "If anyone slays Cain, vengeance shall be taken on him sevenfold." So "the Lord put a mark on Cain, lest any who came upon him should kill him."

And "then Cain went away from the presence of the Lord, and dwelt in the land of Nod, east of Eden." And he "knew his wife, and she conceived and bore Enoch; and he built a city, and called the name of the city after the name of his son Enoch" (Gen. 4:9-17).

It is of little importance whether this story conforms to factual reality. We will leave to the historians such remarks as, "Geographers know of no land of Nod." When I first read it, that sentence set me to dreaming. Unknown to geographers! And what kind of land would it be, this Nowhere land, which is not a place but a lack of place, the opposite of Eden, another country unknown to geographers?

For these stories are neither historical nor aetiological, but

1

theological — which means that they come from God and concern
God. And if the story of Cain is significant, it is not because Cain
is at the origin of the human race, or because Cain may be the
father of the Kenites, but because it gives us God's view of man,
or rather God's view of certain attitudes and activities of man.

The condemnation which Cain is to bear is being a fugitive
and a vagabond. Until now, only God's protection has enabled
life to go on, and this protection is seen in a certain stability, a
certain familiarity, between man and nature. Cain has shattered
this serenity. He has introduced insecurity, the taste for blood, for
vengeance. And the condemnation pronounced by God is only
the inevitable result of Cain's act. Cain has broken the relationship between man and the world, and so he will necessarily be
a fugitive and a wanderer. He will no longer have natural protection, and, as he himself perceives, "whoever finds me will
kill me." Cain no longer has a home, either human or geographical, because murder destroys the home. And he who no longer
has a home is condemned to death. A fugitive and a wanderer,
he is even worse off than someone already in the grave.

Then God put a mark on Cain and assured him that if he
were killed, his death would be avenged. This hardly makes
sense, it would seem. Some assurance! To be avenged *after* you
are killed. Surely this is not what Cain wanted. Furthermore,
God is standing before a man who is in open revolt and who in
the normal course of events will cease believing in God. What
chance is there that such a man will take God's word seriously?
Cain receives a sign of God's protection, but of what import is
that sign? He would prefer a more obvious security, such as the
one he destroyed by his crime — family security, a relationship
with animals and things, a familiarity with men and places. But
it is impossible for him to retrace his steps, there are no possible
amends to make. And such is exactly the dramatic significance of
Cain.

He is under God's protection, and that is what will enable
him to live. Without that protection, Cain would vanish in his
wandering, in his perpetual homelessness. The mark that protects
him is both real and prophetic, and that is what guarantees its
worth. However, Cain does not want to believe in it. He does
not want to and, in fact, cannot believe in it — because he leaves
God's presence. This does not mean that he goes away literally,
but spiritually. He no longer believes in this God who seems to
have condemned him because he had supremely insulted him.
So Cain has no way of knowing that this mark (which he cannot
see) will suffice to protect him, even in the depth of his sin, from

his disobedience, from his separation from God. And now Cain will spend his life trying to find security, struggling against hostile forces, dominating men and nature, taking guarantees that are within his reach, guarantees that *appear* to him to be genuine, but which in fact protect him from nothing.

THE TRAGEDY OF CAIN — THE HUMAN CONDITION

And so Cain went away from God's presence and lived in the land of Nod, east of Eden. The three things are identical. The land of Nod is a literal translation of the Hebrew "the land of wandering" (but why make into a proper name what is not?). The irony of our text: Cain living in the land of wandering. Someone will say that such an irony could not come from a Hebrew writer of that time. Let us not be so sure. Neither should we be so sure that it does not express God's irony.

But is it really irony? Is this phrase not rather an expression of how incurably precarious Cain's situation is? This Cain who wants a home, and can have none, who is forever the man going somewhere, but where? The seed of all man's questings is to be found in Cain's life in the land of wandering, always searching for a place where his need for security might be satisfied. But the only place he finds is that very country characterized by being uninhabitable.

And the ancient story means the very same thing when it speaks of the east of Eden. The East. The country where the sun rises, the point of departure. But one does not stay in a starting place, one leaves it. And now Cain is forever fixed at this starting place. His eye and its desire must always wander after the land where he will direct his steps, but he can never finish his journey for he lives at the point of departure.

The east has an exact meaning in the Scriptures. It is both the road man takes in his futile search for eternity, and the one he takes when he obeys God's call. These two great ways are parallel and show the relationship between the different attitudes of the human race. On the one hand, those who wanted to build Babel came from the east, just as did the marauders who throughout history oppressed God's people.

But on the other hand, Abraham also came from the east, as do all those whom God calls (Isa. 41:25, for example). Moses and the Levites stood on the east side of the altar. The Wise Men came from the east. This long history is in reality a prophecy of The Great Arrival from the east that will accomplish all that man is awaiting, all that he has been awaiting since Cain settled in his symbolic East.

One particular is added: east of *Eden*. We now know where Cain turns his eye and his desire. Towards Eden, towards the lost Paradise. Now it is no longer only the situation brought about by Adam's fall, a situation bearable through patience, a situation where Adam's security is assured by a natural order which Cain was to disturb. Now it is absolute *insecurity*, man's situation to the absolute degree. And thus Cain's fall raises his desire to a higher pitch, that obscure anguish planted in his heart's inner recesses. No longer is he satisfied with a shadow of eternity — now he wants eternity itself. The farther he is from it, the more his condition drives him back to it. He will take permanent leave of his wandering so as to bring himself closer to the absolute. But he cannot rid himself of his human condition, and thus his departure can never be anything but a journey that never reaches port.

But the goal of his journey is given to us even more exactly. It was after he had gone far from God's presence that Cain began his life in the land of wandering. How can we not associate the two notions when the text does so? It is God's absence which is the never-ending sting planted in his heart. Where may God be found? Suddenly to be face to face with God, this is the only way to stop the Wandering Jew found in the heart of every man. The search for home, the search for Eden, is in the end a constant desire for God's presence. But the search appears to be without hope. How well we know that the Lord closed Eden to Adam and put Cherubim at its gates, and that these Cherubim have very little to do with Raphael's pink, chubby little cherubs. These Cherubim are terrible fighters, flashing fire on every side, bringing terror to men's hearts when they intervene in earthly affairs. Obviously Adam could by no means in his possession — even by his holiness, if he had any — gain entrance. And Cain's situation is even worse. We are told very precisely that he is to be a wanderer and a vagabond. As such he can find no rest. He is therefore condemned to a perpetual searching for God's presence, the God with whom he wanted nothing to do and in whom he does not believe, and his very condition keeps him from ever finding him. Whatever he does, he cannot succeed, and that is the hopelessness of it all. And now he tries something else, something that will disturb his situation and make it even worse.

Cain is completely dissatisfied with the security granted to him by God, and so he searches out his own security. However, this search is no different from his first desire for God's presence, and his security can only be found in God. It is only when he believes in God that he will be able to believe that the mark placed on him (and in fact on every one of us?) is an effectual guarantee, because it is an integral part of God's word (his pledge). But of course Cain does not understand it the way God does. And as for his security, he will find another way to procure it. And another way to satisfy his desire for eternity. He will try to take care of his own needs in these areas. He is about to take the wrong road, where every step leads further from God. But is it possible to be further from God than Cain? No, the road does not really lead further from God, it leads to the mirages of man's heart because it leads to temporary satisfactions of the thirst for eternity and rest.

Once settled in his country, Cain does two things to make his curse bearable: he knows his wife sexually, who then gives him a son; and he builds a city. The first act does not concern us. Only notice that it is the same as Adam's when he is expelled from Paradise, the act which had the result of bringing Cain into the world. It is man's desire to find life, eternity, again. He transmits his life to his children.

The second act concerns us directly. This first builder of a city thinks of his action as a response to his situation, an effort to satisfy his deepest desires. He will satisfy his desire for eternity by producing children, and he will satisfy his desire for security by creating a place belonging to him, a city. The direct relationship between the two acts is revealed in the identity of name given to the city and to the child.

The city for Cain is first of all the place where he can be himself — his homeland, the one settled spot in his wandering. Secondly, it is a material sign of his security. He is responsible for himself and for his life. He is far from the Lord's face, and so he will shift for himself. Cain sought security not so much from God, whom he was trying to escape, as from the world, hostile since Abel's murder. The world was perhaps difficult after Adam's fall, but it was not yet marked by murder. Now it is. The city is the direct consequence of Cain's murderous act and of his refusal to accept God's protection.

Cain has built a city. For God's Eden he substitutes his own, for the goal given to his life by God, he substitutes a goal chosen by himself — just as he substituted his own security for God's. Such is the act by which Cain takes his destiny on his own shoulders, refusing the hand of God in his life. And if someone thinks I am drawing unwarranted conclusions, let him remember that this city is called Enoch.

The city is called Enoch. "Enoch" means "initiation" or "dedication" (*chanakh*: to dedicate, inaugurate, initiate). Cain dedicates a new world: "Enoch," as opposed to *Reshith* in Genesis 1:1. Inauguration, as opposed to creation. Initiation, as opposed to the garden paradise. The city as opposed to Eden. It is certainly not unawares that Cain gave this name to his creation. Now he also is going to make the world over again. This unsatisfying world, this world from which perfection is excluded, where Cain introduced all possible pain, Cain is now going to reconstruct. In fact, the word should not be "reconstruct," but "construct." For in Cain's eyes it is not a beginning again, but a beginning. God's creation is seen as nothing. God did nothing, and in no case did he finish anything. Now a start is made, and it is no longer God beginning, but man. And thus Cain, with everything he does, digs a little deeper the abyss between himself and God. There was a solution for his situation, but the solution was in God's hands, and that is what he could absolutely not tolerate. He wants to find alone the remedy for a situation he created, but which he cannot himself repair because it is a situation dependent on God's grace. And Cain accumulates remedies, each one a new disobedience, each one a new offense. Each remedy which seems to be a response to a need in Cain's situation, in fact sinks him even deeper in woe, into a situation ever more inextricable.

Cain begins — that is, he reduces God to a hypothesis, to the domain of the superfluous and the unreal. Just as history begins with the murder of Abel — since before death there is no way for us to learn man's history, and the death that resulted in the fall first manifested itself as murder — so civilization begins with the city and all that it represents. With Cain's beginning, with Enoch, we have a sure starting place for all of civilization. Paradise becomes a legend and creation a myth. Now we have something to which we can fasten our history, and the ramparts of the Canaanite or Peruvian cities give us a sure material knowledge of *homo faber*. Thus we are satisfied, and Cain was truly correct when he said that he was beginning. He is the murderer, and the one who will realize man's wisdom, who will transform the *homo proto sapiens* into *homo faber*. It may be said that before him, there was only God. But by Cain's act God became the one no longer adequate for the life, the will, the thought of man.

And this fits in well with the exact meaning of "Enoch," which is "initiation and the beginning of utilization." Cain takes possession of the world and uses it as he wishes, with the goal in mind that we have already indicated. Cain creates the art of craftsmanship. He carves stones and thereby makes them impure, unfit for use in an altar for God (Ex. 20:25). It is man's high-handed piracy of creation that makes creation incapable of giving glory to God. Cain bends all of creation to his will. He knows full well that by God's order he has received dominion over creation, and he assumes control. He forces creation to follow his destiny, his destiny of slavery and sin, and his revolt to escape from it. From this taking possession, from this revolution, the city is born.

What appears to me remarkable in this brief and rich declaration of Scripture is that it is true no matter what position one adopts toward the Bible. If it is God's revelation, here is what God thinks of the affair. It is God giving us his appraisal of man's action and the profound meaning of the construction of the city. And we must accept it for all history, for this is how God sees this story. And we must believe that God's appraisal is truer than the scientific knowledge we may obtain.

If the Scriptures are only an historical text, dependent on older documents, themselves dependent on myths created at the dawn of consciousness, our texts are also meaningful because they tell us what man wanted to do when he created the city, what he was hoping to conquer, what he thought to establish. And this narrative of the origin of the city is essential, for we see there in its purest state, and expressed simply, the feelings of the builders. Such feelings are no longer evident in our modern day when the prodigious complexity of the world hides the simple plans of the never-changing human heart.

* * *

Before going on, we must lay to rest a possible misunderstanding. City versus country. We are in no way putting the city on trial or making an apology for the country. Our only intention is to discover what the Bible reveals concerning the city. Nothing else.

Cain and Abel. Baudelaire is wrong when he speaks of the race of Abel. There is no such thing as the race of Abel, by the very fact that he is justified by a free act of God and there is nothing in him of itself righteous. "Righteous Abel," says Matthew. What luck! So there is a righteous race! No such thing: Abel died leaving no children, a fact full of meaning. He is unable to transmit his righteousness. And it would in fact be useless for him to have children, for his righteousness is nothing other than the act by which God accepts his sacrifice. What is important is that we cannot conceive of Cain without Abel, or of Abel without Cain. They are tied in with each other, and they are tied in with humanity; and we should probably say that they are both tied in with every man.

City and country. There is certainly no symbolism associated with the comparison. Cain is not the city and Abel is not the country; but the relationship between them also illuminates (but not exclusively) the relationship between the city and the country. All of man's history is not limited to the history of the city and its progress. But they have nevertheless intermingled, and neither can be understood alone. The two realities are realities for God, and only in him can we know exactly what they are. But the problem becomes serious when the city kills the country, when Cain kills Abel. When that happens, man and history are so thrown out of kilter that nothing can modify the new situation. But — and here is what is important — it can be no other way. Cain could not stop being himself. From the beginning he had to kill Abel. The city, so mediocre, so puerile with its poorly carved blocks artlessly stacked one upon another, with its scanty population still rustic in nature — this city was, from the day of its creation, incapable, because of the motives behind its construction, of any other destiny than that of killing the country, where God put man to enable him to live his life as best he could.

*   *   *

But may it not be possible to give this same role to the city? Perhaps those geographers are right who are looking for its site. Perhaps those historians are right who are searching out its date. Perhaps things are "simpler than all that" and there is nothing in the Scriptures about the city except a few notes due to the clumsy pen of a Jewish scribe. After all, we have no right to construct an entire theory on the basis of a word, a sentence from the Bible. What cursed devotion to literalism!

To the reader scandalized by these first pages, I would give a double answer. First, he is doubtlessly right if we are faced with only a sentence or a word. But perhaps such is not the case. Perhaps there is a harmonious teaching throughout the Scriptures. Perhaps from the first book of the Bible to the last there is the same judgement, the same evaluation of the city. And then, if such is the case, if we find this judgement rendered at every period for seven or eight centuries, and in every possible way, we are obliged to see in it something other than the effect of an agrarian mind sceptical of the city, or the accident of narrative. If we discover a doctrine of the city, complete, coherent, with an undeniable bearing on man's life, his destiny, his relations with God, and at last his salvation, if we discover a history of the city, incorporated into the Lordship of Jesus Christ, we will then be obliged to admit that it is a question of something other than the invention of a professor bent on a new theology. All this we will perceive bit by bit.

The second remark I want to make is that the first time the word "city" is mentioned, we should be struck by it. The city is *'iyr* or else *'iyr re'em*. Now this word has several meanings. It is not only the city, but also the Watching Angel, the Vengeance and Terror. A strange association of ideas. What was able to induce a people (the chosen people) to call this first rampart, this first collection of houses, a name which can mean Vengeance and (associated but contrary in action) Terror and the Angel who watches? The chosen people, bearer of and witness to God's promise, that people whose tongue is surely the best suited to speak of the mysteries of God and to announce in his clearness but also in his incognito him who was to come. The entire Scripture proclaims that the life and thought of this people had a meaning (not because they were better, but because they were chosen) and its language also has a meaning. We cannot easily turn away from this association of ideas, especially since it fits in well with the general idea traced above. And without carrying it any further, we must admit that the city is not just a collection of houses with ramparts, but also a spiritual power. I am not saying it is a being. But like an angel, it is a power, and what seems prodigious is that its power is on a spiritual plane.

The city has, then, a spiritual influence. It is capable of directing and changing a man's spiritual life. It brings its power to bear in him and changes his life, all his life, not just his house. And that seems a fearful mystery. Fear of the nomad before a fortress town? But also fear of the chosen people before a power of unknown origin, before a power dangerous for the promise and its bearers. But how is this possible in something that is purely material? Cain put all his revolt into it. Man puts all his power into it and other powers come backing up man's efforts. The mystery of purpose. Adam's purely material act. Unimportant. But what is important for God?

The city as power. Terror and Vigilance. A rampart against hate and a sign of wrath.[1]

---

[1] The following are the words based on the root *'r*:

   (1) *'ar*, the masculine substantive meaning "city." This is the term used to designate a (or *the*) Moabite city granted to the descendants of Lot. But this same word also means "enemy," in a spiritual sense: God became Saul's enemy (I Sam. 28:16); and the Psalms speak of the enemies of God (Ps. 139:20). The relation between the two words is explicitly shown in word plays between "city" and "enemy" (e.g., Ps. 9:7).

   (2) *'iyr*, the verb "to burn," in a moral sense — i.e., "to become angry,"

II. NIMROD

The entire history of the city has its beginning in Cain's act. All the builders were sons of Cain and act with his purpose.

The next builder we hear of is Nimrod, the first on earth to become a mighty man. We know very little about him, but we do have one essential piece of information: he was a son of Ham (Gen. 10:6-8). Ham, the impure son, the one who disobeyed one of God's fundamental laws, and the one upon whom a curse was laid. Once again the city is to follow upon a curse as the act by which man tries to escape the curse. That curse weighing down on Ham's shoulders finds its immediate response in the founding of cities. "May he be the slave of his brothers' slaves." From the very fact that he is condemned to slavery, he will become powerful, and his power will assert itself in building cities. Once again man's response to God's curse. And it is absolutely accurate to say that man's power is first of all the result of hardening his heart against God: man affirms that he is strong, conquers the world, and builds cities until God comes to judge the world. Some exegetes, in fact poets, explain Cain's curse in this way: "The Israelites invented this myth to justify their own conquest of Canaan, and to explain how, from the very beginning, the Canaanites were destined to be in slavery to Israel."

Fine. But if that is so, how is it that from this same Ham came forth the first man to be powerful on the earth? Going from

---

"to tremble."

(3) *'ur*, the verb "to stay awake," "to be watchful."

(4) *'iyr*, the feminine substantive meaning:
  (a) "city," in a very general sense and used very frequently;
  (b) "guard" or "sentinel," usually with respect to the security of a city;
  (c) "passion," whether of fear or of anger, although the idea of fear is the more frequent.

(5) *'iyr*, the masculine substantive meaning "guard" or "angel." This meaning, which is found in more recent texts, is obviously derived from the second meaning of the preceding word. Just as guards give security to a city, so do angels. Thus it is a question of guardian angels, vigilant angels. The later development of this sense is easily understood, since it became a part of Hebrew angelology. But the angels of Hebrew angelology are usually condemning angels (Dan. 4:10 [v. 13 in the RSV] and Dan. 4:14 [v. 17 in the RSV]) or evil angels in revolt (Enoch 1:6). They are never guardian angels in the traditional sense and although they are spiritual powers, they always play a baleful role.

All this does not constitute a formal proof, because the etymology of *'iyr* is unknown. It is probably a Canaanite word adopted by the Hebrews when they came into Palestine and began living in cities. But even if the comparison between these words does not give scientifically valid results, it nevertheless had to be made.

one conquest to another? And how is it that Canaan, whose son
was Sidon, established a great kingdom? And that, in comparison
with Nimrod, as well as with Sidon, Israel was only a small
people? They may try to get rid of Nimrod by relegating him to
"an independent tradition." But the ruse is a bit clumsy. And
we perceive a realism and a truthfulness much more authentic
when the Scriptures show us that God's curse is inoperative until
the day of judgement, that it in no way keeps man from bringing all his activities to a successful conclusion, and that it almost
seems to be an encouragement for his activities. For when man
is faced with a curse he answers, "I'll take care of my problems
alone." And he puts everything to work to become powerful, to
keep the curse from having its effects. He creates the arts and
the sciences, he raises an army, he constructs chariots, he builds
cities. The spirit of might is a response to the divine curse, and
one could almost say that such a spirit would never have existed
if there had been no curse in the first place. However, the curse
stayed on, and one day it burst forth for all to see in an event
that may be understood as the assurance, a forewarning sign given
to the earth, of the last judgement. One day it was seen in the
fall of Babylon. Another, in Canaan vanquished and a slave, the
type of all those who will be punished in a greater war.

However that may be, Nimrod typifies this situation. The
first to be mighty. But something else is known of him: he was
"a mighty hunter before the Lord." Yet, this detail may hang on
an incorrect translation, for it is not at all certain that *tzayidh* is
to be translated by "hunter." Does it really make a difference
that he was a hunter? Some, of course, will argue that hunting
occupied an important place in the life of the Assyro-Babylonians.
But this is a poor explanation, premised on the conviction that
myths are anecdotal narratives comparable to our novels, in which
it is thought proper to accumulate details "from life" to make a
better story. Is it a useless, incidental bit of information? It is
rare to find unnecessary details in a myth.

And the incongruity of this detail becomes even more apparent if the two terms are brought together: "hunter before the
Lord." What is the Lord doing here? Of what concern is it to
him that Nimrod was a mighty hunter? What does being situated
before the Lord add to his being a hunter? Perhaps we should
first consider the second part of the phrase: Nimrod is "before
the Lord." That is said precisely to indicate to us that he is oc-
cupying a man's place, and to give us the proper setting of the
man and his act. It is a common expression to indicate man before a Lord who is judge and sovereign. This is not the father

calling his children to him. This is the God of terror to whom offerings are brought, before whom the earth is silent and powers crumble to dust. The effect of the preposition "before" is to mark separation as much as presence. He is before the Lord, which means that everything he does is seen and known by the Lord, but that he is also radically separate from him. They are in each other's presence, but not in face-to-face communion as Moses was. There is an abyss between them as there was between God and Adam after the fall. So we learn that Nimrod's action is not neutral, indifferent, but that God has his eye on him. We must at the same time do away with the idea that this "before the Lord" may be a kind of approbation of his action as though the Lord were sanctioning it. In reality, Nimrod is separated for the Lord.

But how can his being a hunter so interest the Lord that the connection between this act and God has to be pointed out? We will understand this remark better if, instead of "hunter," we translate "plunderer" or "conqueror." Then the different parts of the portrait of Nimrod come together. A spirit of conquering might before the Lord. Not only is Nimrod animated by this spirit, but he puts it to work, and that is impossible outside of the Lord's presence. The establishment of the first empires, military conquest — all this certainly takes place in God's presence, but with what separation from God's will!

And Nimrod's power will be established not only by his plundering, but by his cities, for that is the last item of information given us about Nimrod. He is the great builder. "Babylon, Accad, and Calneh, in the land of Shinar were the cradle of his empire [or the beginning of his domination]. From that land he went into Assyria, and he built Nineveh, Rehoboth-Ir, Calah, and Resen between Nineveh and Calah; that is the great city" (Gen. 10:10-11). Of course, historically speaking, Babylon and Nineveh and all the other cities were not constructed by one man. But our text is not meant to give us historical information.[2] It is a teaching about certain peoples, some would say. But, in fact, it is about *cities*. For peoples are not mentioned here, only cities. In any case, the descendants of Nimrod are characterized by this text as being city-dwellers. They have an urban civilization. Now these two verses were not added to Nimrod's story as an extra

---

[2]This is why it is not so very important to argue over the exact translation of verse 11. We translate, "he went into Assyria and he . . ." — continuing the thrust of verse 10 concerning Nimrod on into verse 11, which seems to follow the development of the text. Others (von Rad, for example) think that Assur is another king and that he built Nineveh. However, von Rad also admits that it is around the mythical personage Nimrod that all these traditional elements from diverse sources were grouped.

historical appendix. On the contrary, they follow a clearly established cadence and give the culmination of his activity, the infallible consequence of his first acts: spirit of might, conquest, construction of cities. The city is thus tied in with the will of man whose characteristics we have already stated and which we will meet again.

But we have taken a step forward. The city is now a center from which war is waged. Urban civilization is warring civilization. Conqueror and builder are no longer distinct. Both are included in one man, and both are an expression of that desire for might which is revolt against the Lord. The Scriptures have given us here one more secret about the city. And our modern world hardly gives it the lie. What world could better demonstrate the parallel between urban civilization and warring civilization than our own, a world where the city and war have become two of the poles around which the entire economic, social and political life of our time move. Nimrod. But Nimrod is not alone: "Nimrod before the Lord."

* * *

We have seen the man. Now his work. Babylon and Nineveh require particular consideration. But all the cities he constructed were marked with the same stamp — power. Nimrod settles down in the land of Shinar, where he builds and whence his conquests for war and the construction of new cities are launched. Who is Shinar? He who throws down, the shaker. The sign of fury and of roaring. The land of Shinar is the opposite of the world of peace. It is the land of piracy and destruction. All this, already apparent from the word itself, may be found down through this country's history, even if it is not identified with Babylonia. It was around the king of Shinar that the coalition spoken of in Genesis 14 was formed, the coalition which triumphed over all its enemies, captured Lot, and thereby ran afoul of Abraham. Abraham vanquished the king of Shinar, and Melchizedek, king of Salem, came out to bless Abraham: the king of righteousness, the prince of peace, the complete opposite of the king of Shinar. Throughout the adventure of the people of Israel, the presence of Shinar is clearly the presence of a spiritual power, of a temptation to evil. It is an object from Shinar that caused Achan's terrible sin (Josh. 7), the transgression of the Covenant. And it is not by accident that such is the case, for this country is typically the country of idols and sin. That is where Nebuchadnezzar took the vessels of God's house to incorporate them into the ser-

vice of his own god (Dan. 1:2). Daniel purposely calls the country
Shinar instead of Babylonia, for he wanted to emphasize that this
was a land of thievery and plunder. And if someone does not
want to believe that this country is symbolic, he only has to read
again in the fifth chapter of Zechariah: The prophet saw an ephah
rising up from the land of Israel, an angel throws a woman —
the sin of Israel — into the ephah, and then he covers its mouth
with a leaden weight. Then the ephah full of sin is to be carried
into the land of Shinar where a house will be built for it: "And
when this is prepared, they will set the ephah down there on its
base." Shinar, the land of sin. No other interpretation is possible.
And, after Cain, it is the cradle of urban civilization, Nimrod's
home, the beginning of his domination.

The cities are Erech, Accad, Calneh, Rehoboth, and Calah.
Symbolically, they are the city of eternity, the city of wideness,
the city of force. All of nature's dimensions are found there:
time, space, energy. These names are the symbol of man's taking
over the qualities they represent. Man conquers, and as a kind of
boundary-marker he raises up a city, the memorial of his conquest. Man conquers time, space, power.

But Resen, the great city, meaning "bridle," "bit" — what
is its significance here? We must not forget that the horse was the
first force of nature domesticated by man and put in his service.
Remember that the cavalry was one of the most fearsome of
weapons. Remember that for the Hebrews the horse represented
power and was a symbol of an advanced civilization. Thus, the
name "Resen" takes on meaning as an extraordinary reminder of
"the noblest conquest made by man," of that fantastic history of
man which begins with the horse and leads to splitting the atom.
For from the use of the horse for utilitarian purposes, to the use
of electricity, there is a difference of science and quantity, but
not of spirit and will. The bridle and the bit — the first means
invented by man to subdue natural force. There is no difficulty
in understanding that the first act of any new civilization should
be commemorated by a city, that the city is very precisely the
best symbol of that new civilization. And it is easily understood
why exegetes and translators want to make "the great city" modify
"Resen," and not "Nineveh." Resen is doubtlessly not the great
city of history in any genuine sense, but she is the great city in
the sense that she represents the human power glorified in her.
She is the city of technique, of invention, of domination over
nature.

The history of these cities does not belie their names. They

show the reign of man given over to his sin, to his idols; they
are the place where the chosen of God are held captive.

Calneh, whose power is terrible, is placed there as a warning
to Zion. (Watch and pray, for temptation is coming.) Calneh, the
reign of violence, ready to pounce on Jerusalem, because Jerusalem is asleep in her delusive peace (Amos 6). And if Calneh
is best suited for this mission, it is because she is the kingdom of
idols (Isa. 10:10). She is only one city among others. She is not
a symbol of *the* city, but she has a mission among the cities: she
is to be the launching pad for aggression against the church. Just
as Calah, too, has her mission among the cities, that of being a
place for the deportation of the church. The king of Assyria,
Tiglath Pileser, took Israel captive to Assyria, and the place of
captivity was Calah (II Kings 17:6). These accidental characteristics of cities of secondary importance will reappear often in
symbolic names, but we can already perceive the extraordinary
declaration that the city is the great enemy of the church. The
city is also the "assembly," the "gathering together," but is exactly
the opposite of the church assembly; it is the place where the
church is held captive and is a prey for war and threats, a place
where it is in combat not against flesh and blood, but against
idols, against that spiritual power which is the essential characteristic of the city.

* * *

The center of Nimrod's kingdom is Babel, Babylon. "The
gate of the gods," say modern exegetes. "The place of confusion,"
says the Hebrew exegete, basing his interpretation on the root
"Babel." All we know of it is the famous tower which was supposed to go up to heaven. But the tower is not the central element in the narrative. The two facts around which this myth is
built are the city and a name: "Come, let us build ourselves a
city, and a tower with its top in the heavens, and let us make a
name for ourselves." But, said the Lord, "Let us confuse their
language." "And they left off building the city" (Gen. 11:4-8).
The tower is only a part of the city, an episode in the story.

The point of the story is the problem of the name, and the
city and its tower are the means of obtaining the name. How important a name was for an Israelite is well known. It is the sign
of dominion and has a spiritual quality. God gave a name to the
first man. Man in turn named all the animals. Thus a relationship is established in which the one named becomes the object
of the one naming. The rebellious people are tired of being

named, of being the recipient of a name. They want to name themselves. In fact, they want to *make* a name for themselves. For it is not enough to give oneself a name, the name must be earned. It must mean something. To make a name for oneself has nothing to do with the modern expression referring to a reputation; it means becoming independent, and that is what their attempt at building meant. The people wanted to be definitively separated from God. They knew well that in spite of their revolt they were still tributary to God, that God was still their Lord, that God was still the one naming them, "calling them by their name," just as with Adam right after the fall. Like it or not, they still belonged to God. And that is what the people wanted to eliminate. Their revolt is ever so much more profound in this myth than in that of Prometheus to which it is often compared. It is much more than taking over God's power. It is the desire to exclude God from his creation. And it is this solidarity in a name, this unity in separation from God, which was to keep men from ever again being separated on earth. And the sign and symbol of this enterprise is the city they wanted to build together. It was in this, man's environment, built by man for man, with any other intervention or power excluded, that man could make a name for himself. It was there that his pretension of becoming a subject, never again to be an object, could be realized. The cities of our time are most certainly that place where man can with impunity declare himself master of nature. It is only in an urban civilization that man has the metaphysical possibility of saying, "I killed God."

And again the city's double role becomes apparent: it is both the place where man's conquest is affirmed and the memorial to that conquest. The two phenomena of spiritual conquest and the construction of a city give rise to each other. It is because the city is such a place that man's triumphant march without God can take place, and it is because of this triumphant march that the city is a necessity.

We pointed out above that a city marks man's every success. And a city must also mark the advance against God: she is a tower in order to seize for herself what belonged to God, she is a wall to protect herself against God's interventions, she is stone blocks to fold within her bosom that conquest. "Let us go and build a city." Let us go! The conquering step of man towards the city of his independence and pride! The conquering step of the subject now taking over all of creation and his own destiny by his name, and there is in fact nothing that can keep these men from realizing their plan. In the order of things established by

God after the fall in order that the world might go on, man is
in fact master of things, he can make a tower up to heaven of
bricks baked in the fire and bitumen. He can also make a name
for himself, for no natural obstacle keeps him from manifesting
his pride to high heaven. Such is the nature of this entire enterprise, of every one of man's enterprises. Sin always eggs him on
to use things over which he is master in a way conducive to a
spiritual destruction that nothing, in the natural order of things,
can stop. Such is the city. But this new teaching does not do away
with what Cain's experience has already taught us. For they built
this city "when they migrated from the east . . . into the plain of
Shinar." And thus everything adds up bit by bit: Cain migrated
from the east to build Enoch; Nimrod built Nineveh in Shinar.
And this city of Babel is also the place where men wanted to
settle down so as no longer to be wanderers on the earth, "so as
no longer to be scattered over the face of the earth" (v. 4). And
it is the place of sin. Here, then, we have the progressive enrich-
ment of the myth, with no contradiction because it is in truth the
expression of revelation.

"Come, let us build a city," man said (v. 4). "Come, let
us go down," said God (v. 7). God's action corresponds to man's.
To the desire in the creature for spiritual conquest corresponds
a desire for order from the Creator, he who knows that man's
spiritual conquest can lead only to one end — spiritual and material death. For any separation from God is death. And if man
says honestly, "God is dead," then that man is also dead. And if
God can no longer call man by his own name, then man is dead.
And if all relations between man and God are broken off (really
broken, not just broken in the imagination or the sentiments or
the pretensions of man), then man dies.

But because God wants his creature to live, he keeps the
break from happening. Man absolutely cannot get rid of God because he cannot keep the subject of all things from really being
that subject. He cannot keep himself, subject in the world, from
being an object before God. Despite all the conspiracies that
the trees in my garden may hatch up among themselves, they
cannot keep me from calling them by their names and from
picking their fruit when it is ripe. "Come," says God, and the
subject is once again revealed as subject. But God does not smash
or destroy. Babel does not crumble under the lightning flash. The
problem is a spiritual one, and Babel is only a symbol. To man's
desire to make a name for himself, God responds with the confusion of tongues. Its name is to be Babel. Confusion. Our text
gives this etymology for Babel, but the experts say that this is not

the true etymology. They are doubtlessly correct. But if it is an error linguistically speaking, it does make perfect sense in terms of the myth.[3] That is exactly what the myth has in mind, that is the truth it must express.

The name "Babel" is therefore symbolic of the whole story. Man certainly did not expect his project to take such a turn. He did not anticipate that the name he wanted to make for himself would refer to a place of noncommunication. For this, far more than the creation of rocks and languages, is the meaning of the story. "Let us confuse their language, that they may not understand one another's speech." This has always been interpreted as a desire to explain the different human languages. Perhaps so, but certainly the expression used is singularly awkward to say that. A separation into several tongues is not mentioned but rather a "confusion of their language." It is not stated that man will speak several languages, but that he will no longer understand what others are speaking. The emphasis is not on speaking as such, but on understanding. Just as in the story of Pentecost, it is not stated that the apostles spoke *all* the languages of those present, but rather that, "speaking other languages," they were understood by all. The existence of different languages is doubtlessly a condemnation expressed in the Babel story, but we must go far beyond such an interpretation. It is not only the material fact of the foreign tongues which is important. The material fact

---

[3]I hesitate to use the term "myth," for at best it is obscure, appearing in many diverse forms. From the conscious myth of the Greeks to Sorel's conception, from the biblical myth to the "twentieth-century myth," from the legendary myths of the Indo-Europeans to the Bultmannian, there are vast differences in form, meaning, and value. Barth's criticism of any conception of myth in the Bible is in truth valid only for a relatively minor part of the different possible meanings of this word. He is attacking the mode of interpretation of the Bible used by the historical school, also by form criticism, and finally by Bultmann. In order to be precise, every author should give his definition of "myth." When I use the word I mean this: the addition of theological significance to a fact which in itself, as an historical (or supposed to be such), psychological or human fact, has no such obvious significance. Its role is therefore to make a fact "meaningful," to show it up as bearing the revelation of God, whereas in its materiality it is neither meaningful nor of the nature of revelation. This is how myth operates. It does not destroy the historical reality of the event, but on the contrary gives it its full dimensions. In the myth, God assigns a name to a people who would like to make a name for themselves and quite naturally assigns a name taking its meaning from his act, from the confusion of languages, but also a name with meaning for the whole story, which is one long confusion — the confusion between man's power and God's, the confusion and obscurity of man's plans, the confusion of man's desire by God.

is only an outward manifestation of the spiritual phenomenon of men ceasing to understand each other. They cannot really communicate even when they speak the same language and use the same words.

"Let us make a name for ourselves." They all have one language. And they have undertaken to make a name for themselves. A humanity capable of communicating has in its possession the most terrible weapon of its own death: it is capable of creating a unique truth, believed by all, independent of God. By the confusion of tongues, by noncommunication, God keeps man from forming a truth valid for all men. Henceforth, man's truth will only be partial and contested.

It is remarkable that this fact, one of the most fundamental in human history since the fall, this fact which is the exact response to the flood, occurred in a city. And that the city itself has become its symbol. In and because of the city, men can no longer understand each other and get along. This general human condition reached its high point in Babel, and it is so because Babel was to be the place of unity for the human race, the home of human truth. The city — the place of noncommunication among men, the place where the immense irony of God hides. The result of this confusion is dispersion and a halt to construction. The city is not destroyed, but the builders separate and stop building. There is no other solution, because what they have lost in the affair is the meaning of the city they were building. When men no longer understand themselves, the city which was the seal of their understanding loses all meaning for them. And henceforth it will always be so. Men can live in their towers, they can build their skyscrapers and their giant cities, they can cover the world with a web of interlocking cities, but these have no more meaning for them. Babel will never be finished. The city is only one stone on top of another; a fortress here, a cathedral there, then a house and a slaughterhouse, it is no longer for man the proof of his spiritual power, it is no longer a clear, conscious attempt to make himself God. Never again will men say: "Come, let us build a city and make a name for ourselves."

The city is still this spiritual power, this place and this entrenchment. But man no longer knows it, and each attempt at establishing a city is met by the failure of his unconscious designs. The city has dotted history with its repeated failures, the noncommunication of man, the dispersion of the races. They came from the east, condemned to perpetual wandering, they wanted to stop and build themselves a place to be their own. They were dispersed to all the winds of heaven. No longer could they understand one another. God said, "Come."

* * *

Babel, Babylon. Seemingly we pass from myth to history. But it is only an illusion. The two overlap, both because this history is that of the chosen people and because those who wrote it were only writing to bear witness for God. Babylon only follows up what was foretold in Babel. And if Jerusalem was destroyed by Babylon, if Israel was exiled to Babylon, it was not due to hazard, it was a response to Babylon's inner nature, a necessity. Israel captive in Babylon. It is in no sense comparable to the captivity in Egypt. It did not mark the people in the same way. One is the shadow of sin. The other is confusion. Two different captivities of the church. What an extraordinary adventure is the chosen people's, bearer of the promise, bearer of a revelation for the whole world, shut up — for a time — in the very center of confusion, in the city, in noncommunication.

It is when her message becomes universal that the church runs into this difficulty. She is not the captive of armies and walls, she is not held in check by deserts and administrations, but it all bears the name of Babel; she is a prisoner in the world, in the city, the absolute synthesis of all that is worldly, all that is noncommunication, all that makes the Gospel impossible to share. So then she laments and prays her psalms. Then she faithfully waits, and Daniel is powerless in the midst of the city of confusion. Until God intervenes, until the tyrant has a dream, sees a vision, until fingers of fire write on the wall. Then their ears are opened by God and the church is no longer captive, she speaks, and Babylon ceases to be Babel, for a while, for one man. And then, afterwards, the captivity begins again. After Daniel receives the purple, he gets the lions' den. This city is truly the place of the genuine captivity of the church.

We will find Babylon again in our task of following God's curse on the city down through the Scriptures. But before going on we have one more thing to learn. Babylon is not *a* city. She is *the* city. And this is particularly important when we look back on what we have said about Babel.

Babylon, the great city, or Babylon the Great. The biggest in the world. No one can rival her, not even Rome. Not because of her historical greatness, but because of what she represents mythically. All the cities of the world are brought together in her, she is the synthesis of them all (Dan. 3 and 4; Rev. 14 and

18). She is the head of, and the standard for the other cities. When the wrath of God is loosed, she is struck first. When she is struck, all the other cities are struck in her. The blame laid on her shoulders is applicable to every city. Each city has one aspect of the leprosy of the cities, but she has them all. Everything said about Babylon is in fact to be understood for the cities as a whole. As all the other cities, Babylon (representative of all the others) is at the hub of civilization. Business operates for the city, industry is developed in the city, ships ply the seas for the city, luxury and beauty blossom forth in the city, power rises and becomes great in the city. There everything is for sale, the bodies and souls of men. She is the very home of civilization and when the great city vanishes, there is no more civilization, a world disappears. She is the one struck in war, and she is first to be struck in the war between the Lord and the powers of the world. A city greater than a simple city — the finishing of a work that can in no wise be finished, which man starts over again indefinitely with ever the same purpose and the same success. Babylon, Venice, Paris, New York — they are all the same city, only one Babel always reappearing, a city from the beginning mortally wounded: "and they left off building the city."

Nineveh is completely different and has a different destiny, although she, too, is a city and exhibits the characteristics of a city. What gives her a particular meaning is her status as the city of repentance. We will meet her again under this form. But for now, Nineveh is also the city of Nimrod, perhaps more than any other, the daughter of the conqueror, the rebel.

Nineveh, the bloody city, "full of lies, full of violence, no end to her plunder" (Nah. 3:1). The connection between the city and war which we have already noticed is carried here to its highest point. Nineveh is nothing other than the nest of a brood of rapacious birds. She is so warlike that she is almost presented as the personification of war. And Nineveh was truly so, historically so. But this takes nothing from the fact that it is a city which is the homeland of war. In Nineveh we find the city's other side. We saw in Babylon the city as the synthesis of civilization. In Nineveh we see the synthesis of war. Two forms. *The* two forms of man's spirit of power. Strong in her chariots and cavalry, Nineveh can say, "I am and there is none else" (Zeph. 2:15). A city sure of herself — who then would dare to destroy her? Because she is a city, she is powerful. Because she is warlike, she is of necessity a city. Why a city? Why not simply a man, the man of the city?

We must certainly not attribute the conception to a weakness of the Hebrew mind, tempted to personify everything. Sociologists know that every city has its own personality, and that a man's mental make-up changes when he goes from the country to the city and again from one city to another. It would be irrational to refuse to see this. But Nineveh, the city of blood and conquest, is first of all a city. Her spirit, the angel who dwells there as the god of fortresses, is introduced by Daniel in his later prophecies (Dan. 11:38). We are dealing with a problem that is primarily spiritual. The city is a place of physical war, but also of spiritual war. And the men who live there are sacrificed to her destiny. She is the bloody city and men are only her soldiers, her means, her chattels. The power of the city over man. She is condemned, but it is her men who die (Nah. 3). It is impossible for us to be stronger than the strength revealed by God as ours.

Although we may admit gracefully that we are dependent on each other, we dislike its reality. We dislike being included in a group condemnation. We dislike even more being only one building block in that whole called a city, being so interdependent, not only on men but on an abstraction, that our death is decided by the acts of the city.

"Dead bodies without end . . . [we] stumble over the bodies." We think of our cities leveled by bombing. Of all the dead who had done no wrong. All the innocent dead, buried under the ruins by blind airplanes, of all the children who had committed no other crime than that of living in the city. Terrible interdependence from which it is impossible to escape. Cities destroyed because they were a power. Cities denuded because they were full of assurance. Cities wiped out because they said, "I am, and there is none else." Bloody cities, where the industries that manufactured the airplanes and the mortars were crowded together, where the workers spat out their health in factory smoke. Where all the pleasures of mortals were heaped together. The terrible judgement constantly repeated throughout history. "He will make Nineveh a desolation, a dry waste like the desert" (Zeph. 2:13). And nothing can eliminate this solidarity with the city.

Of course the farmer is dependent on other factors, has his own sins, takes other risks. But his destiny does not appear from Scripture to be so inescapably bound in with an environment which is only the work of man. And what a work it is! The very fact of living in the city directs a man down an inhuman road. He is taken into the service and the worship of a somber goddess.

"And I heard another voice saying, 'Come out of her my

people' " (Rev. 18:4). "The angels took Lot and set him outside
the city" (Gen. 19:16).

III. ISRAEL

And now the spotlight turns and lights up another facet of
history. Pharaoh was also a great builder, but Scripture does not
mention the cities he constructed, because what we need to know
about the city and the motives which drive men to build one has
already been indicated. Pharaoh would teach us nothing new,
his cities are the same as Cain's and Nimrod's. But Pharaoh
interests us now because the chosen people were involved in his
creations. After observing what the city can be, what it means
for a man to build a city, the lens now focuses down and pin-
points the conflict as it is carried to its highest point: the city in
its relations with the chosen people of God. It is to be one of
the invariables in the life of this people, and the history of God's
grace will be tightly interwoven with the history of this people
who, like the other nations, marked its progress with the construction of cities.

The first time we see the chosen people building a city is
in Egypt. Until that time they were nomads. Whenever they were
in contact with cities, it was as foreigners. And the city was
hardly favorable to them. They had to flee Sodom and Gomorrha.
It was in Salem that Dinah's seduction took place. Jacob could
not remain in cities belonging to Esau and his descendants (Gen.
36). And finally, there was the city of Pharaoh where Joseph was
captive, and where the entire chosen people were subsequently
captive.

Israel was everywhere separate from the city. He was a
wanderer and had no share in the creation of the city. He did
not share its spirit, was in fact a foreigner without a place, and
soon found it necessary to cut himself off from it. All he knew
how to build was a pile of stones to the glory of God — Galeed,
the Witness. He did not build for himself, but to draw attention
to someone else, to serve as a witness (Gen. 31:47). He did not
build something to be useful, or for his defense, or to affirm his
power. He built to be a witness to a covenant, a covenant and
not a separation. Nevertheless, this covenant is also a separation
because as of yet there is no question of the perfect covenant
established by God, only of the covenant established by men
chosen of God, doing their duty, but still only men. And that is
why Galeed is also the separation between Laban and Jacob.
But a separation in peace, with a common faith. No longer is

it separation with a proud affirmation of self, but with mutual respect because both are dependent on one God. For Galeed is also called Mizpah: the Lord will be present. And so Israel's first construction is a monument to the one present: the Lord. And they shared a meal on this pile of stones. A covenant meal, a first communion in the presence of the Lord. But this Galeed is not a city. All of Galeed's qualities exhibit a fundamental opposition with the city. It is at the disposal of someone other than man, it bears witness to something other than man's power, it is useful for nothing. It is nothing but a pile of stones and that is all that God's people know how to build.

The historians would say that the chosen people did not know how to build cities because they were only shepherds and had not yet reached the level of Canaanite civilization. That is no doubt true; but the historical reasons seem empty when compared with the brutal fact that the city has the undeniable significance we have tried to point out, and that the first time Israel is mentioned as building something, it has an entirely different meaning.

Up till now, whenever the children of Israel had to stay in a city it was a city they had not built (Deut. 6:10), either because they were incapable of building or because they knew the danger of becoming builders. However that may be, such was apparently the most desirable state for them — people guided by God into great and beautiful cities they had not built. But were these cities not condemned? Can the people live there without being incorporated into them? They become an object again instead of being a power. They are stones piled on top of stones, houses beside houses, instead of being the Angel, Vengeance, and Terror. What a reassuring outlook! We find ourselves before something with which we have already met. But it is true for the chosen people and for the chosen people only. They did not build these cities. But they will learn to build. They also will take the common road, or rather they will be forced into it — not voluntarily, not after a rebellion, but in captivity, in the land of sorrow, in Egypt.

"Pharaoh said to his people, 'Behold the people of Israel are too many and too mighty for us. Come, let us deal shrewdly with them . . . .' Therefore they set taskmasters over them to afflict them with heavy burdens; and they built for Pharaoh store-cities, Pithom and Raamses" (Ex. 1:9-11). The first time! The people did not want to. It was not an expression of self, of pride. It was because they were reduced to slavery, because heavy burdens were imposed on them, that they were led to learn how to build a city, and to do the actual building themselves. It was in slavery that Israel and the city were bound together. And not by chance. Egypt is traditionally the land of slavery, not only because Israel's period of slavery is situated there but also symbolically by its very name *mitzrayim*, the land of sorrow, of suffering.

Mizraim, son of Cain. How singular his destiny! Condemned to slavery, cursed by his father (Gen. 9:25), and yet he becomes the master, reducing to slavery the one who was supposed to be his master. What an upset of a proclamation of God's word! But also what a singular unity in the revelation that makes Nimrod the builder and Mizraim the builder both descendants of Cain. Both of them, going different ways, establish a city building on the curse by which their ancestor was condemned. So it was in Mizraim that the children of Israel were slaves, in the very land of mortal sorrow, "of the shadow of death." And it was also in this country that the children of Israel learned to build cities and were changed by what they learned. Never again will the cities built by the chosen people be an act of the chosen people. They will always be a reminder of slavery, of the sorrow in which the art was learned. And the art is always accompanied by the reminder. When Israel built their own cities, it was always for them the sign of a curse, and the proclamation of slavery renewed. And the prophecies of those long-haired prophets who were a constant reminder of the innocence of the nomadic life as opposed to urban life were based on that first apprenticeship: Israel bound herself to slavery, and, even more, to the land of sorrow and sin; by the cities she built, cities that were always the imitation of what she had learned in Egypt, before the deliverance. For the greatest significance is in the fact that Israel was initiated in this art by a king other than God. The people whom God chose for himself obeyed a worldly king, a king whose power was the most impressive of his time, the king of the land of Mizraim. And the power of this king forced the chosen people into ways not meant for a people of God.

A part of this people's slavery (far from God, no longer able to obey his will although they still love him — Gen. 2:23-24) was to build cities. They were used only for that. Moreover, what is said about these cities reveals to us a new aspect: they are granary cities for Pharaoh, and as such are only another aspect of man's power. Economic power taking its place beside the others. Still the same idea, still the same goal. For Pharaoh is the first to have thought of economics as a political science, who conceived of organizing an economy. So another great enterprise is connected with cities. Thus, each time we notice a new step by man in conquest and autonomy, the step is consolidated by a city going up whose mission is to mark the limits of the new power. And by this process the people of God are drawn into the same cycle. What they learn from the world involves them in the world's enterprises, and military and economic enterprises will always be reduced to the problem of building a city.

But the act never has the same meaning for Israel as for other peoples. In fact, God's constant effort is to denude this act of the meaning given to it by men. But it is particularly difficult for men, even when belonging to the chosen people, to accept God's reworking of things, to edify the world by their acts without bearing the bitter fruits of disobedience. Taken into the world, taken into Egypt, the people of the Lord have difficulty getting rid of the dross, especially since they are really captives, really obliged to follow the politics of the world. And by building Pharaoh's cities they not only assist him in his economic plans, but they also accomplish, perhaps involuntarily but certainly to Satan's profit, another abominable thing: they build Pi-Thom, "the house of Thom." Thom was an Egyptian sun god, one of the main gods of the fourteenth century B.C. in a complex and intellectual religion that was one of the most perfect theologies ever opposed to God's plan.

And thus Israel is caught in a spiritual trap set by Satan, and instead of building up the house of the Lord, they are forced by the city to build a house for the adversary. This adventure has been reproduced at every turn of God's work because it is impossible to completely refuse the world's work and be immune to the spiritual bearing of that work. And God must continually intervene in his people's involvement and warn them of what is happening, for, alone, their eyes are blind to the reality of their involvement.

God addresses himself both to the act and to its meaning. He takes upon himself the act and gives it a new meaning. On the one hand he warns them that "Unless the Lord builds the house, those who build it labor in vain" (Ps. 127:1). But that is no more than an appeal to man to make him recognize the depth of the vanity of his work. You who are building cities, he says, and who have placed in them all human certitude, who have condensed all human effort into the city, which is the synthesis, the symbol, and materially the greatest act of human power because it is spiritual — you must understand that it is all empty and in vain, and that all cities from the beginning until now are emptiness because God did not build them. But on the other hand, God brings about what he says. When he affirms that "unless the Lord builds the house, . . . " it is not as a simple hypothesis, a rhetorical and impossible condition, but as a statement of fact that God can build the city. For "God will save Zion and rebuild the cities of Judah" (Ps. 69:36). He will act in two phases, both of them clearly indicated here: God will both accept and save the city built by men with blood (Mic. 3:10), men who learned in error and slavery how to build Zion. Thus the Lord himself is going to substitute his work for man's, and he will build lasting cities, different cities, the true cities of Judah, cities which will be under another sign and controlled by a power other than Cain's. But this is a hard lesson to learn, and the people of God often refused to accept it. They tried to evade the problem, they followed the other nations and built their own cities — with the same importance as the other cities, and yet with an added feeling of despair because they were the peculiar people.

Israel conquered the cities of Canaan and settled within their gates. But when Israel took over one of these conquered cities, they did not restore its political importance. They moved into an inhabited place, after exterminating its inhabitants, but did not know how to get the most out of city life. Only Manasseh became a part of an ancient federation of cities with their populations (Shechem, Tirza).

In Manasseh the cities retained their political orientation and Canaanite influence was dominant. And what was the result? Gideon, the judge himself, makes an ephod, an idol which he proposes for Israel's worship. He makes "Baal of the Covenant," whose sanctuary is at Shechem, as we would expect, and whose name by a terrible play on words recalls both the traditional god of the Canaanites and the covenant Lord of Israel. Such a horrible mixture is the normal result of the occupation of a city by Israel. We find the same progression in the life of Solomon. And even more important, Gideon's son Abimelek, starting with these very same cities, undertakes the conquest of Israel in order to establish his kingship and work out a Canaanization of Israel based on kingship as practiced in the cities of Canaan. He wants to dethrone the Lord God in order to make himself the Lord of Israel. The same old plan. And soon the children of Israel are no longer content with living in old cities. They go to work building for themselves, building and rebuilding. They rebuild Jericho — symbol of power, for she was a fortified city. Jericho, before whose walls Israel celebrated the Passover; Jericho, which was destroyed by a miracle, a miracle that made a nomadic people bearing the eternal truth of God, anointed with God's power. Jericho, whose destruction is also (and in the opposite sense) the symbol of the defeat of the spirit of power and of all that the city stands for. And now Jericho is rebuilt by the chosen people.

How subtle the temptation was, finding as it did a place at the very heart of God's work. After all, it is natural to argue, the people of Israel had to fortify their borders, they had to en-sure that the fords of the Jordan were closed. The reconstruction of Jericho took place just at one of Israel's greatest moments, when King Ahab was triumphing in the establishment of a power-ful state. But over the ruins of Jericho, after the miracle, Joshua had declared, "Cursed before the Lord be the man that rises up and rebuilds this city, Jericho! At the cost of his first-born shall he lay its foundation, and at the cost of his youngest son shall he set up its gates" (Josh. 6:26). Some 400 years later, Hiel of Bethel did rebuild Jericho. But "He laid its foundation at the cost of Abiram his first-born, and set up its gates at the cost of his youngest son Segub, according to the word of the Lord, which he had spoken by Joshua, the son of Nun" (I Kings 16:34).

Was Jericho deserted for 400 years? That is unlikely. It is improbable that Hiel built the city up from nothing. Jericho was inhabited long before, probably since shortly after the division of Canaan into lots, because Jericho was included in Benjamin's portion and even then was called a city (Josh. 18:21). It was certainly inhabited at the time of the judges, especially in the judgeship of Ehud since the king of Moab took the city of palms in his day (Judg. 3:13), and also at the time of David. But it is of little importance whether or not houses were added to houses to form a place of habitation. That Hiel's work was probably only one of enlarging, rebuilding, or fortifying has no relevance. The fact remains that he is the one who founded the new city, be-cause he was the first to decide consciously to do so, because he ran the risk of the curse, because he wanted it to be a powerful city, and because he chose human modes of decision (political power, a military garrison) in spite of God's word. In other words, he chose the particular position among the Goyim of builder. And his act led to the same results as their acts, only more dis-astrous. He is cursed, and cannot save himself from the curse. In Joshua's prophecy there is neither choice nor redemption. Perhaps it is true, as scholars say, that the sacrifice was part of the foundation rites. It was probably thought necessary to drive out the demons who traditionally haunted ruins. We know that it was common practice, not only among the Semites, to lay the first stone of a new town on the body of a human sacrifice of-fered to the power of the city in order that his spirit protect the city. And there is no reason to reject the tradition (which no ex-

cavation could confirm one way or the other) that the sacrifice
was the eldest son of the founder. Again we find, as with Enoch,
that, as works, the son and the city are considered equivalent.
Once again we ask how one could refuse to believe, with this in
mind, that the city has no inherent spiritual influence? But we
must refuse to draw any conclusions whatsoever from these magical customs, which can only be described as errings of primitive
peoples. *Our* cities need no foundation sacrifices, for by their very
existence they swallow up and destroy the vital forces, both material and spiritual, of the millions of men sacrificed to them.
But that has no convicting power because it has not received
meaningfulness as the Word of God. So we must not insist on
the horror of these sacrifices in their connection with the city but
on their meaning here in the story of the Book of Kings. Because here they have lost all the magical significance traditionally
attributed to them.

In Joshua's saying, what is most important is the curse itself. This is easy to understand since it is directed against the one
who would try to reconstruct what God destroyed, and who is
thus going directly against God's will. The curse means God's
withdrawal, and according to the promises made to the children
of Israel, must take the form of material calamities. This curse
will therefore have a material sign: the sacrifice of the eldest and
youngest sons. The sacrifice is there only as a sign, a sign that
reveals certain things: first that it is Hiel and no one else who is
the fulfillment of the prophecy, and second that it is his act and
no other which has been cursed. Certain historians, unsure as to
why rebuilding Jericho should be cause for a curse, but never re-
luctant to speculate, have proposed (with great virtuosity trans-
posing a nineteenth-century attitude to the eighth century B. C.)
that the custom of child sacrifices may by Hiel's time have disappeared from use among the Semitic peoples, and that the conscience of the people, scandalized by Hiel's act, explained it by
inventing the prophecy of Joshua and his curse.

However that may be, this explanation seems to me much
more difficult to accept than the biblical story, pure and simple.
In order for it to be valid, some important questions would have
to be answered. Why did Hiel resurrect a vanished custom? Why
did he risk shocking the conscience of his people by doing something that was probably not very pleasant for himself? (For up
to the present, the acceptance of child sacrifice by the parents has
been explained only by assuming that it was imposed on them by
ritual, tradition, and the collective conscience.) Why did he carry
out a religious rite that had no more magical worth? The his-

torians' explanation runs up against difficulties so weighty that one is obliged to consider it a fantasy.

But in fact Hiel's act is meaningful in itself. What it makes manifest is that Hiel is gauging his conduct according to foreign custom, for this rite is not essentially Israelite. He adopted, when he began reconstruction, the scorn that a foreigner might have for Yahweh's acts; he disrespectfully abandoned the traditions of Yahweh's cult. In that, we should add, he was only following the example of his king. But it is exactly with that attitude that he is victim of the curse. It is not the act itself of reconstructing Jericho that is condemned, but all the meaning that is contained in the reconstruction. The reconstruction refuses the word of God: when Hiel rebuilds Jericho he abandons Yahweh, and the sacrifice of his children is the bloody proof. That is why he is cursed. And whether Joshua once pronounced the curse, or whether the historians are correct, the significance of Hiel's act is the same.

Nonetheless, the fact cannot be hidden that this teaching is given concerning the founding of a city. Moreover, the story shows us a new aspect of the tragedy. Up till now we have always found man *expressing* his condition by becoming a builder, man giving himself a new being in an undertaking meant to dispossess God. Here, for the first time, we find a man putting himself in that situation because of the city. And the necessity appears so immense, and the city seems so seductive, so good and true, that he does not hesitate to risk everything, himself and his family. From any standpoint the city is useful — as a fortress, as a stone-city, as a center of commerce or administration. She is so useful that man is ready to disappear in order that this obvious usefulness exist. Such a man was Hiel. The fords of the Jordan had to be guarded. So sons are sacrificed, the curse is accepted.

Standing before a city, man finds himself faced with such a perfect seduction that he literally no longer knows himself, he accepts himself as emasculated, stripped of both flesh and spirit. And acting so, he considers himself to be perfectly reasonable, because the city's seduction is in fact rational, and one really must obey the orders of reason.

Let us go back a few years in history. The first great building king in Israel is Solomon. David was always a peasant king. Whether by faithfulness or by simplicity, he was not an urban king, in spite of his skill in choosing his fortresses and his capital. Biblical history keeps the title of builder for Solomon: "Solomon built the house of the Lord and his own house and the

Millo and the wall of Jerusalem and Hazor, Megiddo and Gezer
.... And Solomon built Gezer, Lower Beth-Horon, Baalath and
Tamar in the wilderness of the land, and all his own store-cities,
and the cities for his chariots, and the cities for his horsemen"
(I Kings 9:15 ff.). But it is here that Solomon's first unfaithfulness
may be noticed. He founds his cities in slavery. And, forgetful
of what happened in Egypt, forgetful of the Mosaic legislation
for slaves, he enslaved "the foreigner who is within . . . [his]
gates" for his purposes of power: "these Solomon made a forced
levy of slaves." There is no condemnation in Scripture for that
act, and we can limit ourselves to pointing out the fact without
searching beyond its obvious meaning.

But there was more in it than that. We can already see in
these verses his attraction for what was foreign, for the foreign
power which brought about his downfall and condemnation. If
he rebuilt cities, it was partially thanks to Pharaoh, who pulled
back from some of them, like Gezer, and who gave Solomon
certain strongholds which he put to use.

Moreover, it is striking to notice how fragile these cities
built by the great king were, and how prone they were to destruction. One has but to read through the history of Israel to see how
defeat after defeat was the portion of Hazor, Beth-Horon, Gezer,
and Megiddo. So much for the politics of fortresses, proven vain
by history.

But in the story of the founding of these cities, one fact must
detain us. The first of these cities, built after the Temple, was
the Millo. And there an event came about which truly symbolizes
the breaking up of Solomon's life. Jeroboam was the construction
chief on the Millo. One day, when leaving Jerusalem, he met the
prophet Ahijah wearing a new cloak. "The two of them were
alone in the open country, and Ahijah laid hold of the new gar-
ment that was on him, and tore it into twelve pieces. And he
said to Jeroboam, 'Take for yourself ten pieces; for thus says the
Lord, the God of Israel: Behold, I am about to tear the kingdom
from the hand of Solomon, and will give you ten tribes. But he
[Solomon] shall have one tribe, for the sake of my servant David
and for the sake of Jerusalem, the city which I have chosen, because they have forsaken me, and worshipped Ashtoreth the
goddess of the Sidonians, Chemosh the god of Moab, and Milcom the god of the Ammonites, and have not walked in my ways
. . .' " (I Kings 11:26 ff.).

An astonishing event, occurring precisely at the time when
Solomon, having built the Temple, succumbed to the desire for
power and riches and began building cities. Therefore, it was well

before the apostasy at the end of his reign that he was abandoned, because he put his confidence elsewhere than in the Lord, because, after closing the breach in the wall of Jerusalem, a right and proper thing to do, he began a work designed to protect himself humanly, the construction of the Millo. Perhaps it is only a coincidence, but one must agree that it is rather an astonishing one, and that it was exactly when he began the foundations for a city that he was accused of having abandoned Yahweh for Ishtar, Chemosh, and Milcom! And this happened at the zenith of his reign, before the visit of the Queen of Sheba, before the construction of high places for new divinities. Now the relation between the cities and foreign gods is even more strongly marked by the very names Solomon gives them: Baalath and Beth-Horon, cities devoted by their very names to the false gods invading Israel. This relationship between the city and false gods in Israel is invariable. Says Jeremiah, "Your gods have become as numerous as your cities, O Judah!" (Jer. 11:13). The reference here is probably only to cities bearing the names of gods, but we must never forget the importance of a name: giving a name to a city is giving it the very being of the name it bears. So the detail that Solomon was condemned because he gave himself over to idols is not given in vain; it would be if its purpose were to give an explanation. Solomon's act is not exclusively religious, it has taken concrete form. He worships foreign gods and he builds cities which are consecrated to them. Thus Solomon's actions correspond with the explanation given for them by the Chronicler, and the parallelism of his deeds is even more striking when we see the same man building the house of the Lord and the house of Baal. After building the Temple, he expands his activities in order to find the power soon made manifest in the cities and devotes it to his idols. Someone will doubtlessly say that the Temple itself was shot through with oriental culture. But its meaning is of another nature. Another reminder that it is not only the materiality of the act that counts (although it also counts), but rather its spiritual quality. And the spiritual quality in the construction of a city is undeniable here. Solomon's first act of disobedience to God is the establishment of cities. The precise point where Solomon abandons Yahweh and stops making use of his miraculous wisdom is that point where he decides on a politics of power materialized in cities. Afterwards, he can still dazzle the Queen of Sheba with the remnants of his wisdom. Nevertheless, he has already been rejected. In truth he is the king of disobedience: for although other kings after him denied God, following after human folly and wandering from faithfulness, no other had the gift of wisdom, no other was called to build the Temple. Others will fall as low, but none from so high. He will himself escape for David's sake, but his house, Rehoboam, must suffer.

Rehoboam is also a builder, the greatest besides Solomon. Rehoboam, whose reign was characterized by schism, as Solomon's was by disobedience. Three chapters of the Chronicles are devoted to him. The first tells of the division of the sacred people into two groups because of Rehoboam's blundering. The second tells of his construction of cities and of his idolatry. The third, of his war with the king of Egypt, and of his defeat and death. Thus, what was successful about his reign, for the men of his time, was the great number of cities he erected. "Rehoboam built fortress cities in Judah. He built Bethlehem, Etam, Tekoa, Beth-Zur, Soco, Adullam, Gath, Mareshah, Ziph, Adoraim, Lachish, Azekah, Zorah, Aijalon, and Hebron in Judah and in Benjamin. He made them into fortified towns. He strengthened them and put commanders in them, and stores of food, oil, and wine. He put shields and swords in each of them and made them very strong." Then Rehoboam had many sons and he placed them in his cities. "And he dealt wisely, and distributed some of his sons through all the districts of Judah and Benjamin, in all the fortified cities: and he gave them abundant provisions, and procured wives for them. When the rule of Rehoboam was established and he was strong, he forsook the law of the Lord, and all Israel with him" (II Chron. 11:5 to 12:1). This is the history of Rehoboam. And in him we find the same pattern as before, the natural life-pattern for most men, but extraordinary to find here.

Rehoboam, the king rejected by God. Rehoboam, who ensures the separation of the kingdom by his vanity, his youthful pride, his hardness, his spirit of power. Rehoboam, ready to reduce the people liberated by God to slavery, in order to serve his politics. Rehoboam, who, after God has taken away a good part of his people, tries to regain by his own means what God has removed. So he builds cities. He is missing ten tribes; he replaces them by twenty cities. But they were tribes of the chosen people: now he has only fortified cities, full of spears and swords. For God's promise he substitutes a shrewd military policy. Inordinate compensation for the decisions taken by God — inordinate because it is ridiculous. Rehoboam's powerful cities will be swept away in a day, after so much slavery and trouble, because he sought his own security. He breaks with God, and cities are built to compensate for the break. Men are broken apart from each other and dispersed, and cities are to take the place

of the break, as a sign of regrouping. Go into a city and you will
be united again. Crowd yourselves together behind your walls.
You will bear the same arms, taste the same dangers, undergo
the same famines, the same slavery. *Thus* will you be united
among yourselves. But the lost unity of spirit cannot be found in
dead stones. There is a schism within the sacred people, the
people who are chosen; and that is perhaps where the greatest
scandal of King Rehoboam is situated — in his desire to substitute the sign of power for divine election. And it is not gra-
tuitously that we speak of power, for the text itself says, "When
he had become powerful . . . ."

We will replace the chosen people by powerful cities. They
are to be accepted as equivalent. That they were in fact considered equivalent may be seen in the story of the priests and
Levites who sought refuge with Rehoboam, with the faithful,
"and who strengthened the kingdom of Judah and made the
throne of Rehoboam sure." The first use of the church for the
greatness of the state? Thus the city plays the same role among
the chosen as among the other peoples. She has the same symbolic quality and spiritual energy. Yet, within Yahweh's chosen
people she takes on a greater and more significant meaning. Her
specific bearing on the church will be seen again under Asa and
Jehoshaphat. But with Rehoboam, her full divisive character
stands out, as it did among men before the chosen people existed.

"Rehoboam put his sons in them . . . ." Here is another detail connecting the rejected king with the primitive builders. He,
too, proceeds to unite cities and sons. He, too, counts on the
double foundation of his human power and patiently builds up
what will be his downfall. For apparently he is faithful — as
long, that is, as his cities are open and his children small. He
takes in the priests and Levites whom Jeroboam had mistreated,
and apparently he worships the God of his fathers. He is every
bit the successor of David and Solomon — a successor with a
vengeance: "I will do as my father." This seems to be Rehoboam's
only purpose and his only capability. "He whipped you, I will
chastise you with scorpions. He built cities . . . . I will build
even more."

Throughout the history of the church, such a mixture has
been repeated: between faith and tradition, the tradition of the
Fathers and the tradition of the fathers — introducing into the
church itself all the forms of security offered by human wisdom
against the insecurity of faith.

Thus Rehoboam refused to continue in the insecurity of
his reduced kingdom — two tribes at the mercy of every invader.

He would not entrust them to the only grace which could strengthen them, because he was following in the footsteps of his father. But the full significance of his action will be seen only when Rehoboam considers himself strong enough. Then there is no need even of an apparent respect for God, a God without whom he can readily get along, now that he has twenty cities and twenty-eight sons! Once he has power, there is no reason to keep the mask; realistic politics is resurrected in all its glory. And so he makes a conscious connection between city and power.

Rehoboam built cities in order to become powerful, and once he was powerful, he rejected the Lord. This is not simply a pious story. Nor is it a simple psychological reality. It is something much farther reaching: the other result of his rejection is a deep reliance on temporal considerations. Rehoboam's foundations are no longer sunk in that soil where God placed his chosen people. Rather, he has placed his foundations on material realities. And such is the meaning of the city: she sinks her foundations into material considerations or, more exactly, into temporal considerations. This does not mean that she is materialistic — we have seen the opposite — nor that she excludes intellectual and spiritual life from her gates, but that all of this takes its force and its meaning from an exclusively temporal basis. There is opposition between the Lord and the city. By her own nature the city breaks with the divine nature of creation.

But having chosen the game, its rules must be observed. Having desired temporal status, its rules must be accepted. The best man wins. Rehoboam has to learn this the hard way: his first undertaking turns into a catastrophe. Shishak, king of Egypt, came up against Rehoboam and "took his fortress cities." The Egyptian king began his work right where Rehoboam's pride and glory were concentrated, with what caused him to leave God. The stakes of the game were his cities, and that is where Rehoboam had to recognize that he was not made to live only for temporal considerations. That he lost the battle because he had disobeyed God, as the Chronicles state, is certainly true; he lost playing the game of this world's princes, because he, as king of the world of grace, was precisely the one incapable of playing such a game.

Shishak is not content with a first demonstration of power: he goes up to Jerusalem, takes it, and spoils the Temple. The story is significant, and provides an element we must remember in the curve of the history of cities for the people of Israel. The place of the construction of cities in the curve is as follows: the construction of the Temple, the construction of cities by Solomon, Solomon's rejection, the schism, the construction of cities by Rehoboam, the looting of the Temple. An extraordinary progression of antitheses between the city and the Temple. Relying on the temporal leads to looting the Temple — a normal progression that has often been followed.

However, not all kingly builders were rebellious kings flouting God. Both Asa and Jehoshaphat were builders, and they were among the best kings Israel had. Asa, in fact, announced his decision to construct cities with a pious speech full of good intentions: "And he said to Judah, 'Let us build cities, and surround them with walls and towers, gates and bars; the land is still ours, because we have sought the Lord our God, we have sought him, and he has given us peace on every side.' So they built and prospered" (II Chron. 14:7). Jehoshaphat followed in his father's footsteps. He also was conscious of his belonging first to God and of the necessity of subordinating his means of power, his cities, to God.

But if pious kings who have never been rejected can take up this art, until now reserved for the rebel who turns from God to count on himself, is this not saying that a single inner disposition is enough to change everything? Is this not saying, as a widely accepted and reassuring theory has it, that nothing is bad in itself, that all depends on the use one makes of things? Had Cain been a saint, he could have built a city with impunity. The Scriptures here prefigure the "Everything is pure to those who are pure" principle that Jesus taught. Even the things of Satan can be done by those who have been purified by God's grace. Could one not argue that this is exactly what Asa is expressing when he says: "We can build cities now because we began by searching out God, by loving him, by obeying him, and God accepted this by giving us rest"? Rest, the sign of peace with God and of his grace granted to man. So because they were chosen of God, these kings could build cities. The cities lose their power because God has taken from them their spiritual armor. But it is no less true, the argument continues, that although the city has become neutral for the recipient of God's grace, she is objectively what she always was. This means that the city herself does not become good or an instrument of goodness, salvation, and perfection. Rather, she is deprived of her ability to attack and ruin the one who puts all his confidence in God. For such a man, the constant significance of her spiritual power is robbed of its sting. But for all others she is still the same power, the same instrument of the world. The nature of the city has not changed, for the nature of the world does not change.

Such is the great illusion of many well-intentioned people, who think they can succeed where Jesus failed and who think the world is getting better: "The best ideas are accepted, they find their way into government circles. Everyone wants justice. Everyone is for the individual. Everyone comes to man's defense. Everyone is religious. Christian virtues are honored, especially by the state. And so the world is converted." How innocent such people are! Judgement has been rendered once and for all: "The Light came into the world, and the world did not receive it." There is no use trying again. And if you see the powers of the world so well disposed, when you see the state, money, cities accepting your word, it is because your word, whether you are only a man of good will or an evangelist, has become false. For it is only to the extent that you are a traitor that the world can put up with you.

The illusion of improving the world is due to a confusion between "Everything is pure to those who are pure" and "The pure will make the world pure." The use of money by a Christian does not pervert the man, but he does not make money into a means of sanctification! So it is with the city. Moreover, we went too far when we said that the city had totally lost her sting for pious kings. For despite the holiness of Asa and Jehoshaphat, she had preserved her power, at least her power to tempt. The cities remained the symbol of the spirit of power, and although at first Asa was able to perfectly submit all his actions and victories to his faith, although he was not trying to satisfy himself, although he accepted complete dependence on God, nevertheless, little by little, the attractiveness of power asserted itself in him. He allied himself with foreign powers, with the king of Syria. And a whole string of coincidences formed around this alliance: at the same time he was fighting with Israel, he contracted an alliance with the foreign king, and he built new cities (Geba and Mizpah). So we still find the influence of the city in Asa's betrayal. For there is no doubt that he betrayed the Lord, as the accusations of the prophet Hanani show: "Because you relied on the king of Syria, and did not rely on the Lord your God . . . ." The same pattern, repeated again and again — the construction of new cities, schism, power and betrayal. So even for King Asa, the city was able to introduce its temptation into the very heart of his piety. His situation is of course very different from Rehoboam's: instead of building cities in order to become powerful and abandon Yahweh, Asa builds cities to be of use to the people of God. But even this is dangerous, an opportunity more dangerous than any other for him to be separated from the Lord, and without trying to establish a cause-to-effect relationship, we can still see that this is in fact what happened. And an accidental fault became a permanent condition, for he began to persecute the prophet and oppress the people. And "even when ill, he did not seek the Lord, but sought help from physicians." So he relied on temporal considerations to his very death.

IV. LET US BUILD

When the history of these kings of Israel is examined, a curious thing stands out. Of all the historical books, only the Chronicles give an account of the construction of cities. The books of Samuel and Kings are almost silent on this matter. This fact furnishes us with new information. First, the books of Chronicles are more recent. Written between 400 and 200 B.C., they are far from their original sources. This does away with the argument, traditional for the last half century, which explains the condemnation of the cities by reference to the prophets: Basing their opinions on pious tradition, it is said, "The prophets consider that the desert period, that of the nomadic life, was the time of Israel's holiness. For that reason they are enemies of the city because it symbolizes the betrayal of the nomadic life and therefore of holiness." But this explanation is astonishingly simplistic. Not in the least did the prophets condemn the cities because of their vision of an ideal past. They saw with their own eyes what the new world was, the corruption of man in the city, and their condemnation of it was based on a revelation of God's will for man. And starting from there, they were able to give a tableau of the ideal past, which is a normal procedure for a religion in which God expresses himself in history: God spoke in Abraham's time and in Moses'. But they did not all connect this past with the nomadic life! Elisha upheld the peasantry in their struggle against the city, but never the nomads. And Isaiah and Jeremiah champion neither the nomads nor the peasants, and they are the very prophets who condemn the metropolitan centers. It is much too simple to believe in a unanimous "pro-nomad" attitude among the prophets, to credit them with social or political motives in their attacks on cities. The motives common to all of them are completely other, and the nomadic ideal played only a secondary and supporting role in their prophecies. This interpretation is obviously confirmed by the Chronicles, which took up the prophets' condemnations several centuries later. The Chronicler never speaks of the desert. His point of view is entirely different. He is too far from the nomadic period to miss it and desire to go back to it. He is writing in a period when the predominance of urban civilization is no longer in doubt, when it is brillant and has spread to the entire surrounding world. Nevertheless, his attitude toward cities is the same as that of the prophets, but less explicit, less explosive, less grandiose.

There can, however, be no doubt that the Chronicles consider the city as one of the predominant forms of man's opposition to God. That is already obvious from what we have written, but even more so from the overall orientation of the book. Its stylized schema is well known: a strict separation between the good acts and the bad acts of the kings of Judah, as an explanation of their success or failure, and a rigorous conception of the life according to God's will, a life which has its immediate rewards. In this stylization, all details considered useless are left out. Nothing is brought in that is not useful for the point under demonstration. So we must believe that the construction of cities, constantly brought into the Chronicler's narrative, is of no secondary importance. And since this fact is connected directly with betrayal and punishment, there can be no doubt that in the writer's thoughts, the construction of cities is in itself an expression of separation from God. And if the Chronicler emphasizes this relationship more than the other historians do, this is because his conception of good and evil is somewhat social or political — exterior as it were. More than any other writer, he considers Israel's political actions to be the act of a church. Sin for him is not so much a personal, individual act, as an act of the whole people, with the king as its synthesis. Sin is a social act of the king. Alternatively, so is holiness. Thus, what he explicitly represents as the principal element of justice is the cult practiced in Jerusalem, in the Temple; he represents, that is, a rather exterior act, but an act whose roots and principal demonstrations are in the social life. He puts very little emphasis on the moral or purely spiritual qualities of the cult. And his conception of sin is exactly the same. Sin is for the Chronicler principally a political act of disobedience to God — worship on the high places, covenants with foreign peoples, marriage with foreign women, and similar acts.

With this in mind, we can understand why the Chronicles differ from the other books in emphasizing that certain kings were builders. For one of the chief concerns of the writer is to recount social and political actions in terms of his judgement on their author, and with the explanation in mind that he is proposing for their author's destiny. But in the last analysis, the inclusion of cities in the cycle of good and evil, and precisely in the history of Israel, brings up the question of the meaning of the city for the chosen people. For this is the people who conquered Canaan under God's guidance, who took cities and inhabited them; it is difficult to condemn them, for this is only the fulfillment of a promise in Deuteronomy. As they became a true state, they fortified more and more cities; and in so doing, they were acting with political wisdom, according to normal politics and apparently not in disobedience to God. And if it is absolutely necessary, considering what we have seen in Genesis, to see in this act the symbol of revolt, what is particular about it? What particular note does the construction of a city add to the story of Israel's disobedience? Was all that the prophets had to say about idolatry not enough to characterize the revolt of the people of God? Is this not a useless effort to establish the significance of one human act among others, since the worship of idols in fact includes them all?

I am rather inclined to believe that we have here details with a specific purpose. For in most of Israel's sins, we see the result of a clear choice between right and wrong; there are no humanly valid reasons for Israel to choose evil. There is no decisive reason, for example, for Israel to choose the Baal cult to Yahweh's. Rather, the opposite is true as the prophets constantly remind us: reason would lead them to prefer Yahweh since he has already shown his power and his love for his people. So if the people leave God, it is an aberration which can be condemned by reason and by experience. This aberration brings before our eyes the corruption of the human heart in its purest state, we might say. For it shows that man, even when he has every reason to worship God, still prefers not to recognize him. And this is already for us an indication that as long as the human heart has not been transformed by the Holy Spirit, it is impossible for him to be convinced of God's excellence, either by experience or by reason. Man acts reasonably in every area but one: that of his relations with God, where he acts contrary to all reason and knowledge because the roots of his heart are bad.

But for Israel the symbolic meaning of the city is totally different. There we no longer have a gratuitous act, but a reasonable one. And reason seems to be on the side of those who build cities. Surely this is no choice between God and Baal, but simply an act of wise administration. It is right and proper, is it not, when one is chief of state, to build fortresses? It is right and proper to cover the principal access routes into the country and to keep watch over them. It is right and proper to establish commercial centers at the main crossroads and to put storehouses there, just as it is proper to have an army and equipment for war. And so we are face to face with an undeniable necessity. And when the prophets teach the contrary, they must be teaching madness, something which there is every reason to refuse, for it cannot be disobedience to God when history shows it necessary. Thus the people of Israel must face the undeniable proofs of the world. Apparently there is no choice. The stream of political, military, and social necessity is so overpowering that superhuman strength is required to struggle against it. No asceticism or exercise of human power can overcome it — only the holiness that comes from God. And although the power is given to overcome it, there is no way of escaping it. God's people cannot withdraw into heaven, there to carry out a divine policy and refuse all the world has to offer.

Here they are at war not only with their own heart, but with their human life, inseparable from military and commercial considerations. And it is this necessity that is expressed in the problem of the city for Israel. It is expressed more sharply than any other problem facing the nation, because there is no way out. If Israel wants to continue life as a people (and God himself requires it of them, because of the promise), they must go along with certain conditions of the life of a people. They cannot, according to human judgement, live always and exclusively by depending on grace. Now these conditions depend on the Prince of this world, and it is with him that Israel must deal. The spiritual power of the city must therefore clash with the spirit of grace. Such is the central problem that the city represents for Israel. Such is the problem for every man who wants to live by the grace of Christ. And what seems both tragic and disconcerting is that there seems to be no theoretical solution to satisfy this problem. There is no theological demonstration for one to follow. The answer comes with life, day by day, in the conflict between the world's necessity and the liberty given us of God, between the world's wisdom (which we can never totally set aside) and the folly of the cross (which we can never totally live out).

* * *

The greatness of the scriptural doctrine of the city seems completely out of proportion with what the city really was in the tenth century B.C. One may conjure up all the explanations he wants, the fact will still be astonishing. There had doubtlessly been, and still were, civilizations surrounding Israel which were

almost exclusively urban. The Chaldeans and the Assyrians were
essentially peoples of the city. It is also doubtlessly true that
Israel judged the cities, with their grandeur and splendor, by the
legends which had course among the nomads, and we must also
keep in mind what even the smallest city could mean for a people
of shepherds and wanderers. All of this must have contributed
to a mythical conception of the city, surrounding it with an aura
of sacredness. It is also true that Israel was rapidly "urbanized":
by Saul's time there were about 400 cities in Israel and they
clearly dominated the country. Nonetheless, all of this is de-
cidedly insufficient to explain the biblical teaching. There is such
profound understanding of urban reality that it appears to be
taken from an observation of our modern cities. The consciousness is there of the city as a world for which man was not made.
How to explain it? The Canaanite cities with which the Israelites
were first in contact were only the necessary wall made with great
blocks of stone roughly shaped and assembled, with wooden
towers and a few meager houses. A sparse population lived in
primitive houses. But this does not complete the description of
the city. The Canaanite city is but an extension of rural life with
its qualities and mentality, and is economically dependent on it.
The Israelite town is no different with its few thousand inhabitants at the very most. It is not a closed society, withdrawn in itself, independent, autonomous, giving birth to its own sociology
and psychology, radically different from the rest of the country.
But what is astonishing is that the Scriptures speak of the city in
exactly those terms, whose complete reality we only know today.
In that sense the biblical doctrine is truly prophetic. Working
with what was not yet the monster-city, the Holy Spirit brought
to man's knowledge the reality of what he was undertaking, which
was only to become a reality centuries and centuries later. The
Holy Spirit showed man the depth of his work and God's judgements on it. He did it from the very beginning, in spite of man's
inability to understand it then. For it is obvious that the man
writing the first few chapters of Genesis could not have understood the reality of what he was then recording. And there is no
reason to be surprised that until now virtually no one has paid
much attention to the existence of the city in the light of God's
revelation concerning it. Man's situation has been such that the
prophecy could not yet be a reality. For it to become reality, it
was necessary — besides the action of the Holy Spirit illuminating
the text — that man come face to face with the monster, although the monster's full form is visible only when prophecy
shows it up. This meeting of man with history was necessary for

the prophecy to be seen in its full light — in Jesus Christ and nowhere else, as we shall see. The truth was no less present beforehand, but it was yet hidden.

Chapter Two

THUNDER OVER THE CITY

THE CITY HAS BEEN BUILT. AND NOW IN THE ENORMOUS, unswerving resentment that the city constantly manifests against God in every human civilization, one part of the great struggle between sin and grace, between God, the city, and man, is about to be enacted. Each participant has his own attitude. The city dweller becomes someone else because of the city. And the city can become something else because of God's presence and the results in the life of a man who has met God. And so a complex cacophony raises its blaring voice, and only God can see and make harmony of it.

I. THE CURSE

The city arraigned before God. The immediate result is a curse, a curse on the city itself rather than on its inhabitants. The notion of the city as an entity in itself may seem completely nonsensical, but perhaps we should not draw this conclusion too quickly. Even our most realistic politicians, after all, admit without hesitation that the *state* has a life autonomous and independent of the life both of the men and the organizations making it up. The state, in which the pretensions of fascism were praised and to which we all accord the honor of our attention, has all the appearances of a being in its own right. And if we go to the other extreme of the political scale, it is no longer the state, but the collective whole which has a spiritual quality whose virtues must be venerated and which is completely different from the mediocrity of the elements making it up. In communist thought the collective whole is much more than just the union of a certain number of men. It is not formed just by addition — the coming together of individuals makes up a mystical body. What shows up most clearly the mythological character of the collectivity is the problem of property. Give property to each member of the collectivity and the abomination of capitalistic private property will reign. But gather these properties into one, belonging to the same people grouped together, and the marvel of collective property will reign. And the latter system is not preferred because of some economic or technical superiority, but only because of the mystical regard for collectivity. Finally, lawmakers themselves are disposed to mysticism, for they recognize that a business corporation, a labor union, or an inheritance are individual beings — reasoning beings, morally responsible beings who appear for the simple reason that men have formed a union around things. This simple uniting with a common goal is enough to give birth to new legal rights independent of the individuals being united.

And so God speaks not to the inhabitants of the city, but to the city itself. He speaks as to an adult, who knows what he is doing. Or rather, God speaks sometimes to the city, and other times to its inhabitants, but with different words for each. When speaking to men, God calls them to him either by promises or by threats; but in any case, he is waiting for them to come to him, one by one, and his presence is for them a sanctifying presence, even when he condemns. But when speaking to the city as a specific being, God has words only of condemnation — and of condemnation leading not to conversion, but to death. The city is cursed. She is condemned to death because of everything she represents. And she pulls her inhabitants down with her (this is what makes their relationship so complex). Her angel is the angel of the abyss or rather the perverted angel of light. It is remarkable that both times the Scriptures speak of this fallen angel, they refer to him as the angel of a city. "How are you fallen from heaven, O Day Star, Son of Dawn! How are you cut down to the ground, you who laid the nations low. You said in your heart, 'I will ascend to heaven. Above the stars of God I will set my throne on high! . . . I will make myself like the Most High.' But you are brought down to Sheol!" (Isa. 14:12-15). Here the reference is to the angel of Babylon, and so to the destruction of the city itself. "I will cut off name and remnant," says the Lord. "Son of man, say to the prince of Tyre, 'Thus says the Lord God: Because your heart is proud, and you have said, "I am a God, I sit in the seat of God in the heart of the

walls," yet you are but a man, and not God, though you consider yourself as wise as a god. You are indeed wiser than
Daniel, no secret is hidden from you; by your wisdom and understanding you have gotten wealth for yourself . . . and your heart
has become proud in your wealth . . . therefore thus says the
Lord God: Because you consider yourself as wise as God, behold, I will bring strangers upon you, the most terrible of the
nations. They shall draw their sword against the beauty of your
wisdom and defile your splendor. . . . In the presence of those
who slay you, will you say, "I am God"? You will be but a
man and not God in the hands of those who kill you' " (Ezek.
28:1-9). Traditional exegesis has seen in this prince a spiritual
power, the very angel of Tyre. We can easily see, in fact, that
the condemnation is pronounced against the spiritual representative of the city. For it is not the inhabitants, but this particular
being who bears the penalty for his own sins: "For three crimes,
even for four, I will condemn Damascus to destruction. For
three transgressions of Gaza, and for four, I will not revoke the
punishment. For three transgressions of Tyre, even for four. . . ."
And this condemnation of the city, its punishment, always consists of sending a fire (the sign of the curse) into the heart of
the city, to the center of its power, destroying by the curse that
for which the city was built (Amos 1). Every city must suffer
the effects of the curse; it is always considered a good and holy
work for Israel to utterly destroy a city (Num. 21:2), for this
is an act of God. Never a word of hope, never a word of forgiveness for the city as such, for it is the terrible manifestation
of the Day Star which deceived men. And it is because the
Almighty Lord, the prince of the heavenly hosts, is destroying
the powers of him who was placed on the mountain of God
and covered with every kind of precious stone, it is because
Yahweh is throwing him down from that mountain and condemning him to the fire of destruction (Ezek. 28), that the
cities he has created, produced, multiplied, are in turn broken.
They were the instruments of a domination which their builders
sought out and served with groping hands and blind eyes. Thus
the life of the city is dominated by a curse — not only because
of its human origins, which we have pointed out, but because
of its spiritual presence, because of its relationship with the
"protecting cherub with outstretched wings" (Ezek. 28:14).

    And this gives us a new and enriched understanding of the
city. Dealing with the "urban problem" are sociologists and
lawmakers, urban specialists and politicians, architects and
economists, humanists and revolutionaries, and they are all

looking for a moral solution, a legal solution to the multitude of inhuman problems brought up by the city. Clearly, solutions are called for. What we need is a law to tell us what to do and how to do it. And while the search is going on, the vampire does its work and calls for more fresh blood. And new throngs of men take up residence under the rule of the curse. They work, they live the city's unchanging, inhuman life, now irretrievably their life, with no way out but the cemetery. Men innocent with all the world's unconsciousness, who are under the effects of the curse, who feel it and suffer, but who go on, because "what good would it do to try anything else, it's the same everywhere you go." Others try to find solutions — far from those who are suffering — and their solutions are impossible for the sufferers. And the bright star, the Wormwood star, continues his work, imperturbably getting just as much use out of the urbanists' wide avenues, children's parks, paid vacations, workers' apartments, public transportation, and disposal systems as out of slums and tuberculosis.

And the Christian, like everyone else, is looking for a solution in laws. What should the Christian position be regarding these problems (which we call "the problems of modern life," instead of giving them their permanent name)? Arrange things somehow, make city life possible; moralize the city, its leisure time, its work, its dreams. This is how Christians plan. What to do? God has revealed to us very clearly that there is absolutely nothing to be done. God has given us no commands with regard to the city. He affords us no law. For the city is not an inner problem for man. God can say to us, "You shall not commit adultery," but he has never said, "You shall not live in the city." For on the one hand we have a personal attitude with a man, which he can modify according to his readiness to obey God's commandments. And on the other, the city is a phenomenon absolutely removed from man's power, a phenomenon which he is fundamentally incapable of affecting. For man is not responsible for making the city something other than it is, as we have already seen. There is nothing to be done. And the problem does not change. It is still what it was when, forty or fifty centuries ago, they built up those thick walls of clay whose foundations still subsist. For God has cursed, has condemned, the city instead of giving us a law for it.

The curse is not for one city only. How convenient it would be to evade the problem by saying, "That was the opinion of the prophets cursing Judah's enemies," or "it is only by accident that the king of a city was identified with the prince of this world." But such an attitude can never be anything but a dishonorable defeat, an excuse for not becoming involved in the debate in which each of us must take part, whether we like it or not. For there can be no doubt, every city has been cursed. The prophets — and they are not alone — scan the entire horizon and attack every city with unbelievable perseverance and single-ness of purpose. The texts are numerous, and whether the city is friend or foe, the judgement is the same. If there is a formal unity in the prophecies it is here! But the judgement is from God. Which means that it is an affair between God and the city. Which means that it is a unique act of God, although it is ever repeated, and that it is on this act that the prophecy is founded, and not on any set of morals. Our first task is to listen and not to act. While we victoriously flourish our solutions for the city's problems, the march of history empties them of meaning with tragic ease. All this is because we have substituted meddlesome virtues for the prophecy we must ever hear anew against those dear cities where our lives have run their course. And it is against our sins and our very selves — and to be taken in no other way. In order to understand the history of the city and the situation as it now exists, we must take into account not only its beginning as a human enterprise, but also the curse placed on it from its creation, a curse which must be seen as a part of its make-up, influencing its sociology and the habitat it can provide. This curse is not only that placed on the entire world, but is a special curse on the city, both as belonging to the world and in itself. It is the curse expressed from one end of the Scriptures to the other by, "I will destroy, says the Lord."

*   *   *

This curse with its different modes and causes is stated more precisely as regards one city: Babylon. And so we must state the problem as it concerns Babylon, for she, as we have already seen, is the figure of all other cities; she is The City in the Bible. The author of Revelation has not resorted to a camouflage to get the Roman police off the track when he speaks of Rome as Babylon. His only goal is to make manifest the continuity of revelation. What was said by Isaiah, Ezekiel, and Jeremiah about Babylon was not for that unique city only. The same words are said of Rome, which took Babylon's place. And so revelation goes on, Babylon always the center, because of the exhaustive quality which we have recognized as hers. And when Revelation takes a city as the symbol of the human power to be destroyed, that also is not due to any accident. It is not because the historical circumstances made Rome the center of the Empire, but rather because in her all of human civilization is symbolized and summed up. She is the sum of man's spiritual effort, she represents not only the city but the condemned power behind the city. And the triple conjunction of events that we have already mentioned is expressly outlined in the first passage of Revelation dealing with Babylon (Rev. 14:6-12). Three angels are speaking. One announces God's glory and the nearness of the judgement. The second announces the curse on Babylon, which is already fallen and destroyed — Babylon the great city, which made all nations drink of the wine of the wrath of her fornication (the city as a corrupting power in the midst of the nations). The third announces the judgement of God on men, placing before them the choice to be made between the beast and the Lord, and the possibility of being saved: "I heard a voice from heaven saying, 'Write this: Blessed are the dead who die in the Lord henceforth.'"

We have yet to see whether Babylon is condemned because she is a city. But at least the coincidence is striking. In her are concentrated all of man's condemned activities. In her also are all cities condemned.

After the seventh angel poured out his bowl, there was an earthquake "such as had never been since men were on the earth. . . . And the great city was split into three parts, and *all the cities* of the nations fell, and God remembered great Babylon, to make her drain the cup of the fury of his great wrath . . ." (Rev. 16:18-19). Babylon the great city, and all the cities, are wiped out. And for anyone who may doubt the purposely symbolic and representative nature of Babylon, it should be sufficient to recall another passage in Revelation, which refers to "the great city which is spiritually [RSV: allegorically] called Sodom and Egypt, where their Lord was crucified" (Rev. 11:8). This verse shows clearly that the name "Babylon" must be understood spiritually, that the great city includes Sodom, which we have yet to study, and Egypt, whose role we have already tried to grasp.

It is true that the great city mentioned here is not explicitly Babylon. It is clearly Jerusalem, since it is identified by the crucifixion of Jesus Christ. But in fact it is not all so simple. We must first take into account the fact that whenever the great city or the haughty city is mentioned in the Old or New Testaments, the reference is to Babylon. Next, we are not here dealing with a geographical place, but a spiritual location, and in this

spiritual sense we must understand it as Babylon — and Jerusalem becomes Babylon precisely because that is where Jesus
was crucified. And, finally, we must remember how often, throughout the Scriptures, Babylon and Jerusalem are connected, as
inseparable as the two sides of a hill, as two forms of a single
reality.

So all that is said about Babylon can be applied to every
other city, to today's cities even more than to any cities known
by the seer. It is said for the great city, whatever its particular
name may be. The city is at the hub of a state (And once
again it is not just through poetical inspiration or for reasons
of narrative that Babylon is represented as a queen with spiritual
powers in both Daniel and Revelation: neither is it by accident
that she is closely associated with the beast coming up from the
sea, which is to be understood as the state), and is condemned
along with the state, but nevertheless on her own — not as a
simple agent or part, but as an autonomous, specific power having
her own destiny as thrones, dominations and principalities are
thrown down. In the clear vision of the Lord's Spirit, the truth
about Rome is the truth about Moscow, about Berlin, about
Paris, and about Washington. How astonishingly, ridiculously,
incomprehensibly important is the capital. Paris falls into Hitler's
hands and the war is finished. Moscow must be defended to the
very limits of the country's forces, otherwise resistance is at an
end — everyone knows that the retreat behind the Caucasus is
but an empty boast. As though all the vigor of the state were
concentrated in the "great city." Although the nation is still
partially intact, when the great city has fallen further resistance
is out of the question! Of course there is the matter of prestige,
and the necessities of organization, and the concentration of
resources. But perhaps this is not the complete explanation:
when the Bible presents the great city as a synthesis of the state's
power, it is perhaps for reasons entirely different from these
natural considerations. However that may be, it is enough for us
to realize that the fall of an empire is in fact stated in terms of
the city, the great city, perpetual Babylon.

*   *   *

It is truly because of everything she represents that this
curse has been pronounced against Babylon. The life of a powerful city is but a constant succession of revolts against God. Her
life is the normal result of her origin and development. In Isaiah
we see her constantly immersed in war, blindly following the

way of blood and oppression, obedient to a sort of fatality originating in her birth, which, as we have seen, was also connected with war. And when she falls, the nations can breathe at last: "Since you were laid low, no hewer comes up against us." The city and her prince were constantly making of the world a desert, causing kingdoms to totter, plundering the nations, leading prisoners into perpetual captivity (Isa. 14).

We could find many causes of war — ontological, economic, technical — but the Scriptures affirm that the agent of war is the great city. There is no such thing as a great agricultural war. A rural people is never a ravenous people. They may make migrations, but not wars. War is an urban phenomenon, as the city is a military phenomenon. Perfecting one leads to perfecting the other. And this view is upheld by the world in which we are living. Tomorrow's city will be underground because of the necessities of war. It will be even more characteristic than today, and its destiny will be even more tightly linked with violence.

But this is not the only relationship. Revelation transfers to Babylon what Isaiah says of Tyre: the great city is inseparably connected with money. "All the merchants of the earth were made rich by the greatness of her wealth." And when the city falls, "All the merchants of the earth weep and mourn for her because no one buys their cargo any more, cargo of gold, silver, jewels and precious stones, fine linen, purple, silk and scarlet, all kinds of scented wood . . . and bodies and souls of men. The merchants of these wares, who gained wealth from her, will stand far off, in fear of her torment . . . " (Rev. 18:11-15). These are almost the same terms used by the prophets for other cities. This should not astonish us. There is not even any reason to emphasize the absolute unity between the city and riches, commerce, the amassing of wealth and the development of profit. This is just one more facet of urban civilization and is characteristic solely of it. As soon as commerce develops, a great city is made necessary. At the height of the Middle Ages, the cathedral cities became open cities, and the ports of origin of the first European ships became trade centers, as well as the first cities to colonize and the points of departure for military conquest. We must not jump over the city during these historical developments and pass without any transition from the economic beginning to the full-blown political or military establishment. The relation between the two periods is not direct; it can only come about through the intermediary of the social and spiritual link provided by the presence of a city. And not only do we find the city at the crossroads of the political and economic ways, but a nation's moral attitudes are formed there also. She is literally the social repository of sin: Sodom is only one example; the great city is an exhaustive summary. She holds a golden cup full of the abominations and lewdness of her prostitutions. She makes all to drink of the wine of the wrath of her fornication (Rev. 17 and 18). This means that she excites sin to a passion, that she lives her sin not as a sinful man, overcome by sin, feeling his misery and weakness and wanting to be released, but as a power able to live only in her fornication, voluntarily dashing headlong toward her truest environment, pushing sin to its limit in the pride of her power and freedom. She causes men to take part in her corrupt communion of blood. There can be no doubt that the wine which she makes men drink is for John on Patmos the negative counterpart of the cup of communion in Jesus Christ's blood. And it is precisely because John can see in her actions a spiritual communication comparable to that of the communion that he calls her "the mother of harlots" (Rev. 17:5). Not because all sinners are united in her, nor because the inhabitants of the great city are especially sinful, but because, to those who accept her law, she communicates her power of sin and wrath. Thus at the crossroads of three definite areas, the city constitutes the same being, represents the same force. She is the second creation and wants autonomy. In all her activities she affirms that her strength is all-sufficient: "A queen I sit, I am no widow, mourning I shall never see" (Rev. 18:7). So she vaunts her power, even against death. She needs no one. Her base of power is no mere human being. She is her own reason for existing, in herself a sufficient power, a sufficient law. It must be very clear that in his act of building, man gave birth to something stronger than himself. And it is neither the founder nor the inhabitants of the city who say so, but rather the city herself, in her personality independent both of men and of God. She says, "Forever will I be sovereign." She sits in confidence, and says in her heart, "I am, and no one else! Never will I be a widow, and never deprived of children." She can say in her freedom, "No one can see me." Here we touch the heart of her reality. She withdraws within herself, and spiritually becomes a closed and isolated world, as materially she is shut in by her walls. She has no knowledge of the outside world. She wants nothing to do with spiritual opening. She excludes God because she is for herself her own sufficient spirituality. There can be no agreement between God and her absolute world, shut up in death. "I am, and no one else!" This is not the proud statement of a man. This is the assertion of spiritual power, the affirmation of man's work which has gotten out of his hands and has claimed her own particular life.

How ridiculous is man's vanity, strutting around, declaring that these things have no power, no life of their own. "Everything comes down to the use you make of it. Keep cool. It's not so bad. Whenever I want to," man says, thrusting out his chest, "I'll put everything back in order. I just need to expand my mind some more, I just need to get a grasp of the technical problems involved and everything will go back to normal." The childish words of the king of Babylon. In spite of the word of God sent to him, and because of this very Babylon and all that she represents, he can say only one thing: "Is not this great Babylon, which I have built by my mighty power as a royal residence and for the glory of my majesty?" (Dan. 4:30). No, king of Babylon, this city is no longer yours. She has been taken away from you. And because you want to find her again, to marry her, make her sins yours, and use them as your weapons in her march against God, you will become like the beasts, you will eat grass like the cattle of the field. "His body was wet with the dew of heaven until his hair grew as long as eagles' feathers, and his nails were like birds' claws." A marvellous story (given for another purpose, we must add) which incidentally provides an insight into how resolved man's pretensions are with regard to the great city. "God cannot come in here." The "Gate of the Gods" is in reality Babylon's border. And that is why their relationship can only be based on a curse. God can enter only by breaching the wall. God's voice rings out seven times against these ramparts and, at Jericho, the walls crumble. In Babylon, the spiritual walls tumble down.

Into every aspect, therefore, of the city's construction has been built the tendency to exclude God. This explains one rather astonishing series of statements which we must emphasize. The constant message of Revelation shows us the perverting influence of the city not only on its inhabitants. The kings and merchants of the earth also become perverted in contact with her: "With her have the kings of the earth committed fornication" (Rev. 17:2). It all happens as though the political and economic powers of the earth were seduced and perverted by the great city. Kings, though they seem no worse than anyone else, are enticed by her into sin, just as the merchants, whose business in itself is not condemned, are lured by her into a perversion of their very function on earth. Under her influence, their business is limited to luxury items, to those things not necessary for man's life but for the seductive power of the great city, so that she might triumph over men by her great beauty. And it is because of their relationship with her that the merchants have run the risk of punishment, and they flee the city so as not to be included in her death sentence. Such valid human activities as political involvement and business become works of death and sin when they are shut into a world which has excluded God in order to glorify, to force, to seduce men. This is no reason to believe that perversion reigns only in the city, that outside her gates business, government, and money are sanctified! But in her we can certainly see the major perversion. Besides, without the city, where would business and government be? In any case, the city has chosen her special role by specifically and voluntarily shutting herself off from any divine intervention. Stubbornly, obstinately, of her own will, she applies all her attention to herself. And her world without God is also a world of gods. If the desert is the place of demons, the city is the place of idols.

We have already noticed how close is the relationship between ancient cities and idols — gods made by men — because they bear the same names. It is precisely by this creation of idols that the city closes herself up to God. Now she has her own God — the gods she has manufactured, which she can hold in her hands, which she worships because she is master over them, because they are the surest weapon against any other spiritual intervention. And so Yahweh's intervention is to be characterized by his destruction of her idols: " . . . and all the images of her [Babylon's] gods he has shattered to the ground" (Isa. 21:9). Bel bows down, Nebo falls! (Isa. 46:1). The basic relationships between the city and her idols is that of magic, and this art of trying to become master over divine power is constantly pointed out to us as characteristic of the city, especially of Babylon. Of course magic is practiced in places other than the city, but she is chosen as typical of all the others, represented as the place where all sorcery is practiced (Isa. 47:9), the place of wizards and witches (Dan. 5).

And it is all intended to seduce men, to keep them from carrying out to the end the search implanted in their heart (Rev. 18:23). There man ceases his wandering and doubt, satisfied not to leave the city in his search for genuine meaning and fulfillment. There he finds a world which he thinks fits him, a closed world where all his needs and aspirations are apparently satisfied, a world where he can afford to rest, where he has found certainty. But all the city's seductions, all the satisfactions she offers, are in fact complete slavery for man, and slavery of the most ignominious sort. We can hardly overlook the meaning of the progression John is developing from the thing apparently most precious on down (Rev. 18): first gold and pearls, then rare tissues, then precious woods and perfumes, then oil and wine, down through items worth less and less, things for sale on every market, and finishing by what is most scorned, the bodies and souls of men.

The man who disappears into the city becomes merchandise. All the inhabitants of the city are destined sooner or later to become prostitutes and members of the proletariat. And thus man's triumph, this place where he alone is king, where he sets the mark of his absolute power, where there are no traces of God's work because man has set his hand to wiping it out bit by bit, where man thinks he has found all he needs, where his situation separated from Eden becomes tolerable — this place becomes in truth the very place where he is made slave. And a remarkable slavery it is since already we see him subject to the power of money and luxury. By his own work he dispossessed himself of what was left of himself; he became an alien — for the benefit of money and government, themselves diverted from their original usefulness. And the place where all these metamorphoses take place — a place well worthy of magic enchantments — is the great city. Professional historians tell us this: "Cities have always been centers for man's progress, and for the concept of liberty." But clearly, in God's sight, cities belong to an entirely different realm.

*   *   *

The curse was rightly spoken. But, the sceptical mind asks, is it really the city that is referred to here? Does all this apply to her? Is Babylon really a city, or is she rather a much more inclusive symbol — the image of sin, the image of the world, the gathering place of evil powers and rebellious men? Surely what John said about Rome, and all the other references in Scripture, must not be taken literally: they are only allegories, hyperbole, rhetoric which must be understood in a very general sense without getting bogged down in details, and this general meaning is that the power oppressing God's chosen people and the church will be destroyed by God. Or on the other extreme, bringing our feet back to historical objectivity, have we not gotten much more out of these texts than they were meant to say? For in the minds of the ancient prophets, Babylon was an historical city. Thus by over-spiritualizing these texts or by despiritualizing them, we end up with the same results.

It is rather easy to deal with the second proposition. It is the classic historical attitude, which, though pretending only to accept reality, in fact hides the truth. Several times already we have given it a partial answer, by showing that the historical situation is also meta-historical, in that it possesses a complete meaning in itself. I should only add here that the biblical authors *always* connected the condemnations of the city with the last judgement, with the execution of God's judgements on the earth before the establishment of his kingdom. The condemnation of the city is typical in nature. May it suffice to point out — from among a multitude of other texts — the nineteenth verse of Isaiah 32, in which the city is mentioned without a proper name in the context of the establishment of God's kingdom: "The city will be brought very low." This reference to the eschatological nature of the city removes any element of reality from the "objective" viewpoint.

The other attitude is much more serious: is Babylon condemned *because* she is a city (the image of all the cities), or for an entirely different reason, spiritual in nature? It is clear, in any case, that the texts give us no authorization whatsoever to go so far as to affirm that Babylon is condemned for being a city. Neither do I believe that I have gone that far. It is quite true that God's condemnation is for the powers of rebellion and sin, the world in the sense of the prologue to the Gospel of John. But with this understanding, the whole problem of the city is still on our hands, and what we have said up to this point stands. Sin is being judged, but through the intermediary of the city. The world is being condemned, but it is symbolized by the city. The powers of hell are being destroyed, but with the city that symbolizes them. The city is taken as sign and symbol, the synthesis of all the rest. The city is chosen to represent all the other powers, and not a mountain (why not the mountain of sins?) or the sea.

Compare this symbolism with Dante's. In fact the symbolic city participates in the nature of the symbolized powers; it is not by accident that the city was chosen, but because of her essential relationship with what God condemns, because she is the symbolic house of the powers of hell, the nest of sin, the "mother of harlots." Once again we find the continuity of the Bible's teaching. As a builder, man put all his resentment and independence into the city; she was not only a material fact, but a spiritual symbol as well. And this is how God treats her in his judgement. We must also keep in mind that to man's synthesis of evil corre-

sponds the synthesis of God which heaps on her head the entirety
of his judgements, making of her a type. All that the city
wanted to assume as hers will be taken from her in the special
logic of God's judgement — incomprehensible to those who are
not his children.

For the city is condemned not only to destruction, but also
to seeing everything taken from her which made up her particular being: "The fruit for which your soul longed has gone
from you, and all your dainties and your splendor are lost to
you, never to be found again" (Rev. 18:14). Her sorcery is
without effect and her subjects of glory are taken away: "These
two things shall come to you in a moment, in one day: the loss
of children and widowhood. They shall come upon you in full
measure, in spite of your many sorceries and the great number
of your enchantments. You felt secure in your wickedness, you
said 'No one sees me.' Your wisdom and your knowledge led
you astray, and you said in your heart, 'I am, and there is no one
besides me.' But ruin shall come upon you, of which you know
nothing . . . . Stand fast in your enchantments. . . . Behold, they
are like a stubble-fire, they cannot save your life from the
flames . . . " (Isa. 47:9-14). And there is no remedy: "Take
balm for her pain, perhaps she may be healed. We would have
healed Babylon, but she was not healed!" (Jer. 51:8-9).

Here we find an extremely serious statement: the city cannot be reformed. Neither can she become other than what men
have made of her. Nor can she escape God's condemnation.
Thus in spite of all the efforts of men of good will, in spite
of all those who have tried to make the cities more human, they
are still formed of iron, steel, glass, and cement. The garden
city. The show city. The brilliant city. . . . They are all cities
of death, made of dead things, condemned to death, and
nothing can alter this fact. The mark of her builders and the
judgements of God weigh her ruthlessly down. And everything
she hoped in is condemned, her walls have crumbled to dust,
her money is scattered, her power is annihilated. She has become the house of the demons who haunt the desert. "The
jackals will howl in her palaces and the wild dogs in her
mansions."

Throughout the Scriptures we find the same judgement falling
on all who live in cities. It is executed not only on the city
herself, but also on all those who participate in her life. It is
not man's pride that makes the city, but the city as a symbol
of pride drags along in her fall all those who have materially
and spiritually united with her, who glory in her greatness and

who put their confidence in her riches. Men are condemned not
only for their particular sin, but also for having participated in
the evil power socially characterized by the city. After the decree
against the city, the summons against her inhabitants: "A sword
upon the Chaldeans, says the Lord, and upon the inhabitants of
Babylon, and upon her princes and wise men! ... A sword
upon her warriors, that they may be destroyed ... and upon all
the foreigners in her midst!" (Jer. 50:35-37). Then the prophet
declares the relationship that exists between the city and her
inhabitants as concerns her false gods: "For it is a land of
images. They are mad over idols" (v. 38). This connection is
a constantly reoccurring element in prophecies against the city.

The constant element in all this is God's response to the
builder's pretension of furnishing for man a permanent home,
for shutting himself up in his proud solitude, with his proud
self-protection. The city was built as protection for man. It
turns out that she is nothing other than his ruin: the word of
God pierces her ramparts and she takes all her inhabitants down
with her in her destruction, precisely because man hoped that
the city would shelter him from all destruction (Deut. 28:16).
Condemned herself, the city brings on man's destruction. He is
not directly condemned but is implicated in her crime by having
sought her protection.

Her condemnation proves to be so heavy, so general, that
all her inhabitants are taken in, even if they were not personally
subject to her power. Thus the people of Israel, during their
Babylonian exile, run the risk of going down with her: "Flee
from the midst of Babylon, let every man save his life, lest
he be cut off in her punishment, for this is the time of the Lord's
vengeance, the requital he is rendering her" (Jer. 51:6). An order
for isolation from the city. The proclamation of the judgement
is addressed either explicitly or implicitly to men, and by that
means God is seeking to provoke a break, material or spiritual,
between man and the city. And its final fulfillment will be the
ruin of the city, her loss of power and men, the supreme punishment for a city: she will no longer be inhabited. "She shall be
peopled no more forever, nor inhabited for all generations."
This sentence is the leitmotiv of every word pronounced against
the city. Against Sodom and Gomorrha, against Babylon, against
Tyre and Sidon. The echo of this break resounds from the walls
of the cities — there is no longer any reason for the city to
exist, for man has been freed from her confinement (Jer. 50:13;
Isa. 13:19).

But when the city is thus attacked in her relationship with

her inhabitants, the end has not yet come, the problem is not yet solved. Babylon is not only the sign of all other cities, but of the world as well. We have already used the term "symbol," but it would be better to say "sign," not to use an easier or more common word, but because this is the precise term to designate the reality of the biblical revelation concerning the city. A sign is an event by which spiritual and even eschatological realities become no longer abstract, but actual. They are presented figuratively, but concretely and effectively; that is, they have an effect. Thus God's judgement on Babylon and the history of his relationship with her are for all time the mirror of his relationship with all cities, because God took Babylon as a sign of all the cities. Whatever the sociological differences between cities, Babylon is eternally a figure of the others, since God made the decision. A symbol established by man can have no permanence, but the sign used by all the prophets has the very permanence of the Word of God.

The city is also a sign of the world's response to God: "The light shone in darkness, but the darkness did not receive it. . . . He came into the world, and the world was made through him, yet the world knew him not." This failure to recognize God's work is present in its purest form in the city, and that is why the city is chosen as a sign of the world's attitude. The judgement pronounced against Babylon is the last judgement, that judgement which takes in the whole world and leaves no position unexamined. When it is said that this judgement is pronounced, it is not a question of the state, society, the country, or the nations, but of Babylon. The last battle is fought in the city of cities. The battle against the world, the victory over the world, is a battle against the city, a victory over the city.

And this is true not only in Revelation, where it is presented most forcefully, with the particular emphasis that all the other powers hostile to God go under with the power of the city, but also in the Old Testament prophets, who had exactly the same vision of these things. Isaiah's prophecy against Babylon is a prophecy concerning the last judgement, and when Babylon is condemned, the world is condemned in her: "Behold, the day of the Lord comes, cruel with wrath and fierce anger, to make the earth a desolation and to destroy its sinners from it. . . . I will punish the world for its evil, and the wicked for their iniquity. . . . Therefore I will make the heavens tremble, and the earth will be shaken out of its place, at the wrath of the Lord of hosts . . . " (Isa. 13:9, 11, 13). One would have to suffer from mortal obstinacy to see in these verses an oriental

exaggeration on the theme of an *ad hoc* prophecy given for
the Babylon of Isaiah's time in its political relations with
Jerusalem! And Jeremiah gives the very same teaching (chs.
50, 51). It is impossible to accept, then, that it may be due to
accident. It is impossible to believe that this symbolism is
entirely gratuitous. If the prophets and Revelation presented the
city as the place on earth where the conflict between God and
the earth is carried to its highest pitch, where all the powers in
revolt gather together, where God's victory is assured, it must
be because the cities — our cities — are a sign of the world's
destiny, because these cities bear in their bosoms all the hopes
of man for divinity!

We have referred to the *judgement* and *condemnation* of
the city in several of its aspects. But we must not forget the
curse, which we have also been studying. These two elements
come together, but are not identical. The curse was pronounced
from the beginning. It is part of the city's very being, it is
woven into the fabric of her history. The city is a cursed place
— by its origin, its structure, its selfish withdrawal, and its
search for other gods. As it develops, every city must receive
and bear the curse on its own account; it is one of its basic
elements. The city is not conceivable separate from the curse,
just as man cannot conceive of himself removed from the
curse of his sin. But for the city there is no covenant as there
was for Adam.

Thus the city's undertakings have already received their
stamp, and man's technical undertakings are no different. This
is the explanation (and the only one) for the prodigious problem
evident in the lag between man's projects and cares for the city,
and their realization.

The city is the product of good will. There are none but
the well-intentioned in the urban effort. Everyone works to
enable man to live better. To give him better homes and leisure
activities. To keep his life from being perpetually dreary. To
get him to meet others and escape from his solitude. To keep
from his eyes his humorless situation. To procure for him better
and steadier work. To remove him from the rigors of the seasons.
To protect him from men who might harm him, so he might
no longer be subject to the devastations of robbers. Then the
fruits of his labor will stay his, really his. To ensure him more
comfort and what are called the joys of life, with all the
guarantees of science, medicine, and pharmacology at his door-
step. To change the powerlessness of him who must watch those
he loves die, unable to do a thing. To enrich him and enable

him to say, "Rejoice at last, my soul, for you have great riches."

The city is without a doubt the product not only of man's effort, but even more, of his good will. In the growth of the tentacular city, in its demographic accumulation, there is nothing but good will. It is not the Machiavellism of a politician (rare the Haussman-type prefects who open up great highways in order to quell a revolution more rapidly), or of a great capitalist (rare the Michelin-type scientists who accumulate their workers in rabbit-hutches), which decides the course of the city's history. Rather it is the engineer's bright eye, the urbanist's broad sweep of mind, the hygienist's idealism which determine its course. Yet, look at the results: even more slavery — which recreation can only make more tolerable. Slavery tolerated. Human relations destroyed in the anonymity of the great city. The radical uncertainty of work — unemployment being essentially an urban phenomenon, found in the country only because of the contagious and gangrenous growth of the city. Man subject to man, instead of to nature. The ravages and uncertainties of modern warfare: during an enemy occupation — another fruit of urban civilization — it is the city that must suffer most. And the slums — replaced by the new slums of modern apartment complexes. Such are the results of man's good will, mixed in with God's curse.

And just as a radio receiver corresponds to the broadcasting station, so judgement corresponds to the curse. The curse at the beginning, and present down through the history of the city. Judgement at the end, also present already, because it has already been pronounced: "It is fallen, is fallen, Babylon the great." The city is one of those angelic powers whose power Christ removed by his crucifixion (Col. 2:15). She has already been judged, but it is not yet known, just as someone may be condemned *in absentia* by a court in a judgement by default and may go on his way unawares, the bailiff being entrusted by the court to notify him of the decision. In such a case, although he has already been condemned, the loser knows nothing of it before he has been notified. So we can pretend to know nothing. And yet he can escape judgement if, after the notification, he repents and declares himself ready to comply; otherwise the bailiff will enforce the judgement. And so the powers of the city, between their judgement and the double-pronged moment of notification and execution, have already been condemned but can go right on playing their role, apparently unconstrained, without any knowledge of what has happened.

Without any official knowledge, at least. For they have already received warnings of the judgement, but they were partial, incomplete, unofficial as it were. And when we are told that Sodom and Gomorrha are a warning for Babylon, we should also listen to the language of today's events.

Another sign of judgement is the indisputable fact that warfare is becoming more and more centered on the city. Whereas at one time the whole territory used to be defended, today it is the city which is under attack. It is true that the capital has almost always been the ultimate goal, but at first enemy armies were met and vanquished out on the field. Later, fortified cities and towns were built, and these then became the immediate scene of battle. At one time, the undefended city usually had nothing to fear, and the taking of a key city was never anything but the ratification of a military victory. The keys of the city were solemnly presented to the conqueror. But today, when a city has entered a war she must be destroyed. The factory city must be destroyed because she is industrial, the administrative city because she is a nerve center, the populated city in order to lower the people's morale and provoke disorder. From every aspect, the city is a target. No longer is it a question of crowning a military victory by subjugation of the urban population, but rather of destroying the urban population in order to obtain the military victory. No longer is it a question of taking the city, but of annihilating it. No longer is it because the city is involved in the war that the air force attacks her relentlessly, but simply because she is a city. The warnings touch closer and closer, preparing the way more and more obviously for the judgement of God — warnings which we must understand as such and not as the play of fortune or a blow to be parried. Hiroshima, an innocent city. Judgement on all the cities. The coming condemnation. It must be understood and accepted.

II. SODOM AND NINEVEH

Men are buried under the ruins of their cities, which are themselves reduced to a desert. The interdependence may seem inhumanly cruel to us, but the fact is that the city is man's work. Man is taken with his work and treated in the same manner as his work. This rubs us the wrong way. We can accept that the angel of the city be condemned, that the walls and houses be destroyed. But not that men go down with her, even if they did create her — that is simply too much! And in fact God does, in his patience, leave man a way out.

God's judgements are not machines which roll implacably on according to set principles. They are not the blade of a guillotine blindly separating the inseparable with the brutal neutrality of cold steel. God's judgements are living things which are adaptable, which can be formed and deformed. They are pronounced, but a means of escape is left open: "I do not desire the death of the sinner, I want him to repent and live. . . . " If judgement has been pronounced on the city, it is because it is a power of death for man. Even in this condemnation God is trying to bring about man's salvation. And if man is condemned with the city, it is because he has become a part of her. But God leaves a way of escape. What he wants is for man to separate himself from the city.

Change the judgement? No, never, because it was decided in advance, in terms of the existing situation. But God includes in the fact of his judgement even the decision man is yet to make — a decision made within God's secret judgement, of which we never see more than the one aspect he announces by the prophets and makes manifest in his acts. Man can, then, choose to include himself in the condemnation of the city, or he can avert the destruction of the city by removing it from the great whole which the cities make up and making it into a community of men on the order of other human groups, acceptably gathered together before God.

In these two possibilities we find the stories of Sodom and Nineveh. For Sodom, God's judgement marches steadily forward. The two messengers of the Lord are walking toward the city. She is to be destroyed immediately *because of the sins of her inhabitants* (Jude 7). "The outcry going up from the earth against Sodom and Gomorrha is great, and their sin is very grave." Not only are these men criminals, they also proclaim their crime with joy and pride (Isa. 3:9). Here the city is condemned not so much for being a city, but rather because of the association between her and man's particular sin. In his revolt man has outdone even the city and becomes himself totally responsible. Once again the problem of solidarity arises. The city is a whole and the city's inhabitants are considered as a whole — as we would say today, a community. The evil of some is the evil of all, but the righteousness of some is also a profit for all. Although they are condemned for their individual sins, they are also all condemned together because they make up the corporate body of the city. This is what Abraham's prayer, his extraordinary bargaining to try to make God abandon his intention, his constant lowering of the required price, teaches us concerning the city: "Will you destroy the righteous with the wicked? Suppose there are fifty righteous within the city. . . . Far be it from you to do such a thing, to slay the righteous with the wicked . . . " (Gen. 18:23-25). And God consents not to separate the righteous from the wicked, not to take the righteous out of the city, not to make some discrimination within the city's community, but to pardon all for the sake of fifty, then of twenty, then of ten! Thus the solidarity of the city is also made manifest in God's forgiveness. The entire city is spared when there is one pocket of righteousness, no matter how feeble, hidden in her midst. And this opens up a possibility for the inhabitants to save their city. Not to save it from the last judgement, not from the univocal condemnation pronounced against the city, but from its execution here and now, on their particular city, on them its inhabitants, from that execution serving as notification of the final judgement.

However, there are not even ten righteous in Sodom. And that is why God's present judgement cannot be revoked. And also why it was pronounced in the first place. And then the very summit of Sodom's sin is reached: God's messengers are sought out for the supreme outrage. Lodging in Lot's house, the messengers of God are threatened by the Sodomites, who require Lot to hand them over that they might "know" them.

An absolutely ignominious accumulation of sin. First, it is what we call an act contrary to nature, more serious in its stark crudeness than secret love. And second, and far more important, according to the text, the guests are subjected to violence, the violation of the rule of hospitality, a right sacred among the Semites: "They have come under the shelter of my roof," says Lot. Even more serious, it was done against angels. Of course, the Sodomites did not know that. And even if they had been told, they would not have believed it, considering the unbelief manifested even in Lot's family. "Lot seemed to his sons-in-law to be jesting" (Gen. 19:14). No, the Sodomites have no desire to know that these men are messengers of God. That is not what interests them.

A particularly striking element in the story is the common will to sin which the Sodomites manifest. The entire city gathers together before Lot's house to force him to give up the strangers. The entire city rises up against these newcomers in a kind of unconscious reaction, certainly to satisfy their desires and hates, but also against a threat indistinctly felt to be present and detestable. God's presence is intolerable in Sodom. The unanimity, the insistence, the violence of their attack are not simply natural reactions. They are in fact mankind rising up against God's intervention, sensed and refused before it is even announced.

Their understanding of the event is strengthened by Lot's attitude. He also recognizes these strangers as angels of the Lord. Not only does he take them in as such, not only does he protect them with his own life and by offering his daughters' virginity, but he also blindly believes everything they say. He recognizes them (but not distinctly or explicitly) as messengers from God. He senses in them Yahweh's power on the march, and he treats and defends them as such.

There is, then, a parallelism to be pointed out in the attitudes of Lot and the Sodomites. We might say that everything happens in their subconscious. Just as Lot recognizes them unconsciously as angels, the Sodomites also recognize them unconsciously as bearers of judgements unfavorable to them. They cannot accept a strange power in their closed world. Their world has no place for God. They can only insult him, treat him contrary to nature, blaspheme and break all the laws of ancient society when he is present.

One could almost say that the Sodomites want to rape and murder the visitors *because* they are God's messengers. The Sodomites are dragged into carnal sin by their spiritual sin. And what brings on the immediate execution of God's judgement is not only that the prince of the city has risen up against God, but that the inhabitants of the city have followed his example. Twice, they had the opportunity to break with *that* angel and to accept the two others. First, when the messengers of Yahweh came to the city gates, the Sodomites could at least have treated them as they would have treated any other strangers. And second, when they were miraculously struck with blindness and stumbled around Lot's house all night long without being able to enter, or even to find the door, they should have realized with whom they were dealing. This miracle should have brought them to repentance. It is true, however, that in their condition God's acts could easily have been understood as Satan's.

Furthermore, this miracle was backed up by the news explicitly given by Lot: "The Lord is going to destroy this city." He gave it to all his relatives, and it is obvious that the news must have spread. But no one responded to the appeal. No one separated himself from the city's destiny. Men consciously accepted it. And all the inhabitants of the city, without an exception, this entire collective whole united under the city's

power, desired death by fire and brimstone. Only Lot — but
even he is no exception. For Lot was a stranger in the city. The
Sodomites themselves rejected him: "Get out of here! This man
came as a stranger, and now he wants to play the judge!" And
if he was separate from the city, he was also a stranger to the
power of the city. He had no part in it, no more than in its
sin. He was not particularly virtuous by nature — the rest of
the story leaves no doubt to this effect — but he recognized the
angel of the Lord, and accepted his judgement and the risks
that were included in such a decision against the world, against
the city. There is hardly any need to add that the judgement of
God was not a law whose effects could never change. It was
simply a sign and a prophecy as are all the temporal judgements pronounced by God against the earth. Then Lot was
taken away and the entire city, with all its inhabitants, given
into the hands of the exterminating angel.

*   *   *

In the story of Nineveh we find the exact counterpart to
Sodom. She also is a city which by nature, perhaps even more
than Sodom, was doomed to destruction: "I will punish the
arrogant boasting of the king of Assyria and his haughty pride.
For he says, 'By the strength of my hand have I acted, and by
my wisdom, for I have understanding . . . . I have gathered all
the earth!" (Isa. 10:12-14).

Not only is Nineveh a city like all the others, but she also
has the particular characteristic, pointed out above, of being the
city of war: "Woe to the bloody city, full of lies and booty —
no end to the plunder! The crack of whip, and rumble of
wheel, galloping horse and bounding chariot! Horsemen charging,
flashing sword and glittering spear, hosts of wounded, heaps of
corpses, dead bodies without end — they stumble over the
bodies!" (Nah. 3:1-3). And because of her wars, because she
identified her destiny with war, this city is also condemned with
all her warriors: "The Lord will send sickness among his stout
warriors, he will kindle a fire which will burn and devour his
thorns and briers in one day, which will destroy root and branch
the glory of his forest. . . . The remnant of the trees of his
forest will be so few that a child can write them down . . . "
(Isa. 10:16-19).[1]

---

[1]Isaiah here uses a traditional and well-known symbolism when he represents the army by a forest and military power by thorns and briers.
The figure is to be found frequently in his book.

Thus Nineveh's end is also decided by judgement beforehand, exactly as was Sodom's. The men of Nineveh are condemned exactly as were the inhabitants of Sodom. They have all been taken in the same trap, they are all in the same basket because of the curse on the city. Doubtlessly this collective punishment revolts us, we who are so accustomed to scrupulous moral weighings and to attentive evaluations of sin and virtue; but in reality the enormity of the city's revolt far outweighs all the conversions that the men of the city could individually muster up. Here we have for the first time what could be called the sign of a social sin, a phenomenon characteristic of our time. The social group which the city represents is so strong that it draws men into a sin which is hardly personal to them, but from which they cannot dissociate themselves even if they so desire. Individual virtues are engulfed by the sin of the city.

The problem is different from that of simple collective responsibility. The following law, for example, is well known: "The fathers ate green grapes and it is the children whose teeth are set on edge." By familial solidarity, the "innocent pay the price for the guilty." Some committed the sin, while others suffer the consequences, and there is no more connection between the fault and its punishment than the one existing between men themselves. This feeling of solidarity in sin is very strong in the Old Testament, but it is not the exact problem brought up by the city. For no one in the city has really committed a completely individual sin. No one, really, has individually violated, by his own decision, God's law or the order necessary to conserve life. But these men happen to be part of a body given entirely to revolt. They are not each individually responsible, but they are as a group. They have not each committed their own particular sin, but they have participated in the sin of their society. What is characteristic of this type of sin is that no one commits it, but it is still committed. This situation is particularly related to that of our civilization. No one does evil, everyone wishes for the best, but evil is still committed. This is what makes it impossible to pin down responsibility, for example in wars or in social ills. And since it is impossible to find the men responsible, a myth is invented.

However that may be, the involvement of man with his city is very clear. Even if an Assyrian is perfectly good, honest, and virtuous, he is nonetheless caught up in the machinery of the bloody city, he is necessarily involved in the social sin of the city, and his individual virtue neither stops nor covers anything. Then it is not enough to take care of oneself as best one

can, with one's own piety and goodness. Neither is it enough
to lead one's own life as best one can. For we are dealing with
a power which is beyond every one of us and which none of us
is able to escape. The Ninevite is involved, like it or not, in
Nineveh's destiny and to that extent gives us light on our own
situation.

What, then, can be the answer to the problem? It seems to
have been given explicitly in the Book of Jonah. Of course,
there is no reason to take as essentially historical reality what is
told us there. Once again we have come to the same crossroads.
What is said about Nineveh in this book is not necessarily historical fact, and it is certain that the altercation between Jonah
and Nineveh did not take place in a given year of the history
of this bloody city. There is no historical trace of Nineveh's
conversion to the true God, and the prophets of the seventh
century (when Jonah the prophet, son of Amittai, of Gath-
Hepher in Zebulun is supposed to have lived) all considered
Nineveh to be entirely given over to heathenism and hostile to
God. But the reality of her conversion is not at stake. Only its
meaning.

This story cannot be real, but it is true. And it is for that
very reason that this text is prophetic. It is not by mistake that
this "apology," as it is called by the exegetes, is counted among
the Nebhi'im. It is true prophecy because it is a true representation of God's judgement and mercy. It is such, too, for many
other reasons; but it is not our work here to point these reasons
out. Nor is it our goal to search out the total meaning of the
story and particularly its "religious message," or its "christological" stamp. Our interest here is with the book's teaching about
the city. That the book is in fact concerned with the city and
not with the Assyrians in general is clear from the text itself,
from beginning to end. The king is called the *king of Nineveh*,
whereas he is traditionally called the king of Assyria. And thus
it is clearly the destiny of the city and its inhabitants that is
described.

When God called Jonah it was not to deliver words of consolation, but precisely the opposite: "Go to Nineveh, that great
city, and cry against it, for their wickedness has come up against
me!" God's judgements will burst forth — they will be made
manifest in the great city just as in Sodom. And for Jonah, there
is no misunderstanding of God's word against the city: "Yet
forty days and Nineveh shall be overthrown!"

But the unpredictable happens and what Jonah proclaims
he has foreseen (but has not!) does not happen, and makes

Jonah look ridiculous. The entire population of Nineveh is converted and repents! "The people of Nineveh believed God, they proclaimed a fast, and put on sackcloth, from the greatest of them to the least of them. Then tidings reached the king of Nineveh, and he arose from his throne, removed his robe, and covered himself with sackcloth, and sat in ashes. And he made proclamation and published through Nineveh, 'By the decree of the king and his nobles: Let neither man nor beast, herd nor flock, taste anything; let them not feed or drink water, but let man and beast be covered with sackcloth, and let them cry mightily to God; yea let everyone turn from his evil way and from the violence which is in his hands. Who knows, God may yet repent and turn from his fierce anger, so that we perish not?' " Here we have the entire answer to social sin. Not reforms first. Nineveh will not, for example, acquire new social structures or a new government. Neither is it because men will *individually* repent and begin leading a righteous, pious, holy life. It is rather the event that seems impossible to us: the conversion of an entire population *and* its government. For the two elements are kept distinct in order to associate them. The entire population of Nineveh has repented, accepted God's judgement, and spontaneously decided on a fast. And the king, on the other hand, that power both spiritual and political, has humiliated himself because of his injustice and his city's criminal ways, and has made a legal commitment to repentance and conversion. Here we see all the elements necessary for the pardon of social sin brought together. This pardon is, of course, obtained only because God had pity beforehand, and we know in whom his pity was made visible.

We must add that the act of a people and her chiefs who hear and receive the word of God does not ensure any obvious and certain result. Accepting God's judgement with faith, as the Ninevites did, is leaving to God complete liberty of action. And that is what distinguishes this repentance from a political deal.

France's call to repentance in 1940, first with the hope that it would help her to victory and then with the hope that it would soften the results of defeat, is but a kind of magic, and has nothing to do with the Ninevites' repentance, which in no way hinged on its results. What is characteristic here is the liberty of God being integrally recognized by the repentant group. If God goes through with his judgement, that is just, in spite of their repentance. If God accords a reprieve, it is for him a "renouncement," an act of pure grace.

Repentance does not condition God, does not tie the Lord's

hands. But "who knows?" And in fact these men did not repent because God consented to grant them pardon. And by leaving God's freedom of action complete, by accepting his judgement even after their conversion, this collectivity made evident the truth of its conversion. Then God pardons. And thus it happens that the extraordinary phenomenon of social sin, the work of no single man, is forgiven when a repentance occurs that is the work of all. (And we must never forget that this repentance includes not only the collective act of the population, but the individual act of each man as well — a governmental act and a spiritual act.) This repentance assumes, therefore, that there has been a realization of that solidarity in sin which exists because society is organized the way it is, and an acceptance of being condemned for acts which one has not oneself committed. This is real conversion.

Then the power of the city is made powerless. The angel of Nineveh is dethroned. No longer can he drag the entire population of Nineveh along behind his every step. The city, that giant octopus, no longer holds its inhabitants in its tentacles. The man of the city is freed. At that moment man can truly dissociate himself from the city. And the inhabitants are not alone in their submission to God; they bring with them their city on which God also has pity. God has pity on the city because of her inhabitants and because of her animals, not too far removed from these men who do not know their right hand from their left: "And should not I pity Nineveh, that great city, in which there are more than a hundred and twenty thousand persons who do not know their right hand from their left, and also much cattle?" God always loves his creation, men and animals and plants (for Jonah is not wrong in mourning the death of Qiqayon), and it is because of this love that he pardons man's counter-creation. Because of the men who are in the city, he pardons the city itself when these men rediscover that they belong to the Lord.

Here we have the first word of hope, the first light of the coming dawn, casting her gray light on the city while the sinister continuity of curses and condemnations goes on. These men are unable to tell their right hand from their left, for they are heathen idolaters who have never heard the prophecies of the true God. But what a strange coincidence we have here once more. Such men are men of the city. They belong to the great city and that is what drives them out of their senses. And when, under the influence of God's judgements, they rediscover the difference between right hand and left, then they no longer belong to the devilish power, and the city has lost her deadly seductiveness.

Jesus' references to Nineveh confirm this explanation. Our task here is not to try to discover the meaning of Christ's words, nor to argue whether or not they confirm the historical veracity of this story or whether they show that the salvation for all obtained by Jesus Christ was already valid for the Ninevites. But what is beyond cavil is that, for Jesus Christ, the attitude of these men is the exact opposite of that of the Sodomites. This story has for him the same function as the story of the condemnation of Sodom. And just as Sodom does not signify the earthly condemnation and immediate destruction of all cities, so Nineveh does not signify that salvation is assured to all cities by means of her repentance. But we are all, all of us who live in cities, here faced with our responsibility. Up till now everything seemed to be going on above our heads, out of our reach: the functioning of the city's power was partially shared by man because he was the builder, but he was involved in it like a miserable tool, nothing but a kind of mechanical starter! And now we are at the center of his adventure both rejected and called, both possessed and freed. We are subjects of the city and involved in its condemnation, and yet we are the possible artisans of her adoption by God.

* * *

The first consoling text! Has there been an evolution in our understanding of the city? For there is no doubt that what we have just studied concerns every city. The Ninevites were chosen for this story because they were foreigners (and the story is meant to show that God's mercy extends to all peoples), because they brought much suffering on Israel (and the story is meant to show that God forgives without taking into account former relations with Israel), and also because they were exclusively urban. What confirms this opinion is the fact that the text was without any possible doubt written after the destruction of Nineveh. Does biblical doctrine vary, then, as opinions change from moment to moment? The same question continually reappears. At the beginning, at the time of the Yahwistic author in the eighth century B.C., Israel, as yet untamed, is supposed to have had an anti-urban attitude simply because they were yet savage. "The Yahwistic author has a kind of hate for civilization which he considers to be a downfall from the patriarchal life. Every forward step in what we would call progress is for him a crime, followed by immediate punishment. The punishment of civilization is found in the labors and divisions of humanity. The search for worldly, secular, monumental and artistic culture at Babel is the crime *par excellence*. Nimrod is a rebel . . . " (Renan, *Histoire d'Israel*, II, p. 341). Then Israel is supposed to have become accustomed to civilization, to have accepted it, and with it, the city. Opinions changed with the social, political and economic circumstances which brought them about in the first place. Unfortunately, this more favorable attitude of the Jewish people at a later date has not yet been proved. If such an outlook is sought in the Book of Jonah, what explanation can be given for the date of this book, probably about the same as the Book of Chronicles which, as we have already seen, continues the tradition of condemning the city. So the opposition is explained by different schools of thought? Probably. But then the change of thought cannot be attributed to the evolution of ways of life. And on the other hand, was there ever really a change of thought? Jesus also laid a curse on the city. And what about Revelation? But from the oldest period there was a tendency, as we shall see, to pardon, to accept the city. Two opposing currents existing side by side? Perhaps, but such an explanation is not altogether satisfying. If it is possible to understand the messages of revelation in their unity, why resort to artificial historical explanations which can only provide apparent solutions while concealing profound discord?

III. BUT IN THESE CITIES . . .

But it is in these cities that we must live. We human beings. We who are Israel and then the church. Such is our environment, as is the world itself. We must not forget that the city is the symbol of the world, especially today, when it has become the synthesis of our entire civilization.

To the captives from Israel, dragged off to the very heart of the city, to Babylon, the symbol of symbols, Jeremiah wrote: "Thus says the Lord of hosts, the God of Israel, to all the exiles whom I have sent into exile from Jerusalem to Babylon: Build houses and live in them; plant gardens and eat their produce. Take wives and have sons and daughters; take wives for your sons, and give your daughters in marriage, that they may bear sons and daughters; multiply there and do not decrease. *But seek the welfare of the city where I have sent you into exile, and pray to the Lord on its behalf, for in its welfare will you*

find your welfare. . . . I will fulfill to you my promise and bring
you back to this place" (Jer. 29:4-7, 10).

In this city we are captives. That is the first thing we must
understand. As Israel in her Babels, the church is in captivity.
And we know that this is even the essential goal of the cities
— to make every man captive. And as with every prisoner, escape seems to be the ideal goal. Get out. Destroy the prison, or
at least get outside its walls. This is the first reaction: if the city
truly came from man's hands for the reasons revealed in God's
Word, if a curse is truly resting on her, then she is the great
enemy of all dwelling on the earth. Moreover, the end has been
announced and we must first of all flee this place of perdition.
We must settle elsewhere, for outside the city the same curse
does not reign. Then we must fight the city, destroy it, revert to
an agricultural, a rustic civilization. If it is true that there is
more virtue in country living, we must bring about God's
judgements with our own hands.

This is a logical reaction, but God is not logical in what
he tells us. And far from asking us to destroy Babylon, he
asks us to preserve her alive. God will bring about his own
justice alone. Babylon will fall by the condemnation decided by
God when God will decide it. He will choose the day and the
hour, and it is not by the hands of men that the act of God will
be accomplished; or if it is by human hands, it will be done
unconsciously, without man realizing that he is fulfilling such a
task. Man's duty is not to execute God's judgements. Man's duty
is not to establish God's justice in God's stead. On the contrary,
all of the Bible's teaching is there to show us that God establishes his own justice. We know that God has condemned the
city, but we have no reason to presume on this judgement,
putting ourselves on a level with God. For are we not inhabitants of the city? And just like all the other inhabitants of the
city, do we not have our own part of the condemnation to accept
since we are all dependent on each other here behind our
walls? Let us avoid such a terribly simplistic notion as a clear
separation between good men and evil men, right and wrong.
The judgement of God is not separation of good and evil, but
annihilation and re-creation. And this makes us completely
powerless to realize any of God's judgements, powerless to
annihilate the power of nothingness which the city represents,
and incapable of re-creating.

Moreover, we have seen the meaning of God's judgement,
and not only do we have nothing to do with its execution, but
neither do we have any power to add to it. God's condemnation

is sufficient in itself; we have no personal condemnation to add against the city. We have no supplementary human reasons to discover — neither favorable to the city, which is directly contrary to the teaching of the Bible, nor unfavorable to the city, which is just as faithless. In either case, we accomplish not God's will but the teaching of the city: we have substituted, by this act, ourselves for God. And when our pretended obedience to God pushes us out beyond his will, our action falls into the long line coming down from Adam, and takes the form, for example, of the sin of Ahaz (Isa. 7). We have no right to replace God, to make ourselves judges of the world's sin. This temptation would lead us to obey exactly that same will which incited the builders to construct their cities. Thus, far from taking God's side by our works which are already cursed, we are in reality, although we think we are destroying the cities, only working on their side.

This is not the road God asks us to follow. Astonished, we see that, on the contrary, our job is to lead the life of the other inhabitants of the city. We are to build houses, marry, have children. What a happy ground for conciliation, for that is exactly what the city is asking of us! What a mediocre vocation, so disappointing in its lack of heroism and so reassuring in its apparent ease! And thus we are to continue from one generation to the next, assuring, it would seem, that very stability and depth which men were seeking when they built the cities. Are we to do nothing differently? There is one thing which is not asked of us, and that is to *build* the city. We are to live in the city already existing. But we are asked neither to materially found a new city, nor to participate in spiritual building projects, that is, to share in that which forms the very being of the city. This must be made much more precise. For we are clearly told to participate materially in the life of the city and to foster its welfare. The *welfare*, not the destruction. And the welfare of the *city*, not our own. Yes, we are to share in the prosperity of the city, do business in it, and increase its population. We are to defend it because our solidarity is there. But it is the solidarity of the captive with his jailkeeper. We must make it beautiful, because it is a work of man. And because it is such, God looks down even on it with love. Who knows if in this cursed environment, man's work cannot also sing to the glory of the living God? This question is now possible since Nineveh repented before Jonah's preaching and a new door was opened.

But we will never understand the incomprehensible contradiction between God's curse and the order given us unless we remember that this city-dweller with this work is already the object of God's good will, that this sinner has already been called to become, against his will, a witness for righteousness. Although he is naturally incapable of understanding anything good and true, he has nevertheless received from God's word (even if he understands nothing of it) his role as a witness, dependent, bound to that word. For he is already the object of God's great work in the resurrection, he already belongs *objectively* to Jesus Christ. This is only an eschatological reality, the meaning of which we have yet to study, but it already exists here and now, and it is in terms of it that we must take the way of obedience while participating in man's work, which in turn becomes an involuntary witness of God's work.

However, this participation cannot be total, with no limiting conditions. It does not consist of integration into the urban system. It is not absolute and eternal goodness. He who would live in such a way would nevertheless remain a captive; the place he works would still be his prison. It would also be a place of non-communication, as we have already seen, making preaching an empty and wasted effort. That is why we are not first asked to preach and convert Babylon, but rather to pray. Involved in a battle on a spiritual plane, a battle comparable to Abraham's battle for Sodom, our duty is to pray for the good of the city. Thus our task is to defend this counter-creation before God. We must ask God to take away this condemnation which we know so well, and herein lies our liberty in relation to the city. It is our accomplishment of this act which shows that we are not captives like the others. This is the exact line of separation between ourselves and the city.

Some are captives of the spiritual power which has embodied itself in the city, and they help to strengthen the city's specifically anti-redemptive tendencies, although by so doing they are physically free and in full accord with the powers of the world, full of success in their projects even though the curse reigns. The others are physical captives, bound prisoners, working against the dominations, refusing to go along with the game as the angel of the city would like, obstinately attached to an incomprehensible faithfulness, and praying for the welfare of the city. But it is a welfare different from that which the city looks forward to and desires. The welfare they pray for means another kind of success. By their prayer, the very meaning and quality of the city run the risk of change. I have said "run the risk of change" rather than "will be changed," for the reason behind the city's construction runs the risk of being eliminated, while the city itself stays on.

But how is such a thing possible? It is beyond human strength, and only at Nineveh is such a thing shown as happening, with God's intervention. But our task is not to spend time pondering this success, but to obey our orders, and by doing so we enter into combat with the power of the city itself. This decision to follow God's orders puts us in a position much more dangerous than any other we could occupy. For our prayer and the action it implies bring on Satan's vengeance. In fact we are exposed to many vengeances whose motives will not be evident. We will be looked upon as adversaries of public welfare or as enemies of the human race and our efforts for the good of the city will be interpreted as a will to destroy it. And the accusation is in fact true if the city is considered only from the angle of its spiritual power. Thus a secret thread is woven into the visible side of the city's fabric, and its design is not clearly seen. But on the reverse side of the city's history, on the inside of the cloth, this is the thread which appears as the surest link, and the true design.

We are asked to act thus not for the city itself, but (and this of course will appear supremely selfish to outsiders) for ourselves. For the church. The city can go on because it contains men who are bearers of God's word. And this, let us not forget, is the exact meaning of Abraham's prayer for Sodom. The only worth of these men resides in the fact that they are bearers of God's word. And the city can go on only because it contains such men. And by them it in turn temporarily becomes a bearer of the Gospel. Our welfare is bound up with hers, and so we must work for it, both materially and spiritually — not for our own peace, our own satisfaction, our own established security in the city, but for the good of the Word we have to announce to the world and which needs to be upheld.

As servants of the Word, we must for its sake accept working with what revolts us, hurts us, and breaks our human hearts, for blind refusal is a disservice to the Word of God, and this Word declares forgiveness with judgement, not a judgement without pardon. And the life of the city is dependent on such an attitude. Jonah was angry when the city was not ruined and destroyed, both because the city was evil and because God's prophecy seemed to be false. Since the facts contradict it, who is to say whether this Word against Nineveh was true or not? Have there not been critical students of history who, to explain the lack of evidence for this conversion of Nineveh, have suggested a pretended conversion? And it is in fact easy to visualize the attitude that the men of our time would take toward a prophecy which is not fulfilled! What an argument against God! And we can understand how sad Jonah could be because of what appeared to be a betrayal of God. Jonah's attitude is ridiculous, but it is nevertheless possible that the first steps toward conversion could have turned into play-acting when the Ninevites saw that nothing happened! At least if fire and brimstone had showered down on Nineveh there could have been an argument. But no salvation, either. And Jonah's task is ours, permanently. We must unceasingly proclaim God's curse and judgement on the city; but we must also pray to God that it will not happen, that he have pity (Should not I pity 120,000 men?), that he grant life to the city, that he make of it something to his glory. We must do this even at the cost of looking ridiculous and being embarrassed.

The life of the city is entirely dependent on this faithfulness, on this righteousness, which is not ours. "By the blessing of the upright a city is exalted . . . " (Prov. 11:11). Here is a power which the builders had not foreseen! But the city is built neither for it nor by it. Nevertheless, God reveals to us that it has a decisive role to play in the city's history, decisive but not definitive; for our situation has not been completely changed. Jeremiah's letter shows us that we are still in a period of waiting. Although we live in the city, our efforts in its behalf are still subordinate to the awaited moment when the city itself will be overthrown by God, when the proclaimed judgement will take effect, when we will leave the city with all those called and chosen of God, when God will take us to our true homeland, out of our land of exile, out of our prison. And then it will be proper no longer to oppose the city's destruction. Then it will be proper to separate ourselves from it. But not before. We must wait.

And this situation of ours is also radically different from that of the other inhabitants of the city, its builders. Theirs is a closed world, a world for which nothing else is expected. A world which is reaching man's perfection. A finished counter-creation, to which nothing else can be added. And inside its walls are men who think they have found a secure home, the only one, their Eden. Man protected against attacks from the outside, in a security built up in walls and machines. Men who live artificially contrived lives (just as artificial as their world of concrete and steel), which go on without a hitch, imperturbably, in three-eight time, and where there is no room for adventure, where nothing more is expected. And it is into this world that we are asked to reintroduce an attitude of waiting — not an empty hope for better days, not a desire for more power and security, but a hope for certain very precise events, known by us for a long time, but out of our jurisdiction because they do not depend on us. Anxiety and hope mixed together. And we must bear them to the heart of the city, where the battle rages. For such an attitude is the very ruin of what the city was built for. Our waiting attitude, if it is constant and true, if it reaches our very hearts, is the very ruin of the spiritual power of the city.

* * *

"Come out of Babylon, my people." This shout re-echoes through Scripture from beginning to end, from Genesis to Revelation, and it can be misunderstood if it is separated from the rest of prophecy concerning the city, if only this injunction is remembered and not everything it implies. First of all, these words are proclaimed every time the judgement pronounced against the city is about to be fulfilled, every time its fulfillment is so near that it can be considered realized. Such was the case when the angel brought Lot out of Sodom: destruction was so near that "as he lingered, the men seized him and his wife and his two daughters by the hand, the Lord being merciful to him" (Gen. 19:16). Hardly was he outside the city when the fire began its work! And the situation is the same throughout Scripture, whether it be a partial, symbolic judgement, or the final, utterly actual judgement, both executed on the city. The situation for the city-dweller is the same, and the order is never given at any other time. "Babylon is taken! Bel is destroyed! Merodach is overthrown," says Jeremiah, *before* declaring: "Flee from the midst of Babylon, and go out of the land of the Chaldeans!" (Jer. 50: 2, 8). And John echoed his words: "The angel called out with a loud voice: Fallen, fallen is Babylon the great," and *then* another voice from heaven says: "Come out of her, my people" (Rev. 18:2, 4). Thus the order to leave the city, to separate from her, is given when the city is already fallen, destroyed, when there is nothing else to be done to preserve and save her. When her judgement has been executed, and when, therefore, the Christian's role in her midst has no more meaning. It is this command from God which we must await. This is essentially what we are waiting for during our stay in the city. How much easier it would be to reject the city now, to refuse her our presence now. But that cannot take place before God's final decision. And so we are involved in her life to the very last minute, and it is not in our power to disengage ourselves; and it is God's present order, as it is now proclaimed in the Scriptures, which assures us of the liberty to come.

All of God's people, then, are called out of Babylon — "Lest you take part in her sins, lest you share in her plagues" (Rev. 18:4). Thus, as long as the city continues, God's people are protected, protected against Babylon's sin. They can live there without necessarily being seduced. They are protected, too, against God's anger, against his judgement. Only at the end will this protection seem to cease, only then will man's solidarity with the essence of the city be reestablished. For at that time final decisions must be made, and when the exterminating angel strikes with his plagues, he makes no distinctions. As when he passed over Egypt, as when he struck Sodom, no one was spared. Every man is summoned to justice, and only flight from the condemned body can bring salvation. But it is also the time of hardened hearts. Up to that time the repentance of Nineveh is yet possible, and God's representatives must work for that goal; but at the end the doors are closed, there is no turning back. And the last act of the people chosen by God is to proclaim this very judgement and its execution, "with a shout of joy declare it, proclaim it, make it known to the end of the earth ... " (Isa. 48:20). The proclamation is that of the judgement — with pardon for God's people when they go out of the city. The order is given to proclaim the coming catastrophe, and the terrible thing is that it is no longer a call to repentance, but the announcement that the judgement will be executed as they leave the city, and the announcement is made with shouts of joy.

Entirely different from Jonah's pronouncement, the words of the church must ever be seen in her own repentance, in her own hope of salvation for all; and her words are declared when she leaves — the greatest moment of hardness of heart among the inhabitants of the city. Then there can be no more conversion. It is that very declaration of the church which closes the door, and this is how God's will as revealed by John must be understood: "Come out of her .... Render to her as she herself has rendered, and repay her double for her deeds. Mix a double draught for her in the cup she mixed. As she glorified herself and played the wanton, so give her a like measure of torment and mourning" (Rev. 18:4, 6-7). Thus the people of God themselves seem to be the executors of his great and sacred works. But the whole teaching of these texts shows that this material and spiritual destruction is not the work of God's people on earth, but of exterminating angels. This act of vengeance and retribution that

the church is called upon to accomplish, is that very proclamation mentioned by Isaiah, a proclamation of deliverance for
Babylon's captives and of her own death, not as a promise, but
as a thing already accomplished and unchangeable. The tears
and lamentations of the kings of the earth will change nothing
and their repentance will go unfinished (Rev. 18:9).

Thus the act of leaving the city and the word which the
church must then proclaim to the city cannot be accomplished
any time, any way, because we want to put on airs of purity.
These things are among the final events, or at least among the
signs of final events, and we bear the responsibility of man's
woe. However, someday we must leave, when the wait is ended,
and then there can be no hesitation. The Scriptures give us remarkable details concerning this departure. It is not an escape,
we will not be leaving as conquered foes driven from the triumphant city that man created for this very triumph, for this separation, for this expulsion of everything which might remind him
of God. Rather, it is only an escape in which the city is being
punished before the last day, as a sign. Thus Lot fled from Sodom,
and in men's eyes this is a flight of fright, before man's anger,
and before the descending fire. But when, on the contrary, the
final judgement has come to execution, then this departure is a
glorious one: "Depart, depart, go out thence, touch no unclean
thing. Go out from the midst of her . . . . You shall not go out
in haste, and you shall not go out in flight. For the Lord will
go before you, and the God of Israel will be your rear guard"
(Isa. 52:11-12). It is not a question of fleeing soldiers, beaten in
battle, but of men withdrawing after accomplishing what God
asked them to accomplish. Contrary to what has usually happened
throughout history, these are not men rejected by the city, but
men who know that their act of rejecting the city is in accordance with God's will. These are men who go out, guarded on
every side, with God marching before and behind, and abandon
the city to herself in the midst of God's wrath. Certainly life
has not been made easier for those who are leaving. Their act cannot ameliorate their situation: abandoning the very place where
comfort and ease have developed. They are on their way to the
desert. There will be no more running water, and they will have
to bend their wills to live by God's promise: "They will not
thirst when he will lead them through the deserts" (Isa. 48:21).
They have not left because they are going to a better world, because they have a choice. Neither is it fear which makes God's
people leave, but rather obedience: "Go out of the midst of her,
my people, and let every man save his life from the fierce anger

of the Lord! Let not your heart faint, and be not fearful at the report heard in the land, when a report comes in one year and afterward a report in another year, and violence is in the land, and ruler is against ruler . . ." (Jer. 51:45-46). This is a fundamental notion. Being perfectly conscious of what God's judgement on the city is, aware of the constant threat of destruction hanging over her because of what she represents, the Christian still has no reason to be especially bothered or fearful about the rumors of his punishment and death which may be current. They are human rumors, human words — perhaps the echoes of an obscure and hidden consciousness of what the city's insult against God really means. They are ominous reminders of the Babels and the Gomorrhas of the past, for man always feels threatened in his counter-creation. Be not afraid, says the Lord.

Jesus pronounced the same words, also in reference to rumors of war: "Let not your hearts be troubled." This agreement emphasizes the fact that we must put everything we know about the city and its condemnation back into the outline of scriptural doctrine, that is, among the final events: the judgement of the city must be understood as a part of the judgement of the world. Christians are called to separate themselves, not fearfully or because of rumors, wars, and rulers, but when God will tell them to do so. How? Their task is neither to try to discover his means nor to speculate vainly. God will tell them how to act when he tells them to act. And when the time has come, God's people will know with a sure knowledge, with a certitude not discernible from the outside, not measurable intellectually, but absolutely undeniable, that the time has come to leave Babylon. Nonetheless, one text might provide us with a sign, which in no way removes the unpredictability of the event and God's own liberty: "Flee from the midst of Babylon, and go out of the land of the Chaldeans, and be as he-goats before the flock . . ." (Jer. 50:8). In this departure our first thoughts are not with how to get out of the predicament. It is not the departure of individuals fleeing before a catastrophe, but the departure of all God's people gathered into a flock. What is astonishing is that in this prophecy those who understand God's will are likened to he-goats, the leaders of a flock. And so, in this departure it seems not only that faithful Christians separate themselves from the city, but that they are the guides for still others — men whom God has chosen in secret and who perhaps have never confessed Jesus Christ or belonged to any confession, but who nevertheless belong to God's people and prove it at the decisive moment by hearing the word of judgement and salvation that the church is announcing to the world. When Noah and Lot preached the Word, they received only mockery. Yet, we must think, too, of Nineveh listening to Jonah's prophecy. When the church leaves the city, she must lead out men who have never paid any attention to the word, but who now receive it — mysterious people whom we will be surprised to see, a people who are around us and whose existence is certified by the word of God spoken to Paul: "Speak, for I have many people in this city" (Acts 18:10).

* * *

Everything we have just said and all these Old Testament texts are in agreement with and explain Jesus' disquieting words: "When they persecute you in one town, flee to the next. Truly I say to you, you will not have gone through all the towns of Israel, before the Son of man comes" (Matt. 10:23). The Word that we have constantly found spoken to the city, containing both judgement and grace, is the word of the cross. It is because of it that he is in fact able to say to the city, man's world, that "the kingdom of God has come near" (Luke 10:11). The place which man wanted to shut up is in fact open. But announcing that news in the city is getting to the very heart of resistance to God.

When we understand what the city represents, we understand better both the order Jesus gave to his disciples to go into the cities, and this other curious reference to the city as the center of crisis: "Go to the cities . . . . Shake the dust from your feet against the cities . . . when you are persecuted in one city . . . ." It is in and because of the city that the critical point of preaching is reached. There are of course many valid critical explanations of these texts[2], but they are not exhaustive. To me it does not seem sufficient to limit Christ's words to the twelve (or to the seventy in Luke) and to speak of a temporary and exceptional mission of the apostles. In fact, Christ's words must be understood by the church as having been addressed to every witness of Christ, and as characteristic of the situation of witnesses in the world. The apostles are not the only ones concerned by the teaching on witnessing (v. 16), on fear (v. 27), on God's love (v. 29), on the choice to be made. How could we believe then that verses 5 and 23 are addressed to them only? But without eliminating any of the current explanations, it would seem that God's revelation concerning the city helps us to partially

---

[2]See a good analysis of exegetical treatments of these texts in Oscar Cullmann, *Salvation in History*.

understand these instructions given by Jesus to his disciples: "Enter no town of the Samaritans, but go rather to the lost sheep of the house of Israel." The message of the cross must be carried to the center of man's autonomy. It must be established where man is most clearly a wild beast. Its goal is less the total number of men, than the entity *man*. Christ's sending his disciples out into the cities of Israel is their most dangerous mission, for it is directed against the heart of the world's power and betrayal. Why the cities of Israel? It is the very bringing together of the terms "city" and "Israel" which is most striking. Israel, a people who bear God's promise, also sought refuge in cities. We have already studied what it meant for Israel to build cities. And here we see the conflict ever manifest in the city carried to its extreme: when man builds a city it is a reflex of a son of Cain; but when Israel builds a city, it is much more than a simple reflex, it is the conscious rejection of the true God, in favor of Cain's security. Thus we can understand both the expression "the lost sheep of the house of Israel," which is obviously applied to the cities of Israel (parallel with the cities of the Samaritans and with verse 23), and Christ's insistence that the Gospel of the kingdom be preached in *that* exact place, since when it is preached there it is being preached at the very nerve center of the world, where the battle is raging most furiously. And that is why the disciples cannot finish their preaching among the cities of Israel before the Son of Man returns. As Pernot translated it: "You will not have finished with the cities of Israel, before the Son of man comes."

There are several interpretations open to us. We can accept an obvious, literal sense. Or we can believe that Jesus was mistaken about the nearness of his return, or that the word means only that Jesus is following his disciples, as in Luke (10:1), or that a distinction must be made between the coming of the Son of Man here and the Lord's return, or that Jesus is in fact indicating that the preaching of the Gospel is a grace solemnly granted to men, which is the meaning of the reference to the "coming of the Son of man."

It is only by seeing in these texts a shaft aimed at the city that we can bring the various meanings back to one. For undeniably Jesus was here showing what would be the Christian's attitude and position concerning the city and his work there. It is not for nothing that Christ's unsettled status is mentioned ("The Son of man has no place to lay his head"), and that immediately afterwards he sends his disciples into the place of man's stubborn establishment (Luke 9:57 and 10:16). It is not for nothing that he asked his disciples to go through the cities of Israel, fleeing from one to another, putting each one of them in a position of choosing, in a position of responsibility (Matt. 10:23). It is not for nothing that he showed that the departure of the disciples was most serious, that their departure, by shaking the dust from their sandals, was decisive in the order of condemnation (Matt. 10:14-15). In fact, all that we found in the Old Testament texts is here in résumé. The situation of the people of God in Babylon is the exact situation of the disciples in the city. This dialectic between staying and leaving, preserving and judging, is centered in the preaching of the Gospel of the kingdom. The entire doctrine which we have so far discovered and received is illuminated by these few brilliant words from Christ's lips. Nothing has been changed, but what was announced is being fulfilled. What was described is being lived. And from this vantage point one can look back and understand the rest.

Whether we adopt the traditional translation of Matthew 10:23, or Pernot's makes no great difference. It is not the translator's art which can make the text any truer. "The cities of Israel" are not the cities of Judah. Jesus himself goes through the cities of Judah and teaches there: "When Jesus had finished instructing his twelve disciples, he went on from there to teach and preach in the cities of that country" (Matt. 11:1). The disciples' mission is outside the country, in the cities where God's people, Israel, may be found living, in those cities where these people have entered into slavery, where they have shut themselves up in refusal and disobedience, where they have betrayed their vocation. God's Israel has now become the church. Around her, the same battle is raging. She is bogged down in the same mud and must take up the same work, a work never finished because the city is the city. Go through all the cities of Israel, comes the command, bringing judgement and forgiveness. Your work will not be done until the Son of Man returns. Even Nineveh converted is still Nineveh, and you, as ever in danger in her midst, can expect nothing other than the Lord's lot (Matt. 10:24) — expulsion from the city.

Chapter Three

LONG WE WAIT FOR THE COMING OF THE DAWN

I. TEMPORAL ELECTION

LIKE THE STATE, THE CITY OCCASIONALLY APPEARS IN history (but is it really in history?) as an instrument of God. The relation is complex, and once again we find it portrayed in Babylon. It is therefore meaningful as a sign. The schema of this relationship is generally as follows: because of the chosen people's unfaithfulness, it becomes necessary to inflict punishment, which is to be understood as the opposite counterpart of God's eternal election; then God calls the king of Babylon who gives himself over to his own nature, that is, to what the city enables him to be and do. The king of Babylon punishes the rebellious people and Jerusalem is sacked, the people dispersed into exile. By his act the king of Babylon is the object of a temporal election, he becomes a servant of the Lord and his city becomes an instrument in God's hands — which in no way alters its eternal reprobation.

This eternal reprobation will exercise such an influence that the city and its king are never able to limit their action to God's order. They always go beyond what he asked of them as a punishment of Israel, or they take the glory to themselves, or they try to do violence to Israel's sacred quality. And because of such acts they are themselves rejected; their temporal election comes to an end in the redemption of Israel and the death of the city: "Because you have not obeyed my words, behold, I will send ... for Nebuchadnezzar the king of Babylon, against this land and its inhabitants, and against all these nations round about; I will utterly destroy them, and make them a horror, a hissing, and everlasting desolations . . . . This whole land shall become a ruin and a waste, and these nations shall serve the king of Babylon seventy years. Then after seventy years are completed, I will punish the king of Babylon and that nation, the land of the Chaldeans, for their iniquity, says the Lord, and will make their land an everlasting waste" (Jer. 25:8 ff.). "All the nations shall serve the king of Babylon until the time of his own land comes . . . . But if any nation or kingdom will not serve this Nebuchadnezzar king of Babylon, and put its neck under the yoke of the king of Babylon, I will punish that nation with the sword, with famine and with pestilence, says the Lord, until I have consumed it by his hand . . . . But any nation which shall bring its neck under the yoke of the king of Babylon and serve him, I will leave on its own land, to till it and dwell there, says the Lord" (Jer. 27:7 ff.).

These texts and many others were addressed to the king of the city and not to the city itself. But we also know that the king, however he is designated historically, is something else besides the political head of the city. He is designated as the spiritual reality, the authority of the city itself. For that reason he fits in perfectly with this world shut off from God, but which God uses anyhow. And God grants him the title of servant (in astonishingly close identification with the Servant of the Lord!), whereas we can see that his role is only to realize the destiny of the city. For it is obvious that by going ahead with the conquest of God's people, the king of Babylon does not know that his is a divine mission. He is only following his political passion, the necessities of war, diplomatic arrangements. This is his brand of politics and so he affirms his sovereign rights. He realizes the ambitions of the city. City of war and rapine, destroying and domineering. City of confusion, place of exile and of the counter-creation — always trying, by one of these means or the other, to kill God's creation. And here is a marvellous occasion to strengthen her position: by ruining the city of Yahweh! Enslaving the chosen people. Such is the very summit of glory for the city in its spiritual destiny. The fulfillment of her builders' greatest desires. But this goal is realized only because she has become (without desiring or tolerating it) the servant of the Lord, because she has received from Yahweh himself a new boundary line. But by her acts she gathers the storm clouds against herself and hastens on her own condemnation. It is as though the Lord were yielding to man's existence: his will has become a will for death. Man and his work, the city, have a

passion for death; man tries to destroy himself, made mad under
the weight of sin. Even without God's intervention, man's work
for others is death, and by this work he wounds himself and
perishes. Babylon, an instrument of vengeance, offers herself as
a sacrifice by her obedience: "You are my hammer," says Yahweh to Babylon, "and my weapon of war: with you I break
nations in pieces, with you I destroy kingdoms! With you I break in
pieces the horse and his rider! With you I break in pieces the
chariot and the charioteer! With you I break in pieces the old
man and the youth! With you I break in pieces the young man
and the maiden! With you I break in pieces the shepherd and
his flock! With you I break in pieces the farmer and his team!
With you I break in pieces governors and commanders! I will
requite Babylon . . . for all the evil she has done in Zion, says
the Lord" (Jer. 51:20 ff.).

And this is what scandalizes us. What outright injustice on
the part of God thus to use an instrument, then condemn it in
his wrath, while the instrument has only done his will. But to
reason in this way is disastrously to oversimplify, to betray a
mind unwilling to bow to revelation. I am not suggesting that
we must bow in the sense of renouncing any comprehension of
the texts, but that we must bow to an understanding as God
grants us understanding, with a desire for nothing else, with no
desire to understand as it suits us. When Babylon destroys the
humblest and truest things of Zion, when she puts both old man
and infant on the same level of death, she is working out her
own desires, she is truly Babel. And if she can do so, if she can
in fact become what she is, it is because God has given her permission, and because of God's judgement against Zion. It is the
disobedience and sin of the church that brings on the excessive
measures of earthly powers, of the powers of city or state. God's
gaze rests on Zion, on his church, and decides the limits of
power he will accord to the powers of the earth to realize their
own tendencies and possibilities. But the possibilities were already there, just as sin exists. God is not using an inert tool, he
is granting a freedom — granting it because of his people's unfaithfulness. All the desires of the builders pent up in their
cities then burst forth, and in the resultant tyrannical domination, the whole world is dragged along to death with the church,
and because of her. And when God turns against this devouring
fire, he is judging not a work ordained by himself, but the work
of enemy powers who while they obeyed their own desires, un-
knowingly also obeyed God's. He is judging powers who took

for themselves the glories of successful destruction, powers who
gloried and rejoiced over destruction and death, powers who
refused to believe that they in turn will one day be judged,
powers who became proudly emboldened in their victories! This
is shown to us explicitly: "Babylon, no more shall you be called
the mistress of kingdoms! I was angry with my people. I pro-
faned my heritage and I gave them into your hands. You showed
them no mercy, on the aged you made your yoke exceedingly
heavy. You said, 'I shall be mistress forever!' You did not lay
these things to heart or remember their end!" (Isa. 47:5 ff.). So
by obeying, Babylon is in reality being disobedient. Because she
is accomplishing God's judgement on the church she considers
that she is herself the judge, and in doing so she is obedient to
her own covetousness; she glorifies herself instead of recognizing
the liberty given her of God. This temporary supremacy is a
chance for Babylon to exercise justice and mercy, but instead
she prefers violence. Instead of sensing in the judgement she is
executing a call to consider her own course, to feel herself judged,
she overflows with confidence. And this is how Habakkuk refers
to her at this moment in her experience: "Lo, I am arousing the
Chaldeans, says the Lord, that bitter and hasty nation . . . . They
gather captives like sand . . . . They scoff at kings . . . . They
take every fortress, then their zeal increases and they sweep by
like the wind and become even more guilty: their own might is
their God!" (1:6-11). But could it be otherwise, could the city act
in any other manner? And once she acts thus, how could she act
any other way? And if she acts thus, how can she escape God's
judgement?

The city's temporal election — which unavoidably brings on
her condemnation — was not meant to go against her, it was
not given to condemn Babylon. God does not want the sinner
to die, but to live. It is not because of the city that God calls
her to act thus, but because of the church. His purpose is not
the condemnation of the city, but the salvation of the church.
Then let her power show itself just and merciful! May she recognize her election! Then she also will find there a sign of God's
grace. For the very fact that God has called the city into his
service — man's exclusive work and a spiritual power in rebellion against God — is a proclamation of coming reconciliation.
What appears to be the cause of her rejection, what sinks the
city even deeper into her curse and her darkness, was meant to
be the first sign of a dawn already beginning to shine, a remis-
sion of her condemnation not yet effected but already promised
and of which some would see a sign in this involuntary service

forced on her by God. But the promise was made because of the church.

And this reveals to us another relationship between the city and the church. There is not only opposition between them. There is also productiveness. For in the presence of God's people in the midst of the city, there is the sign of a possible reconciliation with God: "Among those who know me I mention Rahab and Babylon; behold Philistia, Tyre, and Ethiopia — in Zion are they born!" (Ps. 87:4). Or in another translation of this difficult psalm: "I call on Egypt and Babel as my friends. Behold Philistia and Tyre, with Ethiopia — 'This one was born there.' But of Zion it shall be said, 'Man, every man, was born there.'" Here we have not only a proclamation of universalism as found in the prophets, or of the Jewish messianic hope. This text goes even further. Those most idolatrous enemies of the chosen people, and their cities just as well, are now transformed. I have pronounced, says the Lord. The pronouncement is not something immediately accomplished on the earth, but it is the Word of God and thus will not come back to God without having accomplished its purpose. The city is included among those enemies to whom the Gospel is announced and who are chosen of God. It is on the list of "those who know God." How far does mercy reach? But this knowledge is not enough, for the demons also know God and tremble. The knowledge proclaimed by God is also an election and an expected conversion, to be effected by the action of the church: such knowledge can come to life only in Zion.

This election must be likened to that found in one of Isaiah's prophecies: "In that day there will be five cities in the land of Egypt which speak the language of Canaan, and which will exercise judgement by the Lord of hosts. One of them will be called *'iyr hacheres*, and there will be an altar to the Lord in the midst of the land of Egypt . . . . The Lord will be known by the Egyptians in that day . . . . The Egyptians and the Assyrians will serve the Lord. In that day Israel will be the third with Egypt and Assyria, and these lands will receive a blessing. The Lord of hosts will bless them, saying, 'Blessed be Egypt my people, and Assyria the work of my hands, and Israel my heritage'" (Isa. 19:18-25). It is beyond our purpose to make a complete analysis of this text, but we must emphasize that the city is bound in closely with this election, that it even seems in the case of Egypt to be the spot where the election is made manifest. But ever with the double quality which we have already noticed. One of these cities is called *'iyr hacheres*. This name seems to contain a triple word play. First, it means "a city of the sun," a "city devoted to the sun." It refers, therefore, to a city that is idolatrous. But it also means "city of destruction" (reading *haheres*), which is really a double meaning: 1) "a city which destroys" (and here we find one of the city's invariables), and 2) "a city devoted to destruction." The connection between the two basic meanings is not difficult to understand; since the city is idolatrous, she is destructive, and God's judgements must fall upon her. But it is this very city which is to swear allegiance to the Lord of hosts, and the conversion of all the people of Israel is announced on the occasion of this city's conversion. This is enough to retire the purely historical interpretation of this text which goes as follows: Isaiah is speaking of Jewish colonies in several Egyptian cities one of which is Heliopolis, and he builds up an extraordinary political tableau on the future alliance of Assyria and Egypt, accomplished by the intermediary of Israel. This interpretation is purely imaginative. Isaiah's goal was completely foreign to political calculations. Rather, and very precisely stated, the text is an announcement of God's judgement upon and forgiveness of Egypt, granted first of all to the center of resistance — her cities. The name of one of them is chosen to indicate that his word is pronounced in the very place of idolatry and destruction. Thus, not only do God's people in the midst of the city already serve as God's presence, but much more important, they serve also as the temporal election of the city itself, to accomplish God's work — if necessary against the church — and the promise made to the city. All this is to show forth that the condemnation of the city has not plunged her into morningless night.

* * *

Finally, we may note that the city is called at least once to play a positive role in the order of preservation which is a part of God's plan for the world. Moses received the command to establish cities of refuge in the land of Canaan and this was carried out by Joshua (Num. 35; Josh. 20). The purpose of these cities was to save a murderer from blood revenge when he had no intention to kill, when it was involuntary homicide. The rule of an eye for an eye implies that little distinction usually was made among the facts in a case. Whether or not there was premeditation, the material crime was still there; the punishment therefore, in primitive law, must be the same. And on the other hand, even if legal distinctions had been made, the murderer would still have had to fear blood revenge by the family, since this was exercised without consulting any tribunal or court. A juridical interpretation of these texts would see in the system of the cities of refuge a particularly interesting moment in the development of criminal law: a partial transition from objective evaluation of a crime to personal evaluation. The role of desire in crime is beginning to be noticed.

It is also a partial transition from the system of private vengeance to that of judgement by public courts. For the one taking refuge in a city is not free from all prosecution, only from vengeance: "Joshua" (the date when these cities of refuge were established is of little importance here, whether from the period of the judges or of the monarchy; and whether or not there was any difference between the first cities of refuge and those of post-exilic times makes very little difference) organized a whole new procedure of judgement (which shows a clear development when compared with the first mention of the institution in the Book of Numbers. In Numbers, the principle is established, while here we get the details of application). When the accidental killer arrives before the gates of the city he must stop and explain his case to the elders before entering. If the elders accept him, he will enter and be protected from blood vengeance. Then the killer goes before a court responsible for judging the case. This tribunal must complete the elders' decision and decide the fate of the defendant: If the killing was voluntary murder, the man must submit to punishment; if his act was involuntary, he must stay in the city until the death of the high priest in office at the time of the crime; then he is freed from all punishment. So the law progresses.

But these decisions are not juridical, and we must not view our texts from that angle. Even from a sociological viewpoint, it cannot be missed that this institution is very close to the right of sanctuary found among all Mediterranean peoples. By this right, the murderer could escape both juridical condemnation and popular vengeance by taking sanctuary in certain sacred spots. However, there is a great difference between this right of sanctuary and the Israelite cities of refuge. For the right of sanctuary found among the Mediterranean peoples was valid not only for involuntary homicide, but for murder as well. The right of sanctuary enabled one to escape not only vengeance, but also the condemnation of a regular state tribunal. Moreover, the sanctuary itself was most often a temple, a statue, or a sacred grove. But these considerations are no more than an introduction to the texts themselves.

Their *first* purpose is not to give us information about the institutions of the Hebrew people at one moment in their history. The texts are there rather as a teaching from God. There can be no doubt that they do have a meaning for man's life and reflect God's will to see men saved. But our task does not lie there. What directly concerns us is the instrument chosen by God for this salvation, namely the cities. Joshua chose six cities for cities of refuge. Three were east of Jordan: Bezer in the desert, from the tribe of Reuben; Ramoth in Gilead, from the tribe of Gad; and Golan in Bashan, from the tribe of Manasseh. These three cities — chosen before the settlement of the people in Canaan was finished, since they are on the east side of the Jordan — show that the choice was made rapidly, as an emergency measure. It is probable, therefore, that this institution was considered very important. In Palestine itself, three other cities were chosen: Kedesh in Galilee, from the tribe of Naphtali; Kiriath-arba, which is Hebron, from the tribe of Judah; and Shechem from the tribe of Ephraim. Thus there was one city for every two tribes. They were there to ensure the reign of greater justice, to avoid the shedding of innocent blood. We have before us, therefore, a new function of the city, in contradiction with every teaching we have found so far. Obviously there was a practical reason for the choice of these cities. Geographically they were good places of refuge, and it is true that the city, by its very purpose, with its walls and garrisons, is the place where the most effective protection could be offered to a criminal. But materialistic reasons are obviously insufficient for a people who consider the city to be a supernatural power, and certainly — in any case — an evil power. These convictions must have been especially strong since they were at the beginning of the conquest and the captive cities were Canaanite cities. It is certain that the only justification is found in the order given by God, which is in fact an election: "Therefore I command you, You shall set apart three cities" (Deut. 19:7).

They are to separate three cities which henceforth will have a meaning and a quality entirely different from that of any other city. They have been set apart, as the people of God were set apart, as those God loves are set apart. The cities are holy. And what is particularly remarkable here is that their holiness is devoted entirely to man. In reality, their election was limited to transforming the meaning and doubtlessly the spiritual power of the city (although nothing is said of this) without modifying the function that man had originally prescribed for it. Cain had wanted to protect himself from vengeance for the murder of his brother; the city is essentially protection for a murderer, and here it keeps that quality, but it is now for the innocent murderer.

The city is the place where man is all-powerful, where he establishes his own justice, opposed to God's will. And here we have the opposition of the city's walls to God's law expressed in the formula, "an eye for an eye." But this opposition is just in God's sight and in accordance with his will. The city is intimately connected with murder; she is warlike and bloody. Here also she is connected with murder, but to help an innocent person escape death "lest innocent blood be shed in your land which the Lord your God gives you for an inheritance, and so the guilt of blood shed be upon you" (Deut. 19:10). Thus the role of the city is retained, but its meaning has changed.

One phrase is often repeated in these texts. Protection will be granted to the one who was "not at enmity" in time past with the one he killed. Is this simply a somewhat oblique reference to premeditation? Certainly not. It would have been enough to note the involuntary and accidental quality of the act as is done in the texts, for this involuntary quality implies the absence of premeditation. Moreover, the same text adds that the murderer had killed without intent (Josh. 20:3). What we in fact have here is a new moral element. Only he can claim refuge who had not beforehand been at enmity with his neighbor! This does not mean that he was pure of all sin, but that he may not be condemned, because true murder is enmity. "The one who says 'Raca' to his brother is a murderer," says Jesus. Thus the reversal of meaning for the city is even more obvious — she has become the protectress of the man who has not broken the law of love set up by God at the end of his work as its fulfillment.

And the man may stay there "until the death of the high priest who was anointed with the holy oil" (Num. 35:25). To my knowledge, this is the only case where the death of the high priest is indicated as having a special effect. The high priest purifies others by animal sacrifices, but his own life is not implied in these. But here the death of the high priest frees the murderer from his prison city, from his place both of refuge and of exile (for it is nothing other than exile; only after the death of the high priest can he return to his property — Num. 35:28). Why is it so? The explanation seems obvious. A life for a life! The one whose responsibility is to expiate the sins of Israel with his sacrifices is to expiate, with his death, the greatest sin from the Old Testament viewpoint, murder. The life of the high priest redeems the life of the involuntary murderer, who should have yielded his life for the life of his victim. No animal could be

used for this sacrifice of redemption. In this case it is the life of
him who carries the sins of Israel to wipe them out which is
required. But as the murder was unintentional, the murderer is
left alive to await the natural death of the priest. And it is this
function of the high priest which is referred to in the text where
mention is made of the anointing oil. This death frees the murderer from vengeance. It liberates him from exile, and the city
has then finished her work. How could we avoid seeing a prophecy in all this? There is no reason to belabor the point. But
we now understand that this city has a part in God's plan.

However, "among the thousands in Judah" only six cities
were chosen. And the change of their spiritual character is not
explicit, their role is still extremely limited, secondary. One
could almost say symbolic. Nevertheless, there is more here than
an oral prophecy. What we have are the first fruits of what God
wants to make of the city. Although this role is completely
secondary, it contains all that will be the glory of heavenly
Jerusalem, when the murderer's place of exile will become the
place of refuge for all the pardoned. Thus, in the midst of his
people, God has placed all the signs of his work. He has placed
the mark of his Spirit's triumph. And this is even more true for
Jerusalem.

* * *

II. JERUSALEM

The life of the city of Jerusalem was very special. There
have been many holy cities down through history — Thebes,
Lhassa, Mecca, Banaras, Rome — and from a human viewpoint
Jerusalem is only a holy city like the others, with her own claims
to the title. However, one has only to read her history in detail,
even with no religious interpretation whatsoever, to realize that
her destiny is inexplicably unique, as is that of the people of
Israel. But our task here is not to outline her history or describe
her origins.

Jerusalem already existed when the people of Israel entered
the Promised Land. And, whether by diplomacy or lack of power,
Judah did not take the city from Jebus, the Jebusites kept her,
and she may have been their capital although she seems to have
had no special importance. The true reason for the references
to her in Joshua and Judges (Josh. 15:63; Judg. 1:21) is her
later importance. Jerusalem is a Canaanite city like the others
— a city one avoids so as not to become impure, a city to be
scorned; as Ezekiel says (ch. 16), she is a child of savages ex-

posed in the open from the day of her birth. Historians find great reasons for David's choice of this recently conquered city as his capital. Jebus becomes Jerusalem, and the city of David. We could go on at length about its strategic worth and how easy it was to fortify, about the political necessity of choosing a completely new capital, and of the value of making the political capital what was already the religious capital. But after all is said, these considerations are secondary. What transforms this military city is David's act: in the name of the Lord he made with her a pact of love. David knew the meaning of the city. He was not unaware, even if several of the texts we have quoted are posterior to his reign, of God's teaching concerning the city. Nevertheless, he wanted to make of this city so recently heathen the home of the ark. Up till then, the ark had always been in the country, in private homes, or only temporarily in cities — such as Bethel, Shiloh, Beth-Shemesh, Kiriath-Jearim. But changes of location had been frequent and the presence of the ark was not a blessing for these cities. Most often, the ark was kept outside the city, in a peasant's home or in a fortress (e.g., I Sam. 7:1). But now David is bent on making his own city into the city of the ark, and soon the city of the house of the Lord. His attempts are not without hesitation, however, and the story of the ark's sojourn in the house of Obed-Edom shows that David's conscience was not absolutely clear in this undertaking. When he wanted to build the house of the Lord in Jerusalem, the answer given him by the prophet leaves no room for doubt: "I have not dwelt in a house since the day I brought up the people of Israel from Egypt to this day, but I have been moving about in a tent for my dwelling. In all places where I have moved with all the people of Israel, did I speak a word with any of the judges of Israel, whom I commanded to shepherd my people Israel, saying, 'Why have you not built me a house of cedar?' " (II Sam. 7:6 ff.). This is a kind of refusal to enter the city, to make his home there. And all of Jerusalem's destiny is included, then, in this opposition emphasized by God: "You, David, want to build me a house, and put me in a city. But in fact, it is I, the Lord, who will build you up a house!" And the Lord then grants to David's immediate posterity the permission to build the Temple, but it is really nothing more than accepting David's wish. God's consent is given to him in whom he is pleased, whom he chose and loved and who is henceforth only a mirror reflecting God's pronouncement that he will build up the house of David, will give him a true posterity and will construct the true city. But David was also acting, acting in line with God's action. He was

the instrument of the major sign of election by grace. A city, a
heathen city, a city scorned in the conquest of the twelve tribes,
a city covered with blood, is chosen by God to become the center
of his people, the city of the king whom he loved, the place
where his glory will reside. Jerusalem — the city of the Lord's
Anointed, reconciling the two halves of the chosen people, Israel
and Judah, as in Christ she is established above the division between Jew and heathen. But even here an immense misunderstanding was to take shape around Jerusalem.

Jerusalem is a holy city, holy because of the Temple and
the ark. There is an absolute unity, an absolute bond, between
the city and the Temple. Each exists only by the other. But all
this is only a concession granted by God to David's wish, and on
the condition that there be no misunderstanding of the reality
of things, and that the mirror not be mistaken for the object,
David's work for God's. Thus Jerusalem is in truth Yahweh's
city, but with these words as a constant warning: "I will raise
up a house for you!" And when he has said this, the Lord comes
to dwell in the Temple. After Solomon has finished the building, God fills it with his glory, and Jerusalem's destiny is henceforth unique and ambiguous, that of being one of man's cities
chosen by God. For such is the miracle of God's submission to
an act of man, when this man has been chosen of God and is
himself subject to God's love. God can say of this city chosen
by David, and whose situation is therefore in doubt, "I have
chosen it." God can protect it, respect it, love it. He makes it
truly his, and henceforth what is said of Jerusalem can be understood as concerning not only David's city, but Yahweh's city.
He brings it truly into his plan of salvation, and into every aspect of the history of a people whose march toward the Messiah
he is guiding.

Just as Cain's work turned against him, so did Solomon's
turn out for his evil. In spite of all of Solomon's faults (among
them having built fortresses other than the only one valid for
Jerusalem — the Temple, the holy sign of its election), God was
able to say, "However, I will not tear away all the kingdom;
but I will give one tribe to your son, for the sake of David my
son and for the sake of Jerusalem which I have chosen." Thus
this city becomes an opportunity for pardon. Because David and
Solomon truly consecrated it to God, and because God accepted
this modern version of Abel's offering, he now forgives Solomon.
In that city, God's name and his glory reside. There he lives;
but in order to understand this fact we must not forget the complexity of his choice. For in spite of historical appearances,

everything must go back to and depend on God's action. And
this action has not yet come about. If Jerusalem is a holy city,
it is because she has been justified from among all other cities,
and because she has received the proclamation of the good news
(Isa. 41:27). "I bring near my justice, it is not far off! And my
salvation will not tarry! I will put my salvation in Zion, for
Israel my glory!" (Isa. 46:13). Jerusalem's spiritual history took
several directions: her relationship with the church, for example,
her particular role in the work of God's salvation, the symbolism
of the Temple as a sign of the architecture of the universe, the
date of the Temple dividing the history of Israel in two.[1] But
our only goal here is to study Jerusalem's significance for the
history of the city. What does this unique city planted in the
midst of men represent in revelation?

* * *

Jerusalem is a holy city. But she is still a city. She carries
man's mark, even in her election, even in her adoption by God.
She never escapes from all the characteristics of the city, as is
indicated by the accusations constantly aimed at her, aimed at
the sins she never ceases falling into anew. Her sins are those of
other cities; she acts like them and is condemned like them.

Jerusalem is also a bloody city — built in blood and living
in sacrifices, crime, and war. The terrible curse pronounced against
builders weighs her down also, and God adopted her when she
was covered with blood . . . (Mic. 3:10; Ezek. 16). She is the
city of pride. She also, like the other cities, insults heaven with
her mad desire to plunder heaven itself (Jer. 13:9). City of pride,
of injustice. And we must not, as is so often done, misinterpret
several texts from the prophets by identifying these words with
the history of Israel as found in the Chronicles. We are never
told that Jerusalem was sometimes righteous and sometimes not,
that she was sometimes a city of blood and sometimes a holy
city. What is condemned in her is not an accident or event, but
a permanent attitude. Yet, she is at the same time a holy city,
and this quality is never taken from her. It is not a question of
a single sin, but of a situation. Jesus confirms this. And what
makes Jerusalem's destiny of imperative importance for us is her
crossroads situation.

The great condemnation is pronounced against her because
of her idolatry. On this we have abundant material. From the
most ancient prophets down to the post-exilic, all condemn Jeru-

---

[1]For this detail see Visscher, *Les Premiers Prophètes*, pp. 361 ff.

salem's idolatry, in the midst of the common idolatry of the
people of Israel, as the summit of evil. Ezekiel, for example,
says of Jerusalem, "Your father was an Amorite, and your mother
a Hittite . . . " (ch. 16). Jerusalem's pagan origin is not an invention extracted by force from innocent texts. The prophets
understood that origin clearly. Jerusalem was not built by God,
nor was she built for him. She was thrown out into the fields by
men, as were all the cities, without purification and without
love.

And God came and saw the blood of the murder, the blood
of the foundation rites (Ezek. 16:6), and he built her up. As
did David, fortifying her, beautifying her with a fortress, surrounding her with bastions. But this force and this greatness
were in no wise righteousness and holiness. There was no covenant with her, no love for her. She was naked (v. 7), still in the
state of condemned nature.

And God covered her with his love. We cannot help being
struck by this adoption described by Ezekiel, so close to Solomon's prayer at the dedication of the Temple, bringing so directly
to mind the Lord's presence which filled the sanctuary with its
brilliant darkness. Then God made his city perfect. But sin came
into the picture — Jerusalem's sin. The gifts received from God
she consecrated to the idol. The influence of the city's angel has
outdone the influence of God's gift. She builds high places for
herself, and the substitution made by God is made over again by
the city. The Temple is dedicated to other gods: "You offered
my oil and my incense to likenesses of gods." And following
through with this terrible work which we have already seen to
be particular to the city, Jerusalem sacrifices her sons and her
daughters to idols. The sons of God's people. "You slaughtered
my children and delivered them up as an offering by fire to
them" (v. 21). The tragedy goes on to the maximum of its intensity. Never again will there be a more total repudiation,
never again an adultery more absolute. This becomes obvious
when we think what the city represents and how Jerusalem became a holy city. God's cry of pain, and Christ's cry of pain
will long ring out against such idolatry.

Jerusalem also, according to Ezekiel, brought to a zenith
the sin of the city. Sodom and Gomorrha never committed the
half of their sins, says the prophet: "Bear your disgrace, you
also, for you have made judgement favorable to your sisters;
because of your sins in which you acted more abominably than
they, they are more in the right than you. So be ashamed, you
also, and bear your disgrace, for you have made your sisters

appear righteous" (v. 52). Thus because she is a holy city, Jerusalem's sin is so much more serious, so very complete (and we will see that she has in fact committed the "total" sin), that she makes all the other cities appear righteous. And God must condemn Jerusalem with the other cities (vv. 35 ff.). She wanted to be like the others, and she will in fact be like them. All those to whom she prostituted herself will come to spoil her and strike her. Her condemnation is this act of God giving her over to those to whom she gave herself. God abandons her to those whom she loved. And these avengers will treat her like a prostitute, they will despoil her of all that in which God clothed her. She must return to that state of nudity which was her natural state.

And here we find another important revelation concerning the city. Precisely that work of man which was meant to protect and cover him, to give expression to his desire for power, is in reality naked and miserable. The city is naked, without ornament and without beauty — like a dead body abandoned in the fields. Despite all of man's best efforts, she needs other clothing, other ornaments; the work is like its maker. And the worker's folly is to believe that the work of his hands could be helpful and effective in his adventure, could protect him, whereas the work itself needs to be clothed. Because of Jerusalem's condemnation, repeated again and again down through the prophets' messages, it is easier to understand the order given to the chosen people to leave Jerusalem in order not to go down with her collapse. "Behold I set before you the way of life and the way of death. He who stays in this city shall die by the sword, by famine, and by pestilence, but he who goes out and surrenders to the Chaldeans who are besieging you shall live and *shall have his life as a prize of war*. For I have set my face against this city for evil and not for good, says the Lord: it shall be given into the hand of the king of Babylon, and he shall burn it with fire" (Jer. 21:8 ff.). Here also, God wants to separate man from the city, his people from his city. Jerusalem may be *his* city, but she is still *the* city, and in tragic mockery Jerusalem is submitted to Babylon, before she herself becomes Babylon.

It may be easily understood why there are some who wish to minimize Jeremiah's words and reduce them to purely historical proportions, to localize them to the time and place of the siege of Babylon. For they are so threatening to each of our cities and lives, that it is intolerable. Send it back to 600 B.C. — it's so much easier!

Yet, this curse on Jerusalem is not eternal, and with Ezekiel's prophecy in mind, we can see beyond it to a covenant, a covenant renewed only by grace. Only because of his own love does God reinstate the pledge broken by idolatry (the breaking off of one covenant by the desire for another). Jerusalem will be rebuilt, but we know neither when nor how. And its reestablishment does not seem to be temporal. The decisive action is double: "I will deal with you as you have done" (v. 59). Then the Lord declares that he will establish an eternal covenant, a covenant based on pardon granted by God and Jerusalem's repentance. And in the generality of this statement is to be found the ambiguity of Jerusalem's situation — an ambiguity renewed every time she becomes a holy city again, because of how extremely difficult it is to accept both sentences as ontologically possible.

But the promise goes much further, and here we see a confirmation of the eschatological meaning of verse 61: "Then you will remember your ways, and be ashamed when I take your sisters, both your elder and your younger, and give them to you as daughters, but not on account of the covenant with you." Thus Jerusalem's idolatry had made the other cities righteous when compared with her, and now the pardon granted Jerusalem will be extended because of her to all the other cities. It has already been announced that all the cities will be daughters of Jerusalem, that they are to share her lot, as Jerusalem had shared theirs. For concerning this word "sisters" there can be no doubt: Sodom and her daughters, Samaria and her daughters (v. 55), heathen, perverted cities, idolatrous and rebellious, have all received their consolation now in Jerusalem (v. 54). But Jerusalem will not reign supreme, "not on account of the covenant with you" (v. 61), that is the old covenant, the one setting Jerusalem apart. So it is not a temporal and political domination that is announced here. But because of the new covenant, all the cities will be saved in Jerusalem. She will "receive them in herself," and, by an act of God's grace, will "give" the cities as daughters to the holy city, truly holy now because she has been renewed. But this leads us into new areas.

* * *

For little hope is left us for earthly Jerusalem: "I will break this people and this city, as one breaks a potter's vessel, so that it can never be mended. Men shall bury in Topheth because there will be no place else to bury .... I will make this place like Topheth (a place where idolatry was practiced, made impure by Josiah, an unclean place where unclean bodies were buried). The houses of Jerusalem . . . shall be defiled like the place of Topheth . . . " (Jer. 19:11 ff.). But this very condemnation to uncleanliness and impurity is only a devotion of what is unclean to its unclean state.

Everything in the city of Jerusalem that still belongs to the world of the city, the creation and pride of man, is condemned to be only a devastated cemetery. It is only the shedding as through fire of that tough outer skin so difficult to remove because it is the city's very purpose in existence. The city is still that city where God's name is invoked, and for that reason she is still a sign. Once again, and not by accident or in vain, God wants his name to be invoked in a special city, that his dwelling-place be established in a city. By this means God gets a foothold in man's world. He chooses a city, or rather he lets man choose a city for him (after all the city belongs to man!), and by accepting from David's hands the consecration of man's counter-creation, God intervenes in the world where man wanted to refuse him entrance. And it is by the hand of man himself that it happens. God does not act as a master able to break down the barriers set up by man, to bring down the walls of Jericho, or to break the gates of Damascus. He does not act as a judge, far above every effort of man to revolt against him, a judge able to destroy Sodom and annihilate Babel. God meets man on his own ground, on his own terms. As he meets Satan and his spiritual powers where they are.

God's loving humility is manifest long before the incarnation (of which it is too easy to see Jerusalem as a figure, although it would not be wrong to do so) in his choice of Jerusalem. And by this act God enters into the very heart of revolt and refusal. He did not build himself a city different from all the others, more beautiful and more perfect and more powerful. He did not do something different from man, or desire for himself a pure world separated from anything impure. He took one city among others, a city of heathen, with all the faults of a city. He even chose Jerusalem for motives which historians recognize in David's action, and which are there to show us that Jerusalem was as useful as any other city. She is militarily strong, well situated, and in Benjamin's territory. Her political role and the adulteration of "religion" to politics which took place within her walls are perfect indicators of that nature entirely common to the city.

And God is present, in the midst of it all. He does not transform, he does not purify, he does not give earthly Jerusalem

more righteous politics or a holy army. He is simply where men
do not want him. Cain's immense undertaking is doomed to
failure by David's act, for henceforth man will no longer be at
rest behind his walls. From that moment when Jerusalem becomes the city of God, the city is no longer man's. That in no
way changes the situation of the other cities, but it does open
doors which men wanted closed. Man's wandering must begin
again, his mortal disquiet must reappear, because the God who
was driving him on has managed to reach him even here, even
more surely than in catastrophe or flood. But God's presence
in the counter-creation, by his election of Jerusalem, is not
drained of meaning by the idea of God meeting man on his
own territory, for God had no miracle to accomplish to meet
man there. And David's act is only due to God's love for him.
In fact, this situation in Jerusalem shows us that God is really
present in the work made by man. This is a mystery, and it is
useless to try to explain it. In reality, when man becomes involved in the titanic task of a counter-creation, when he or-
ganizes the world of death, when he builds with dead matter,
stones, bitumen, asphalt, cement, cast iron, steel, glass, alumi-
num, lime, brick, there is still life there. And when man's enormous machine becomes the body of a new spiritual power rising
in revolt like the others against the Lord of creation, that is
where the Lord is: not outside or before, but inside. And he
lets man's work go on. He lets him build immense necropolises.
He lets the angels revolt who have embodied themselves in
cities. But he is there, not excluded, present also in this work,
as Jerusalem is there to attest.

We must go a step further. Jerusalem has even more to
tell us. She became the Lord's city — not only the city where
he is present, but the city belonging to him, bearing his name.
She is therefore his power. She is *'iyr-Yahweh tzebha'oth*. She is
in fact clothed with the power of the Lord. And using the term
we have already used, God has truly adopted her. God adopts a
city. He makes her his. He makes his a work of man. And once
again, he does not change her (although her very purpose is to
announce a change), he does not moralize her (although her very
purpose is to announce a judgement of justice). What man manufactures, what is outside the work of six days, outside of that
creation made for man, outside the garden of Eden, what is
something other than what God had desired for man, what is a
deliberate desire to be somewhere other than where God had
put him, on a plane other than that intended by God — all this
God actually adopts. No longer is he in an attitude of opposi-

tion, but of covenant. This is what Jerusalem announces in such an astonishing fashion. God took all the vices and idolatries of the city and adopted the city; and his Jerusalem is no different from the other cities. But God is already completing his work for man by also doing it for man's creation. For it is not an object to be scorned.

We have already studied enough biblical texts which reveal to us the deep bond between man and his work. No longer is it possible to destroy the city without overcoming man in the same measure. No longer is it possible, without breaking him, to remove man from the environment which he desired for his own. So God, in his love, adopts the environment itself as he saves man. But the adoption is not fully realized. Man is too well entrenched behind his walls: these walls have become too useful as man's instruments and those of the rebellious angel for all to be put back in order simply and immediately.

We said that the curse is fully maintained but that Jerusalem's presence is a proclamation of God's work. Her adoption shows us God's true and final decision toward this work of man. It *is* truly a final decision — in a double sense. First, in the sense that there is no other decision after this one. God decided on the adoption of the city and he made his decision manifest in Jerusalem. He makes no retractions: the curse on the city is truly the next to the last act, followed by the adoption. But in a second sense, it comes at the end of history. Jerusalem continues on through history (perhaps not for all of history as we shall see), as witness to her adoption. But the latter will not be realized for the city, obviously and absolutely, until the time of judgement.

And in his adoption of Jerusalem in history, God goes just as far as he must to make of it a real adoption: he becomes a builder. We have already had no difficulty seeing how closely man's act of building imitates God's act of creating, and also how close a reply to that creation it is. How diabolical the builder's counterfeit of the Creator's act. And this is one of Satan's best tricks when he wants us to see in God the great architect. The architect is the opposite of the Creator. But God in his adoption has not hesitated to go all the way: he becomes a builder. How often has this promise rung out in prophecy: "I will build the walls of Jerusalem, I will make the holy city rise again!" God has taken on the responsibility, and he accomplishes what is necessary for his city, sparing nothing. After the exile, it is in obedience to his orders that Jerusalem is rebuilt — but, for an unforeseen mission. God's words will be fully accomplished only

at the end of time when, according to the promise made to
Ezekiel, it will no longer be possible to build fortifications around
Jerusalem, for it will no longer be possible to contain the innumerable multitude. Moreover, such fortifications will no longer
be necessary, since God himself will be their wall.

Thus in her entire relationship with God, Jerusalem is seen
as the first fruits of the cities. The meaning of this term is well
known, since it is often used in the Bible, and we can consider
the entire history of Israel in the light of this figure. But we
must first know of what she is the first fruits. We have already
seen what action of God was manifest in her, but the Scriptures enable us to take a step further, and we must go as far as
Scripture leads.

* * *

Throughout her history, Jerusalem served as a witness, a
witness city because she was there to show men what God's action was in regard to the city. And we have no excuse for mistakes since Jerusalem is the very city where men call on God's
name. She is a witness city because she forces man to realize
how serious the situation is: if God treats his own city in such a
way, what will happen to the others? She is a witness city because she enables one to see now, here on earth, what God is
doing in secret and will do openly as soon as his kingdom is
fully realized. She is in truth set among the other cities to make
things undeniably clear, to make them visible to all, whereas
they are normally known only to those who understand prophecy.
God's acts in Jerusalem are apparent and signal to all; and because of her, people will recognize what God has done, and she
will be for them a reason for condemnation, humiliation, slavery
and contrition, and a reason for joy and thankfulness. Men will
clearly recognize in her the mark of Yahweh. The entire Old
Testament is bursting with this possibility for natural man to
recognize this evidence, and it is clearly true that Jerusalem was
set up to make evident God's action for the city. This is what we
had in mind at the beginning of this section in saying that it
was enough to read through honestly the history of Jerusalem.
She is first of all, then, a witness to God's judgements and to his
grace toward the city. She is already a symbol of judgement —
of judgement on and for herself, first. All the partial judgements
of history on cities are clearly signs, as we have said, of the
greater judgement announced against them. But this quality of
a sign may always be refused. After all, who among us, looking

on the ashes of Hiroshima, the shell holes of London, and the ruins of Berlin or Hanoi, ever accepted these as present manifestations of a complete condemnation? It is always easy to localize a symbol in time and space and so to remove all its worth. But to do so in the case of Jerusalem is especially emasculating since the proclamation is made that it is God who is acting. And that is why Daniel could say truthfully that "under the whole heaven there has not been done the like of what has been done against Jerusalem" (Dan. 9:12). Nothing may be compared to it, for all the other cities are bastions of men against God, and it is proper and right for them to be bombarded, devastated, annihilated in the horror of a war that goes infinitely beyond all of man's wars. But when Jerusalem, the city of the Lord, is treated in this fashion, it means that God has turned away from his own city. This is the real catastrophe. God seems, by his judgement, to be casting doubt on his adoption. And with that all hope is removed for the other cities.

To the extent that Jerusalem is for all the cities a sign of God's adoption, her rejection is a sign for all of condemnation, and no argument or localization is valid. What seems, then, to be exaggeration on Daniel's part (for how many other cities have been treated more rigorously than Jerusalem!) is the expression of a universal and spiritual reality. And this reality is found to be visible and recognizable for the other peoples, for the heathen. In this respect there are many texts to show that the nations will halt stupefied before Jerusalem's destruction, and will hiss with horror. In Daniel's same prayer we find the peoples considering the curse on Jerusalem, and taking it for themselves (Dan. 9:17).

Not only is Jerusalem in her judgement a sign of the judgement coming to the other cities, but she is the place where the other cities first meet with their judgement. And the encounter between Babylon and Jerusalem is characteristic in this respect. "His rock [his king, his god, his city — Babylon] shall pass away in terror and his princes [his angels] shall be terrified by a sign: this is the word of the Lord whose fire is in Zion, and whose furnace is in Jerusalem" (Isa. 31:9). Jerusalem is the place where Babylon clearly sees her judgement, the place where Babylon meets God's flame, but not according to a simplistic interpretation of the imagery which would see Jerusalem as good and Babylon as evil, and not because the Chaldean armies will be conquered, but because the adoption of Jerusalem makes her absolutely incompatible with the other cities. So it is no longer a question of a struggle in war, but of a spiritual struggle, as is shown by the ambiguous vocabulary and word plays of our text.

The reference is to a veritable spiritual furnace which God placed in the midst of the cities by choosing one of them to bear his name. And it is this sign which terrifies the angels of Babylon, for henceforth this city is irremediably vanquished.

But just as she is the visible attestation of God's judgement, and permanently so, she is also the sign of his grace. For it is the very place where God's grace is manifest, and first of all his grace for the city itself. For all the texts announcing the restoration of Jerusalem are not necessarily to be interpreted in an eschatological sense. There is a distinction to be made here, and a certain number of prophecies may be pointed out which concern the temporal happiness of Jerusalem as a sign of the grace granted her of God, a sign meant for all. God will purify his city. He wipes out revolt and idolatry, and in the heart of Jerusalem he establishes faithfulness. He once more takes possession of her walls, and dethrones the angel of the city who had taken his stand there again. He does it freely, by an act of grace, without changing the city's being or existence, without making her reconsecrate herself or do works or offer sacrifices, for, he says, "not with silver will you be redeemed." This phrase is explicitly aimed at Jerusalem, whose only role is to bear, as a response to God's free gift, her free witness. Not a burdensome witness, a serious, theological demonstration of God's act, but a free witness, shown forth in joy, feasting, abundance, the glorious raiment of him who has received pardon: "Arise, arise, put on your raiment, Zion! Put on your festive garments, O holy city of Jerusalem!" And this order is given to render God's act visible, apparent, obvious for all people and all cities. When desolation and the curse reigned, the ruins of the city spoke aloud, and there was no need to add words or acts to explain their meaning. The very fact of the ruins constituted an interrogation for the other cities. But in the blessing and grace of which Jerusalem is also the indisputable sign, the city herself must participate. She is called upon to proclaim that blessing and grace to the other cities, to show by word and act that the happy event is not something natural, but rather supernatural, supernatural in that it breaks the normal course of revolt (itself done away with) by its very nature as a sign of God's spiritual and eternal act, as an appeal and a promise to the other cities. Such is the mission of Jerusalem for the other cities. "This city," says the Lord, "shall be for me a subject of joy, a praise and a glory before all the nations of the earth who shall hear of all the good that I shall do for them! They shall marvel and tremble because of all the good and all the prosperity I provide for it" (Jer.

33:9). Jerusalem is called upon, therefore, in her destiny as a city, in her reality as a city, to show that the reality of God's grace is for the very object of man's revolt, that the love of God extends to everything made by man, that his election is inalienable and inalterable. For God loves Jerusalem not as man's work, but as the object of his election. The city must serve as a witness of this for the other cities so they may say with the psalmist: "As we have heard, so have we seen in the city of the Lord of hosts" (Ps. 48:8). This is Jerusalem's first role, but her presence has even further meaning and God calls on her to advance.

* * *

The city of confusion! And an absolutely unbreakable bond links Jerusalem and the Word. "For the sake of Zion, I will not keep silence," says the Lord. The restoration reaches everywhere. Where God confused the languages, there his Word must resound. Where man wanted to choose a name for himself, there God decides to give him a name. But this truth must be understood even better, pressed even harder. It is not the Word of God in its totality that is revealed in and by Jerusalem. Jerusalem is not Jesus Christ, as we shall see. Jerusalem listens to the Word, keeps the promise, proclaims it to the world. On her watchtowers are sentinels who keep silence neither day nor night, who are attentive to the Word sent by God, and who repeat it for that city and for the other cities. But the other cities are not attentive to that Word, they do not repeat any message. Here Scripture is very clear. The sentinel awaits the dawn. God's Word proclaimed to Jerusalem is the proclamation of her definitive and glorious establishment on earth, of that moment when all the nations will gather together in her, when she will no longer be the city of a people, but of God himself, when there will be no more Temple, since God himself is their Temple. Jerusalem must live from this promise, she must bear witness to it, and even her historical function as a sign of condemnation and of grace is but a part of that higher mission.

She does not play this role by word or example, but by her very existence. It is not what Jerusalem says or does that expresses her true mission, but her simple presence in the world of men, confronting the cities of men. She is like a catalyst: because she is there, things change. She is like a road sign, changing the route of those who observe her. But the most basic meaning of this mission is that by her very presence she shows the world that there is a final judgement — and that its presence may already be seen in her. She is a city, and as such she must enter the conflicts of history, into its wars and victories. She does business and becomes rich, she becomes beautiful and her people great. She is subject to all the twists of history and to the reverberations of what is happening in Chaldea or Egypt. But throughout this history her only and never-ceasing purpose is to hold up before men not the end of time, but the present reality of what constitutes the end. That is why we said that her witnessing to divine grace and condemnation is an integral part of her eschatological function. She is a city already in existence, but the Word sent to her is in the Hebrew imperfect tense, which expresses an action that was begun in the past, but which is still going on, and will, for Jerusalem, come definitively to an end only at the end of time. When her merits, for example, are mentioned, those announced by and for Jerusalem are future merits: "You shall be called the city of righteousness, the faithful city . . ." (Isa. 1:26). But what she is to be, she is already — yet "figuratively," we might say. And the Word pronounced concerning her which proclaims the fulness of what she will become is not an empty one. Her true responsibility is, therefore, to bear for the world her witness as an eschatological presence.

And this is easily explained if we understand that judgement belongs essentially to the eschatological schema, and that the city by her very nature is doomed to the judgement and wrath to come. Thus the city of the Lord, from the day of her election on, is the place where God makes indisputably manifest all of his justice and his final decision concerning man and his work — man's own little world, forever lost to him by God's act. For the fact that God chose the city to show forth there the presence of final truths removes man's sovereignty over his work. Man can no longer direct it as he wishes, extract from it the use he wishes.

And in the enormous development of our cities, in the growth of urban science, which man considers to be his special domain since the city is nothing else for him but "the House of Mankind" (Le Corbusier), in his desire to make the city the place of his supremacy, may be seen the complete ridiculousness of a declaration already contradicted and the incoherency of someone trying to escape his past. He is no longer master of the city. No longer is she for him a sure refuge, or just a thing. Now she has been redirected toward a goal over which he has no control, no control whatsoever.

One reason is that he is not the one who decided on the

goal, who chose it, who determined its content. And another is that he is not the one who will bring it to pass, who has prepared it, who is driving on toward it. Nor can he keep it from coming about, or even turn it aside or slow it down. He is powerless simply because Jerusalem is what she is, because God, by taking possession of Jerusalem, symbolically took possession of all the cities. This is her function as the first fruits.

But the astonishing fact that man's work, created for a very precise reason, is inhabited by an autonomous power, and that Jerusalem is adopted by God and given another purpose and inhabited by God himself, puts her in a very delicate position: she must, as we have said, announce final truths, but by doing so she shows that her role is to be replaced. Her presence is there to announce that she is not final, that she is not the standard for all else, that she is not righteousness and truth, but that she is only there to be changed, transformed into that other city where righteousness and truth and security will dwell. Her presence announces that all that she is must disappear and that man's goal in creating the city will be found in the city, but in another city, that city which must replace Jerusalem. "In that day this song will be sung in the land of Judah: 'We have a strong city, it gives us salvation as walls and bulwarks' " (Isa. 26:1). Thus the surest thing we can say about Jerusalem is that she is between two epochs. For everything else has its own function while waiting to be replaced. The heavens and the earth are already something while waiting to be "rolled" aside for a new heaven and a new earth to appear. Man now has a life which may have a meaning, which is valid in itself, while waiting to be replaced by the fulness of life and to receive the fulness of truth. Jerusalem, on the other hand, is absolutely unimportant, meaningless, worthless, except as a proclamation of the Jerusalem to come. She is nothing if she allows herself to be separated from her eschatological function.

From whatever aspect she is considered, Jerusalem is but mediocrity in herself. Out of a 600-year history, her political significance did not last more than fifty years at the most. A city with no real political importance, she is for the most part simply a city among all the others on the victory *stelae*. What is Jerusalem compared to the political giants of the Near East? She has no commercial value, she is economically dependent on her neighbors. A laughable city from a cultural or artistic viewpoint. The Temple with all its splendor is a bit ridiculous when compared with the Assyrian palaces! We must not let ourselves be dazzled by the biblical stories. Things must be put back in their setting, and the setting is not very favorable for Jerusalem. A city without a glorious destiny in history, she is not the center of an empire, either military or cultural, she is on the invasion route of every army, vulnerable in spite of her strategic position because she is along the route of the great conflicts of her time. A city without a destiny — this is practically what characterizes her the best! Constantly besieged and changing hands, taken and retaken, with no historical continuity, she finally sinks into the mediocre position granted her by the Arab conqueror. Her only worth is in the Word of God addressed to her. Her only meaning is to testify of a new Jerusalem, and everything announced to her concerning triumph and riches, is *only* announced.

To understand Jerusalem otherwise, is to give oneself over to the illusions of historical objectivity. She is there only to announce her own disappearance and replacement. She is herself a shadow, nothing more, with no solidity in herself: a shadow which vanishes when reality appears. But this makes her no less necessary. As a kind of preparation for the final creation, earthly Jerusalem already has in her the foundation of the new creation: "Behold I am laying in Zion for a foundation a stone, a tested stone, a precious cornerstone, of a sure foundation . . . " (Isa. 28:16). It is in Jerusalem that we may find the foundation of the new Jerusalem. It is in Jerusalem and nowhere else that the final destiny of all men is to be decided and the immovable stone of reconstruction and resurrection is to be established. She is there only to disappear, her only truth is in her death. But in her is found the one thing necessary to pass victoriously through judgement and death. But she is not herself that thing. "I am laying," says the Lord. It is an act of God.

Her mission is something real. It is, in fact, true greatness. And this fact makes her something unique among all the cities even in her present role. Because her presence is a reminder of the end, and because in her is the true cornerstone, in her also is to be found the destiny of the nations and the worth of the cities. Her vocation is to present them to the world, literally to give birth to them in the light of God. It is too easy to identify Jerusalem with the church. Jerusalem is not the church, not even figuratively. What is certain is that Jerusalem is a city, and of this existing city — just as closely linked with the city to come and just as radically different from the city to come as our carnal body and our spiritual body — it is very precisely said that she will give birth to the nations. We must quote all of Psalm 87 with its astonishingly present yet universal bearing!

On the holy mount stands the city he founded!
The Lord loves the gates of Zion more than all the dwelling
    places of Jacob.
Glorious things are spoken of you, O city of God!
Among those who know me I mention Egypt and Babylon;
Behold, Philistia and Tyre, with Ethiopia.
In Zion are they born.
And of Zion it shall be said, "All were born there, and the
    Most High himself will establish it."
The Lord records as he registers the people, "This one was
    born there."
Singers and dancers alike say,
"All my springs are in you."

This psalm leads us directly toward an understanding of the
new Jerusalem, but it is nevertheless spoken to the present miserable city, to the humble servant of the policies of Babylon or
Egypt. But before entering into the study of this new city, we
must examine yet other details from our present viewpoint.

* * *

At the very center of the history we are now about to enter is Jesus Christ, without whom there would be no relation
between the present city and the future city. We should have expected it. We had to touch this point, for this is Jerusalem's last
mission. Her life is one of waiting for her Lord: "Lo, your Lord
is coming!" What makes especially clear that *this* is her attitude
is the fact that her only period of noteworthy influence, the period between the Old and New Testaments, is not recorded in
Scripture. After all, the second State of Israel, so much more
brilliant and powerful than the first, was to fill the Oriental world
with her activities, and the Western world with a certain fear,
and also with an irritation which was to lead to anti-Semitism.
Was this not the great period of Judaic expansion, the social,
economic, and even political expansion of which the Maccabean
wars were the high point? Together they form a whole. And the
invasion of the Mediterranean world by the Jews of the Diaspora
coincided with the invasion of Jewish thought and piety into the
proud circles of Hellenistic philosophy and mythology. Jerusalem
becomes a true capital — political, economic, cultural, and even
religious. She is the capital of a Jewish world in full victory, of
a people who are the most urbanized of all the peoples of that
time. She is immersed deeper than ever in her role as a city.
No recorded history? Just when this people, the smallest of all,

was becoming one of the world's powers, an historical factor of
world-wide dimensions? And this is the mystery, the trap set
and waiting. God's revelation to Israel had always been within
the confines of history, of their particular history. From Abraham
to Ezra, his revelation followed their history step by step. It is
essentially a mediocre history, full of the shattering experiences
and disobedience of this minute people. God's act is expressed
neither in a religion nor in a metaphysical system, but as history.
And just when this people launches into her great period of
history and becomes a world power, God is silent. There are no
more prophets. How sad that those prophets who do speak in
this time are false prophets. At the time of the Great Jewish War,
the people believed in this prophecy: "In that time, the Master
of the World will rise up in Judea." This long 400-year history,
full of laurels and success, has no meaning in the history God is
working out. God is silent. The people builds itself up. The law
is elaborated upon. The theological schools divide into factions.
The writings of wisdom appear. The Jewish religion becomes
more noble, and morality and piety more refined. Yet God is
silent. But here is the other side of the miracle: to its very
foundations the people of Israel stay the chosen people. How
can we tell? By the fact that the people *know* that God is silent.
They have the basic honesty of not wanting to consider as the
Word of God what is not the Word of God. At this time they
build up the canon of Scripture, and without the guidance of
God's Spirit they dare not insert there the story of their present
exploits as though they had meaning as acts of God. They gather
together the texts of revelation dealing with their history. But in
the humility of God's people, they realize that their glorious
present history is not revelation. They gather a few wisdom writings, in Chronicles they reconstruct a past history, but accept
Ezra and Nehemiah as the end of their significant history. And
behind the events, the heroic acts, the high successes of these
400 years, nothing. Jerusalem a powerful capital is only in waiting. That is all that can be said for her.

Chapter Four

JESUS CHRIST

I. THE FULFILLMENT

JERUSALEM WAS WAITING. BUT NOW HER WAITING IS OVER.
Our first concern, however, is not Jesus Christ as an answer to
her hopes. Nor is it Jesus himself in his relations with Jerusalem.
Once again it is the city, but as affected by Jesus Christ. And
the first item of evidence that cannot but appear is that Jesus
Christ in no way modifies the Old Testament message. In this
particular area also, Jesus Christ fulfills but does not change
what was said in the law and the prophets. Everything that was
said finds its true meaning in Jesus Christ but does not disappear
or change. On the contrary, it takes on its true meaning, its full
force, its complete seriousness. Until Jesus Christ, it could be
considered as human opinion. In Jesus Christ, all that the people
of Israel recognized as revelation is certified, as well as accomplished and made clear. The same is true for both the highest
spiritual truths and the strangest or most ridiculous ceremonial
and social laws. Jesus Christ makes no distinction between types
of law (Matt. 5:18; 23:23, 26). The same is true of the universal
bearing of God's Word, including his judgements on the city.

Jesus Christ has no conciliatory or pardoning words for the
cities. But when he speaks to men he has both curses and pardon.
Promises of salvation and warnings. When he speaks to the cities,
he never has anything but words of rejection and condemnation.
He never proclaims grace for man's work. All he recognizes is
its devilish quality, and his only reaction is to struggle against
the power of the city trying to hinder his work. Although John
the Baptist fled the city and Jesus Christ went out to join him
and was baptized in the desert, there are no conclusions to be

113

drawn from this. But after his baptism, Jesus' first contact with the city takes place in the Temple, in the holy city. And it is the Devil who takes him there. We must not see in him a special demon for the holy city. One of the three temptations took place in the desert (the place always longed for by the Jewish people as the place of their past holiness), one on a high mountain (the primitive place for the worship of Yahweh: Sinai, Tabor, the mountains of Samaria), and the other in the holy city, on top of the Temple. Israel recognizes, then, that Satan acts not only in the city, but in all holy places. Of the holy city, Jesus first knew only one aspect: Satan received him there and asked him to prove his divine sonship. And it was in this Jerusalem that the prophets had announced that the Son of God was to be recognized and confirmed. That is where the Messiah is expected, and so Satan uses the holy city as a lure, as a temptation for Jesus Christ. This is why he was taken to Jerusalem. It would seem that this is his first contact with the city — a contact marked with Satan's stamp. It is impossible to affirm that the city here has any positive value; it is rather the instrument of temptation. No more.

But then we have Christ's decisive statement concerning three Judean cities, which is in fact to be understood for all the cities of Judea and for all cities: "Then he began to upbraid the cities where most of his mighty works had been done, because they did not repent. 'Woe to you, Chorazin! woe to you, Bethsaida! for if the mighty works done in you had been done in Tyre and Sidon, they would have repented long ago in sackcloth and ashes. But I tell you, it shall be more tolerable on the day of judgement for Tyre and Sidon than for you. And you, Capernaum, will you be exalted to heaven? You shall be brought down to Hades. For if the mighty works done in you had been done in Sodom, it would have remained until this day. But I tell you that it shall be more tolerable on the day of judgement for the land of Sodom than for you'" (Matt. 11:20 ff.). First of all, this text confirms several characteristics of the city with which we have already become acquainted. One item: the city is a specific being, independent of its inhabitants. Jesus speaks to the city itself and threatens it with punishment, against the collectivity of its inhabitants, of course, but even more certainly against the city as an independent being. He speaks of judgements against the city, and so magnifies what Scripture has already taught us. For it is not a question of the inhabitants, but of the city itself.

Obviously we could find an answer to avoid this reality. On

the one hand, we could say that Jesus is speaking figuratively, using metonymy, designating the inhabitants by the name of the city in which they are grouped. On the other, we could say that Jesus shared the erroneous concepts of his time as to fact, and being a man had limited intellectual and scientific knowledge. His words must not, therefore, be taken absolutely seriously, and in any case not to the letter.

As for the first objection, we must notice a very clear distinction in the texts between those intended for the city and those in which the inhabitants are mentioned. We have already met with this distinction, and in the Gospels we must also contrast our present text with the one where Jesus speaks of the inhabitants of Nineveh. But this argument is not yet clinching. However, the proposed objection does lead to problems that are extraordinarily difficult to handle, if not impossible. If Jesus means by the word "city" its inhabitants, is the human collectivity then condemned with no discrimination? Must we believe that no one in the Judean cities was reached by Christ's miracles? Jesus also speaks of the day of judgement with regard to these cities. If he is speaking of the inhabitants, is his judgement to be limited to those of his time? The text, however, makes no such limitation at all (and to a certain extent is in this detail in contrast with the preceding pericope: vv. 16-19). Is he condemning all the inhabitants of the accused cities for all time? If so, how could we accept such a permanent condemnation? How even could we understand it? In fact, if we refuse to take the city as a specific entity, the text is incomprehensible. And the final blow against the above objection is that the idea of the text does not stand alone — it is not the only one to be understood in this sense. It is, as we have shown, a constant doctrine in Scripture. It would be too easy to rid ourselves of it by saying that all the texts in agreement on this point are using metonymy. What would be the basis for such an argument? What criterion would enable us to give to the texts any but their most objective literal sense?

But then we must meet the second objection: Jesus was speaking thus because he shared the erroneous beliefs of his time. Now it is certainly true that Jesus did share these beliefs; we do not believe that he had any particular light on nuclear physics or the jet engine. He probably believed that the earth was flat, that the sky was an immovable vault, that the "cradle of civilization," as it is so elegantly described, was in Mesopotamia, and that there was nothing outside of the Mediterranean world. But is his teaching about the city on that plane of his-

torical and geographical knowledge? I have tried to show so far
that the city has great *spiritual* significance, that man's destiny is
intimately connected with it, that it is a problem of sin and
grace, rebellion and forgiveness, and that we are not, therefore,
dealing here with simple natural knowledge, but with knowledge
that concerns man's salvation. And if such is the case, we must,
when referring to this order of knowledge, be reticent about
speaking of Jesus' "beliefs." For in this area, there can be no
doubt for those who accept Jesus as the Christ, that he knew
"what is in man, and all that is necessary for man's salvation."
As soon as we begin dealing with truth, what the Son of God
says is valid as truth. This is so even if it can be shown that it
is a question of beliefs from the milieu in which Jesus lived.
What does this mean? Simply that these beliefs are declared true
by Jesus Christ; the sheer fact that they were the beliefs of God's
people is no reason to marvel that they could be true: they were
simply a part of God's revelation to his people. Thus all the
works on "Jesus in his time" which try to show that Jesus offered no original contribution but adopted what the Israelites
believed, must be turned inside out, for if the Israelites believed
these things, it was *because* Jesus Christ fulfilled — not revealed
— them.

Moreover, if we are to reject these "beliefs," on what can
we base our decision? On what grounds can we declare a given
statement of Jesus concerning man's salvation true or false? On
what grounds can we make ourselves judges of truth? On the
grounds of our reason, our conscience, our feelings? But does
the very fact that they are "ours" not make them subject to error, and therefore subject to doubt? Who will serve as surety to
guarantee them for us?

Enough of that. Why go any further in such an inquiry
since from the start it shows how ridiculous man's pretensions
are? What Jesus says about the city is said concerning the city
as such. He places a curse on it because it has not repented. This
we have already understood. But our present text takes us further: Jesus says, "Woe." Not often does he pronounce this word
which is so very final. Jesus Christ, our protector and advocate
before God, turns and says, "Woe." If he, too, becomes our ac-
cuser, who then will protect us?

He does not say the word often, but the list of his curses
reveals a great deal. Woe to the Pharisees who put their confidence in their personal holiness, in their strict observance of
tradition. Woe to the scribes and doctors of the law who put
their confidence in a perfect knowledge of the law and in their

science of sacred things. Woe to the rich who put their confidence in their material power, in the money which enables them to rule the world. Woe to those who laugh, who put their confidence in happiness and who are in quest of earthly happiness. Woe to those who are seeking men's praise, and who put their confidence in public opinion. Woe to those who build the tombs of the prophets, that is, who put their confidence in a spiritual truth which they have killed and which they pretend to conserve and honor by themselves. Woe to pregnant women, to those, that is, who carry a human hope and who, whatever our opinion may be, put their confidence in this hope — which is, moreover, true and legitimate. Woe to him by whom scandal comes about, and to him who betrays Jesus, for this is triumph over God, against God, the declaration of man's autonomy, the banishment of the Lord's messenger. There is no other "woe." And the city is included in this series.

Now what characterizes all these woes brought against completely different beings who seemingly have nothing to do with one another, is that they are all aimed at one attitude of man. In every case, man may be observed putting his confidence elsewhere than in God. In every case, man tries to make himself the center of his life, to put his reason for existing in something he possesses, and which he uses to protect himself against God. The city is placed among man's efforts.

Jesus asks the city to repent. But to repent from what? What is the extraordinary sin of these three cities of Chorazin, Bethsaida, and Capernaum? They are condemned because they do not understand his miracles. The miracles do not lead them to repentance. And we must come back to this question: Repent of what? Of the same sin as other men? But why is Jesus speaking to the cities as he did to the Pharisees and the doctors of the law? And why does he compare them to Sodom and to Tyre, who also had a very particular sin in history? Nothing enables us to say that these cities were particularly idolatrous, as the commentators seem to believe. Their call to repentance concerns the same facts, the same attitude that characterizes all those against whom Jesus' "woe" has been proclaimed — man's confidence in himself, in his security, in his spiritual life, in his power made sure by his own hands. This is what is condemned. Jesus Christ is taking up again the judgement pronounced against the city from the beginning of time. Chorazin and Bethsaida must repent, in fact, of being cities, of being cities in the sense of an instrument used by man to strengthen his confidence outside of God. That is also why he speaks to the city as such, as an independent body, and it is the only time that woe is proclaimed against a thing and not against a man. The city is called upon to repent of all that she is, by her origin, by her material reality, by her spiritual reality, and by her structure and meaning. She is found on the first row of all men's attempts to escape and revolt. The Old Testament teaching is here astonishingly confirmed.

That is also why only miracles are mentioned here. It seems that in the face of the power of the city, words are powerless, and only the miracle is effective — ministry by the miracle. This ministry is not, of course, valid in itself, does not dominate, but serves as a part of the ministry of the Word. It is a miracle that refers to the Word, but which is nevertheless different, with its own particular function. And here it is a question of miracles. Already when Jesus was sending out his disciples to the cities of Israel, he emphasized the importance of miracles. Now we have exclusively the act that had been accomplished for the city: Chorazin and Bethsaida are not blamed for not having listened to words but for not having understood miracles. This bond established between the city and miracles is easy enough to understand. The Gospel miracle is first a manifestation of the power of the Holy Spirit. As a manifestation of power, it is a necessary weapon for the warfare with the power represented by the city. We can see in it a kind of confrontation between two powers. The city as an expression of the spirit of power, herself a material and spiritual power, is vanquished and convicted only by a manifestation of power. The human word has no way of coming to grips with her. It cannot penetrate the city, which, as we have said, is the place of confusion, the place of mutual incomprehension, the place of spiritual separation. The city cannot understand words, and Jesus speaks to her only to curse her. Furthermore, his words are not exactly spoken *to* the city, but are pronounced *against* her, and they do not establish a relation, but serve notice of a schism. All that the city can receive is a fact. She herself is a fact and can submit only to a fact, a fact which establishes proof; and this is the goal of the miracle, as though the Spirit's intervention were not separate from its manifestation. In the proclamation of God's Word, there is the word announced by man and there is the action of the Spirit which can transform it into the Word of God and make it authoritative. In the miracle there is no such separation. Here the Spirit manifests himself clearly, brutally, one might say. And no less is needed to speak to the city; for as both a spiritual and a material power, she can be dominated only by a power which expresses itself by both material and spiritual means, and both at the same time. And Jesus is blaming these cities for rejecting miracles that were great enough for the city to recognize and defer to. She did not want to yield her spiritual power. She did not recognize the power acting in her midst. She did not recognize by the signs shown her that "the kingdom of heaven is near." The Word is spoken, in the city, to people whom God has from all eternity chosen there.

There is another reason why this particular language is used for the city. The Gospel miracle is essentially the restoration of God's order which sin has thrown out of kilter. And the city is a symbol of this disorder. She has within her every disorder because she is the great means of separation between man and God, the place man made to be alone. She is the very center of the world's disorder, and it is therefore useless to speak to her of order. There is a basic lack of understanding. A two-dimensional being cannot imagine three-dimensional space, and we cannot ourselves imagine four-dimensional space. We can calculate what it would be, but we cannot live it. Thus the city can calculate, but not live, any word concerning God's order. But the miracle, the restoration of God's order in her midst, both the proof and the experience of that order (not every miracle, but as practiced by Jesus Christ), can be received and lived. And it is again because the city does not want to live God's order that Jesus Christ condemned her.

Jesus' very words show that the city could have understood, could have grasped the sign. She could also have recognized herself as beaten, as included in a truly new order of things. What she could not do confronted with words, she could do confronted with miracles. She can, when a miracle speaks, change the focus of her confidence to God. The miracle is just that: God's call for man's confidence, and particularly for the city its purpose is to replace confidence in walls by confidence in God's Spirit. How many times did the prophets point up just that opposition! The miracle is ever an expression of God's power acting as a magnet for man's confidence. Thus the curse may yet be explained in this way: In spite of miracles, these cities did not place their confidence in God. And it is, in fact, right after Jesus' acts in these cities that the condemnation becomes final. It must yet be carried to its climax in the death of Jesus, but his death in the city has already been announced in the rejection of his miracles.

II. NEITHER HEARTH NOR HOME

Jesus had no home. His entire life, from birth to death, was a life of wandering. Just when he was about to be born, an event transpired that made his mother leave home. Such is the order of Quirinius: she must become a vagabond. There is no farsighted organization to prepare step by step itineraries. She must leave — Jesus will be born away from home. She and her husband must go back to the city of their origin, to Bethlehem, a little town in Judea — in fact hardly a town. But Bethlehem is also the city of David, where the descendant of David must be born, which gave the great king his eternal worth. And in this very city there is no room for the Christ. How could it be that even in the city of David, there is no room for Jesus? If the world is such as the Bible describes it, it is normal for it to close up when the Son of God appears, as a poisonous orchid springs shut at the touch of danger. There is no room for the Prince of Peace, and he must find a hole in the stable of an inn. He must not be born in a noble home. Men must not put themselves out of their way to take him in, these men of the city. Those who come are shepherds of the field, and travelers. But men settled in the city can only have Herod's idea: he has come to bother us, to trouble us, to change our kingdom and our habits — he must be killed. Herod, a true prince of the city. And from that capital, lightning bolts are launched against the innocent one. Even though they miss him, they force him to flee. When Rome has finished the census, Jerusalem takes over its campaign against Jesus: "When Herod the king heard this, he was troubled, and all Jerusalem with him . . ." (Matt. 2:3). Jerusalem is a city, and its order is no different than any other city's. So it takes measures early to force the rebel and the blasphemer to flee, even if he is as yet only a babe in swaddling clothes. Not yet is he to have a home, for he must flee to Egypt, once again on the road, in search of security. In the city there is no place of security for him. Perhaps after his infancy, Jesus did come to know a resting period, life in one locality, peace; we know nothing for sure, for in the only text we have that refers to Jesus' childhood, he was already twelve, and still traveling, coming back from Jerusalem. This is all we know of his childhood. How surprising it is not to see him settled down as the member of the family, never to see in Scripture the appealing tableau, traditional and imaginary, of the "Holy Family." When we see Jesus again, it is on the road, never at rest, never in one place to carry out a long-term work there. And Jesus is perfectly conscious of this situation: "Foxes have holes, and birds of the air have nests, but the Son of man has nowhere to lay his head" (Luke 9:58). This is certainly no complaint on his part, but his response to the generous gesture of a scribe who declared that he would follow him anywhere. And we must not seek an emotional reaction to Jesus' poverty, to his miserable condition. He did not portray his condition to touch our hearts. Nor was he boasting of his poverty. Nor was his philosophy one of rootlessness. Jesus did not declare that it is the proper thing not to have a home. He was not giving himself as an example. He was not claiming that homelessness is favorable to the spiritual life, whereas the settled condition is not. On the one hand he does not say: "Even the animals have a place to stop and live, but the Son of man is so poor and miserable that he is not even on a level with the animals." Nor, on the other hand, does he say: "Having a place to stop, to settle down, is the condition of the animal. To assume this condition is to succumb to animal temptation. Man is called upon to dominate such a temptation, to tear himself from fleshy bonds and fly off to spiritual adventure, in witness to his liberty." We must go to neither of these extremes. Jesus' words are only a statement of fact: this is how things are. To the man who says he will follow him, Jesus answers that he will have to do a lot of walking. He will have to abandon human comforts and securities, because, as a matter of pure fact, the Son of Man has no place to call home. This statement is particularly precious when we think that Jesus practically never spoke of his earthly condition. And he characterizes it as having neither hearth nor home. When he speaks thus, he is not referring to a simple coincidence or to a temporary circumstance. He does not limit it to "right now." He has no home. Nor does he say, "I," but rather, "The Son of man." So it is his constant situation, as it must be, from which there is no question of escaping. It is the condition of the servant of Yahweh. Now if Jesus attaches so much importance to this fact — which is not a detail of his life, but the condition of the Messiah himself — if Jesus is not complaining that men's wickedness forced him to such a situation, but only describing a simple objective reality, what does this mean for us? At last we see the realization of a complete attitude of wandering. At last there appears before our eyes the one bearing Cain's curse. Cain wanted nothing to do with his sentence. Cain revolted and built the city. It was against man's will that he was nevertheless a wanderer on the face of the earth, broken away from his environment. But Jesus took the full condition of man. Totally man, except for sin. But that means that he had to accept the consequences of sin. We are well aware of it when we contemplate the cross. We are less well aware of it when we think of his life. Throughout his life, he entered into man's slavery, the slavery of his body: he was hungry and thirsty and sleepy. He knew what cold and dirt and tired limbs were. He entered into the slavery of man's condition: all of God's curses pronounced against men from the beginning of the world he knew, he suffered, he took for himself. Thus Cain was sentenced to wandering, and Jesus, too, is condemned to wandering. His ceaseless travels are not because of duty, reward, or pleasure, but because he is fully man and therefore a wanderer like the Wandering Jew. He fulfills in himself the curse which, pronounced against Cain, has never been completely fulfilled because of the means used by Cain. Jesus takes this curse for himself and recognizes that it must have its effect. Thus the Son of Man experiences the fulness of isolation, the fulness of intimacy with nature. He gives his innocent blood, and against him Abel's blood cries from earth to heaven. He accepts perpetual flight to remove the curse from other men, so that man might finally find a legitimate place to end his running, so that the call of chimerical horizons might no longer be a falsehood bound to a curse. Jesus does not seek, then, to protect himself against this curse. He does not follow Cain's way. He builds no city, he finds no sheltered refuge, he settles in no one place. And it is this acceptance which both delivers us and gives Jesus the full knowledge of urban reality that leads him to confirm the words of the prophets. The only protection accepted by Jesus is the world of God, God's sign on him. Cain had had no confidence in this protection. Had it been otherwise, in fact, he would not have been Cain. Jesus does have the confidence. On the one hand, he accepts the curse of wandering, and on the other he accepts God's mark on him to protect him in the world. He knows that if he stays faithful, his father can send twelve legions of angels to guarantee his safety if necessary.

What good are city walls? Jesus takes no part in the city. He rejects her money, arms, sciences. He ignores the capital and the progress of civilization. He knows that the only legitimate rest is found in confidence in God. He knows that if he accepts man's wandering, he is building the kingdom where man will finally be able to come home from his millennial flight and find his full development in truth.

But it is then all the easier to understand why he refuses man the possibility of settling down in the city, why he "sends forth" his disciples, with no respite, why he condemns the city: If man keeps up Cain's reaction, if man continues to take the city as his port and as his security, then Jesus' work is in vain — or rather, man will forever be ignorant of his true port and his true security.

Once again Jesus' judgement (which he could pronounce because he had begun by taking it for himself) is *for* man. Man must some day know where his real interest lies, must some day choose what is most favorable for him — for he has to choose! Fence-straddling is impossible. Jesus' refusal to settle down in a city to carry on there a pious ministry shows us that to do this would be an unforgivable betrayal. It would, for him, be accepting the propositions of Satan. But what madness, it would seem. What a beautiful field of action Jesus could have had in Jerusalem — in his capital, near the authorities whom he could have influenced, near the high priest whom he could have converted, in his country's religious nerve center, at the Temple where he could have preached to the theologians. What an opportunity, to be in the great city, where he had the multitude within reach and all the proletariat he should have sought out! For while Jesus preached often to the peasants and to the artisans of the small villages, he spent a mere eight days with the slaves and workers of Jerusalem, the only proletariat of Judea. What a mistake, what madness not to have seen all the advantages he would have had for his ministry by settling in Jerusalem! But he did not. Jesus chose against the city; he preferred not to accept the glory and amplitude the city would have given him, but rather to stay faithful to his calling of taking on himself the totality of the human condition, and therefore of refusing what man uses to escape the condition God had decided should be his.

When Jesus went to the city it was only to leave soon. Not only did he not reside there, returning each evening to Bethany, but he also left the city to die. He was, in fact, forced to leave it. The demons of the city could not tolerate the Son of God in their midst, and in fulfillment of the law they leagued themselves against him. For it is well known that it was to accomplish the law that Jesus was thus crucified outside the gates. The scapegoat had to be sent out of the camp, into the desert. The bodies of animals sacrificed as sin offerings, whose blood was carried into the Temple, were also to be taken out of the camp, and burned outside the city (Lev. 4). It was therefore necessary that Christ the victim also be rejected, as a sign of his rejection by the law and by the power of the city. For the latter is, with

regard to Jesus Christ, on exactly the same level as the law itself. When Jesus obeys the law, he is expelled from the city,
which cannot take possession of Christ. His death is only the
eternal assurance of the city's actual conquest to be carried out
by God from the outside. But for now, all the powers of the
world and the angel of the city have come out at once, have
gathered before the cross to be in turn nailed to it and disarmed.
And as for the angel of the city, he is by Jesus' act separated
from his army, from his strength, and from his means. He is
drawn outside, as the sin resting on the goat's head was taken
outside the camp. He is forced to follow the Son of God where
he wanted himself to draw the man. He is forced to deprive
himself of his own glory just when he is seeking to deprive
Jesus of his. But all this is yet a secret, for this death *seems* on
the contrary to ensure the triumph of the powers.

Thus Jesus, in his very person and in his entire life, shows
himself to be a stranger to the world of the city. In no way
does he participate in this work of man, he who in all other
aspects participated fully in man's life. And it is precisely because he took on himself the fulness of human life that he refused this false remedy, this false source of help, this false greatness. And it is because he was establishing the Kingdom of
Heaven in the midst of the world that he totally rejected man's
counter-creation.

In any case, this shows us the relationship between the city
and the effects of the miracle. In reality, one cannot evangelize
the city only by the Word. The only way to speak to her is by
miracle. By miracle or by martyrdom.

III. THE MULTITUDE

But these men? For Jesus does not condemn the men in
the city. Jesus' condemnation of the impenitent cities is found
in Matthew immediately after his questions addressed to the
multitude concerning John the Baptist. And he presents to that
crowd their own acts, their own responsibility. But he does not
condemn them. And, completely distinct from his attitude toward the crowd, there is his curse against the city. We have seen
that until Jesus Christ, man was imprisoned in his work, caught
in his own creation. Today's situation is nothing new: man has
let loose forces he cannot master, which drag him along where
he does not want to go. The Old Testament teaches us that such

has ever been the case. Man the creator of the city has become the prisoner of the city, doomed with her to destruction, condemned with her, cursed in her. We have seen that the inhabitants of Sodom and of Gomorrha were swallowed up in their ruin; there was no separation. In fact, the city is one of man's treasures, and man's heart is possessed by the demon of the city. "Where your treasure is, there will your heart be also."

But what appears new in Jesus' teaching is that he does not include man in the city's downfall. Doubtlessly there is no material change: the inhabitant of a city is still materially wiped out in the ruins of his little world, just as in the time of Joshua the inhabitants of fortress cities were dispatched with the edge of the sword. But the final situation, the situation before God, has been changed: man is no longer entangled in his work, because Jesus Christ came for man as separate from his work, because he came to save man considered as though he were outside of his work. And this is why his condemnation of what holds man back, of the seducing city, was so violent.

Although man is caught by his own traps, Jesus Christ does not brush him aside and does not condemn him. In Matthew's text we see Jesus speaking differently to the multitude than to the city. The multitude, the crowd! Such is the form of life in the city. Man can be nothing but a crowd in the city. He is never separate, never physically alone, never one, face to face with himself. In the city we find the strange phenomenon of man separated from himself and others by a sheet of glass, invisible yet present, unbreakable, impassable. Never alone yet deserted. One man in a crowd, this is the constant situation of all of us. A crowd is not just a number of people gathered in one place, a material phenomenon observable by counting the people in the crowd. It is also a psychological, sociological, and spiritual situation which we today usually refer to as a mass. It is observable, then, by the orientation of the mind and not by statistics. A man can be in the crowd elsewhere than in the city, but here he is always and necessarily a member of the crowd. And because he does not have enough room to live, his acts are measured, his voice lowered, his eyes averted. For everything collides with the neighboring walls and immediate presences. He has no silent zone; he lives in a perpetual noise that eliminates any isolation, any meditation, any authentic contact. And soon he can no longer tolerate the judgement of silence. He cannot stand to be constantly seen and heard. Even if no one is paying attention to him or especially observing him, he is under the control of others, of the anonymous Other One. Be-

cause houses touch, odors blend, noises combine, lights do away
with night — for these simple material reasons (so negligible,
it would seem), the man of the city is necessarily a man of the
crowd.

In the eleventh chapter of Matthew, we find this connection
between the city and the crowd. Jesus speaks to the multitude,
then to the city. And his words to the crowd already seem to be
characterized by a kind of pity for their inconsistency and weakness. The multitude does not know what it is doing: "What did
you go out into the wilderness to behold?" The crowd felt itself
drawn to John the Baptist; they left their usual places and went
out in search of something, but even then did not know exactly
what. If they went out in search of a prophet, they did not know
which prophet he was or what kind. They were drawn to that of
which were ignorant. They were obedient to an inconsistent
movement, to an impulsion felt by a crowd rather than by a normal man. They did not know what they were seeking. The crowd
acts without thinking — for a goal which is not clearly conceived.
And Jesus responds to their ignorance. He reveals their inconsistency and explains to them why they act as they do. And this
is how he speaks to a crowd. To a man he responds otherwise:
he speaks to him in other terms.

* * *

The crowd lives with indecision and division. Jesus characterizes the multitude gathered before him as a group of children — irresolute, uncoordinated, constantly wrangling, judging
falsely and recklessly. They are "children speaking to other children." The point of Jesus' words is doubtlessly not to offer a
description, but the description is nonethless there and must not
be neglected — even more so when we consider that this is not
the only time the Gospels show Jesus in real contact with the
crowd, judging it, speaking of it. And Jesus always sees the
crowd in its aspect of incomprehension and indecision.

This may be seen in the story of Jairus, one of the rulers
of the synagogue. When Jesus saw the mourning crowd in front
of Jairus' house, noisily lamenting the girl's death, he ordered
them to disperse, because as a crowd they were simply obeying
a sociological reflex and did not know what they were doing.
They were incapable of recognizing who was before them, incapable of knowing that he was the vanquisher of death. They
scoffed at him. He sent the crowd away, but had no harsh words
for them. It is this constant inconsistency (and there is no need

here to refer to the psychology of a crowd) which seems to draw Jesus to the crowd, which makes him speak as he does, which moves him to compassion.

This multitude has hardly any right to his compassion. When the Gospels mention a crowd, all of man's sufferings are present — his lameness, his blindness, his disease. But we must recognize that a crowd has no other characteristic than its misery as a crowd. In this crowd, according to the chief priests, there are only accursed men, men who do not know the law (John 7:49). It is composed of individually miserable men, despised men who, because they do not know the law, also have no knowledge of the way of salvation and do not lead the pious and righteous life required by God.

The crowd today has not changed its composition. It is still typically formed by those who do not have enough money to live in "residential" districts, by those who must rely on public transportation, by those for whom material considerations take precedence over moral questions, by those who, on the other side of the coin, do not have the moral education or the refinement (not only the means) to want to be distinct from the crowd, to be separate and begin an individual life. It is a well-known fact that both intellectual advancement and conversion to a faith separate a man from the crowd. As soon as he takes an individual position, there is a break in the mass, or at least an attempt to escape, although the conditions under which men live today do not favor an escape. In any case, the man of the city and the man in the crowd (the two areas always tend to overlap, if they are not completely identical) is the same man unversed in the law, accursed, whom the chief priests condemned so violently.

The crowd is thus composed of the most miserable of men, and on the other hand, it is the most miserable way for a man to live. It is as though all that makes up his dignity, his courage, the unity of his creation as a human person, were lost there. It is as though the remnants of his humanity disappeared in the crowd. Miserable crowd — not only because of the men making it up, but in itself, in the body it forms whose tendencies and impulses are infrahuman, but which nevertheless prove to be extremely active and powerful. For the crowd is always seeking. So it is presented in the Gospels. The crowd is seeking as though it were conscious of only one thing, knowing that something is missing, but not knowing what. It has a terrible undefined sense of something's being absent, and desperately wants that presence. We see all this in the simple fact that before the crowd

Jesus is moved to compassion. Is it not remarkable that this
phrase is used only to characterize Jesus' attitude toward the
multitude? Never, to my knowledge, is this phrase used when
Jesus has before him an individual case of suffering. Even when
Jesus speaks to a person and is moved to compassion, that person is a part of the crowd, a person *from* the crowd, and his
compassion is for the crowd and every one of its members. This
is the case when it is stated that Jesus had pity on the two blind
men in the midst of a crowd (Matt. 20:34). As a corollary to
this, we must notice that almost every time Jesus has a crowd
before him, he feels compassion for it, as may be seen in many
passages (e.g., Matt. 9:36; 14:14; 15:32; and Mark 6:34; 8:2).
The precise use of the term is certainly not accidental. Jesus
feels compassion specifically for the crowd, and this implies,
when compared with the other biblical data, the truth of our
description of the crowd. Jesus is thus moved to compassion
because the crowd appears to him a flock of sheep without a
shepherd.

This characteristic corresponds exactly to our description
above and would be enough in itself to justify the notion of
misery. Jesus is moved to compassion because he is faced with
man's lowest condition. But this feeling is not at all the common,
everyday feeling of pity. Jesus is not seized by an emotional
sentiment, the same by which we are seized when in the presence of some misfortune. It is not the pity of subject for object,
with due respect for barriers and distances, which usually goes
from a higher plane to a lower. There is much more than that
here: Jesus is not obeying his human nature subject to feeling,
he is fulfilling his destiny as the Savior. His compassion is the
suffering he experiences for those who suffer. Not only does he
suffer with them, he suffers in their stead. Jesus breaks down
the partition separating the men of the crowd: he goes into the
crowd, bears its misery, its desperation, and its mournful de-
spondency, and makes them his own. His compassion is not only
the act of love, outgoing toward whatever is humble and despised; it is the act of salvation effected at the extreme point of
human baseness. If Jesus is moved to compassion by the crowd,
it is because it is there only that he can see the human condition he is bearing in its naked reality. Thus he can feel the
great emptiness behind man's demand, and he is led not only
to take on that condition, but also to respond to that demand.
And Jesus' compassion seems to have no effect; it has no success in human terms. Although he has before him a crowd with
no goals, wandering like sheep without a shepherd, Jesus does

not become their head. He gives no outward manifestation of being a shepherd to drive and guide the flock. He imposes on them no password, no responses, no orders, no directions. He makes no use of his quickening power. He does not lead the crowd elsewhere. Apparently he leaves it as it is. He heals the sick, he gives men material food, which will perish. And then he sends them away. Rarely does he speak to the crowd. Most often when he speaks it is to a person in the crowd, or else, as at the beginning of the Sermon on the Mount, he speaks to a small group while surrounded by a great many people.

Then what happens? The answer requires an understanding that goes beyond appearances. The most important fact is that by his compassion Jesus makes his condition the condition of man in a crowd. And by this very act, the phenomenon of the crowd explodes, we might say. Everything incoherent and senseless in the mass is found torn to pieces by the presence of awareness itself. The being that the crowd is cannot contain Jesus Christ and is thus transformed. The crowd ceases to be a crowd in the spiritual sense, although it continues materially to be a great assembly of men. But this meeting is also characterized by material changes, particularly by the dissociation of crowd and city. The crowd surrounding Jesus is the dwelling of another spirit, and the full fruits of this spirit may be seen in the day of Christ's triumphal entry, when the crowd recognizes exactly the king it was waiting for, a king able to fulfill its demands, able to transform its mournful desperation into a new and ever present joy.

Jesus Christ disperses the crowd because he can then deal with each man in the crowd. Each person ceases to be an atom in the mass and again becomes individual, separate and complete, not completely alone because each person is in the presence of his Savior and Lord. And that is also the meaning of the miracle of healing, of the feeding of the five thousand — the feeding of the crowd (*one* meaning among others). By healing, by the food given to each one by means of a miracle accomplished for all, there is a kind of individualization within the crowd. Jesus Christ considers each individual in the reality of his suffering, of his demand; and each person is taken from the mass — not separated from it, but delivered from its demons. Thus Christ's victory is within, not only within man (and made manifest in history), but within the crowd. This individual, wounded by the conditions of his life, by his work on a production line, by the constant noise, by the slum where he lives, by the bestial contact of others he cannot shake off, can find a certain unity, a certain healing, a genuine deliverance. But he is still a member of this miserable body, he still belongs to the miserable crowd. And we can already discern the necessity of this situation; for the flock without a shepherd is forever an expression of the suffering Christ took on as his own.

The crowd came, and Jesus did not become its leader to guide it toward a better society, toward the kingdom which he said had come near. It had no shepherd, and apparently Jesus did not decide to be its shepherd. What a strange situation! But if we find it strange, if we do not understand the Messiah's attitude, it is because we do not understand him or the act of the crowd. The crowd came to Jesus. It was not going *elsewhere.* And Jesus was not to lead it elsewhere. Once it got to Jesus, it had reached its goal. With no idea of what it was seeking, nonetheless, once it found Jesus, it had nowhere else to go. Jesus was not to lead it on a long pilgrimage. He is not one witness among others of man's long quest. He is not an indication of the direction to be taken. He is not an example to be followed. He is not a momentary translation of man's permanent hope which has created so many Edens, golden ages, paradises, millennia and communistic societies. He is not preparing the ideal scientific society where every man will have his own place and be happy. He is himself, himself alone, the answer, the goal, and the kingdom of God present on earth. When the crowd comes to Jesus, it is in the kingdom. And this is another meaning of the healing miracles and the feeding of the multitude. Beyond Jesus, behind him, there is nothing — nothing but lies. And more exactly, Satan's lies, who persuades men to prolong this momentary gift of Christ, to make men's cities like things were for an instant when the gathered crowd was healed and filled, spiritually and physically. And this is the tragedy of ideal cities, the terrible problem of modern urbanism, as of older utopianism: not believing that this meeting with Christ is unique, that it cannot be prolonged on earth, that it is only the sign of the hidden kingdom and an announcement of the kingdom to come, not accepting or seeing this as simply a gift of God. And what is given by God can neither be stolen nor imitated by men. Thus, since he refuses the reality of Christ's presence and wants to do better, man can only go beyond, into falsehood. And falsehood is the foundation of both the technician who thinks to make a city the ideal place for man's full development, equilibrium and virtue, and the politician who thinks to construct around giant cities the perfect society where men can get along without God. Man is trying to steal the totality of what God

promised and has only given in part. Man is trying to construct
what *God* wants to construct, and to put himself in the center,
in God's place. Thus Jesus Christ can take the crowd nowhere,
since it is already there. All he can do, after delivering it from
its panic and from its demons, is to send it back home and separate himself from it for a time. But the parting crowd is no
longer the same. For an encounter with Jesus is always decisive.

The crowd came to Jesus, but the astonishing point, clearly
indicated in the Gospels, is that Jesus did not meet it on its
own ground. He did not meet it in the city. Rather we find that
when the multitude had left the cities, they followed Jesus into
the desert (e.g., Matt. 14:13). There are of course historical motives for this and the exegetes have carefully listed them. But
these are of little interest to us here. What is remarkable is to
see the crowd leaving what brought it together, what formed it,
its own domain, to the extent that we can say that in the city
there is always a multitude, out of the city, never. The multitude goes out into the desert, or occasionally to the mountain,
which is the same thing for us. And we must remind ourselves
of the meaning of the desert in biblical thought. It is the place
where the spirits meet.

The desert is the place where human powers must be re-
nounced. In the desert there can be no more trickery, no illusions as to getting out by one's own means, no possibility
of placing hope in natural sources of help. Man is denuded of
all his techniques, of all the possibilities of his civilization. He
is alone, without arms or armor, and then he is both a ready prey
for the demons and in a position to be helped only by God. The
desert, then, appears as a place of trial, because it is the place of
honesty. Going into the desert is the moment of truth. The
desert is particularly the dwelling place of the spirits, according
to the older texts of the Old Testament. This is where the scapegoat is sent, bearing the sins of Israel, there to be the prey of
the demons. But it seems to be even more the place where the
spirits are encountered. The event is the same, the viewpoint
changes. There is no certainty that there are more spirits living
in the desert or that they prefer to live there, but rather that
man, because he is deprived of his amusements and vain sure-
ties, encounters them more readily there. The good ones and the
evil ones, the Spirit of God who led his people through the desert, but also Satan — and the jackals. We see prophets trans-
ported to the desert to receive revelations from God. So David.
So Elijah. So Jesus, to be tempted there as also in Gethsemane.
So the woman of Revelation, who fled into the desert under

God's direct protection. A desert retreat is always a detachment from human powers and an experience of spiritual combat.

Such being the case, we see the crowd following Jesus into the desert. And from the viewpoint of our study, Christ's work there is effective. For it means that he brought man around to leaving his principal fortress, the city, to abandon the work of his power, to taste the dearth of human means (the crowd lacks even food), in order to lead man into the place of renunciation and combat. What characterizes Christ's work for the urban man, for the inhabitant of pride itself, is this detachment of man from his city. Christ introduces a kind of break between man and his world, not only in the sense that man leaves it, but in the much stronger sense that man is denied the possibility of purely and simply retaking possession of his former garments. Never again can he enter the city with the same spirit, the same strength, the same submission, the same destiny. No longer does man belong to the city, exactly as he no longer belongs to the crowd, because his individuality has been affirmed by his encounter with Jesus Christ. He was made separate, set aside when he left the city to go out into the desert. And this is accomplished in a double movement. When he leaves he is freed from the power of the city. The spirit of the city no longer dominates him, because Jesus Christ has vanquished this spirit.

Here we meet a line of thought so prominent in recent theological literature: Christ has conquered the powers, thrones, and dominations, he has despoiled them, but without annihilating them. The city is one of these powers. It has been conquered. And we could ask ourselves if the enormous proliferation of the modern city is not the reaction, the savage response of its vanquished spirit still struggling and building a monstrosity because it has no future. The proof that the city is vanquished is that the crowd is able to leave it to go out into the desert. As when Jesus was on earth and his presence justified this movement, the same departure is still possible today because Jesus has won the victory. We must know with absolute certainty that the circle has been broken, even if appearances are violently contrary to such a belief. Christ's victory is being followed up, and we are responsible for making it manifest in this particular area.

The second movement is the return to the cities. For Jesus sent the crowd back to their towns. But while it is a return, something has been changed beyond recall. There is no means of retreating once the encounter with Christ has taken place. This is so not only because it is an act in the past, which nothing can change, but especially because that fact is continually changing the present, because no one can ever become absolute master of a present that has been modified by that past act. No doubt can be cast on the reality and actuality of that event, and its result is that the man who returns to the city is not the same who went out to see Jesus. He is actually yet in the desert; he is forever situated outside of the domination of the city's spirit. He may physically be there, but he no longer belongs to it. We must not suppose this to be a separation of material fact from spiritual truth, as many Christians do who think they can neglect material things because they are spiritually free. When man comes back to the city in its present state, it is not for his personal satisfaction as a free being, but because he has a material work to do there. The very fact of having escaped the inner possession of the city's mysterious fascination is a serious disintegration of the deepest urban reality. Its only coherent reason for existing is as a spiritual power. When its power is broken, for eternity and in each one of us as inhabitants of the city, the city begins literally to fall apart. And the man who comes back after intelligently separating himself from it works as an acid to decompose the city's bonds. We should have no trouble recognizing this situation, since we have already encountered it in the problem of the Christian's presence in the city, in the midst of the curse. We came to the conclusion that such a situation is truly impossible and intolerable. And it is. But we came to such a conclusion because something was missing from our considerations, something that makes an unbearable and impossible situation a living one — namely the person of Jesus Christ. Not his doctrine, his action, or his example, but his person, with whom we are in communion, and by whose communion these impossible things are realities.

* * *

Jesus points out this separation of man from the city with particular clarity when he speaks of the conversion of Nineveh's inhabitants. Nineveh does not change. She remains the ravenous city, the place of war. But when Jonah preaches, the men of Nineveh seem to detach themselves from the city and are converted. They immediately accept God's judgement and melt at Jonah's first words.

But the story raises a major puzzle. For while it is true that the conversion of Nineveh is a result purely of the grace of God, who had pity on these 120,000 men, and while it is true that Jonah's preaching is not merely human preaching, that Jonah is only an instrument, it is also true that the conversion of the city appears to occur in absolute independence of what we have just discussed — namely an encounter with the person of Jesus Christ. We have already met these facts, and they appeared to a large degree incomprehensible. And they will stay so as long as we keep them locked in their historical or mythical setting, as long as they are considered as specific and are not placed in the immense current of God's action, which is unique whenever it appears.

We have already seen that this story is probably not historical. And if its meaning is as a representation or a sign, it cannot be separated from the thing represented, toward which the sign points. One can dispute the prophetic (and christological) character of historical events, one can say that it is excessive interpretation to see Jesus Christ everywhere in Old Testament history; but it is absolutely incorrect, and intellectually dishonest, to refuse to accept any hidden meaning in a mythical narrative and, if that narrative is in the Bible, any prophetic meaning. In fact, by our very classification of the Book of Jonah we are led to accept its prophetic meaning. Then we must (because it has already been done, because it is the prophetic *consensus omnium* of the chosen people and of the church) place this narrative in the long stream of Covenant history, the history of God's grace and action. Now this history is concentrated in its entirety in the person of Jesus Christ. Every story is one more step toward his person. No event is isolated; all are orientated, not by a will of their own but by an outside force. The difference between any work of art and a biblical narrative is the difference between a watch and a compass. In one the driving force, the worth of the object are found inside. The other is entirely dependent on a magnetic field on the outside. And this is how Jesus Christ himself understood the story of Jonah. He applied it to himself.

Because this narrative is part of God's action through the ages and because Jesus uses it, the myth cannot be considered separate from Jesus. Its real meaning is in him. The Book of Jonah is nothing but a prediction of the Jesus who died and was resurrected after three days, as Jonah was cast up on land by the great fish. Jesus establishes a direct relationship between the conversion of the Ninevites and the miracle of Jonah's sea experience, and this must draw our attention to the fact that the conversion, too, must be connected with Jesus, just as Jonah's adventure is. And the parallel made by Jesus between the conversion of the Ninevites and the nonconversion of the present generation is another confirmation: Whereas the Ninevites accepted the preaching of what was not yet the Gospel, but only a prophecy pointing to the Gospel and given by a man who was not yet the Savior but only his sign, Christ's generation refused the Lord himself. This shows that the conversion of the Ninevites is truly related to Jesus: They accepted conversion when presented with the prophecy pointing to Jesus. Thus, for their conversion they must travel the same path the crowd travels: they must meet Jesus. This is what sheds permanent light on the story of Jonah. This is what enables us, in spite of our human weakness, still to perceive as in a glass darkly the constancy of God's teaching and the unity of this one parcel of truth.

IV. JESUS AND JERUSALEM

Jerusalem waits. In Jesus her expectations are fulfilled, as we have already said. However, what is true from the messianic point of view entails strange and serious consequences for Jerusalem the city. Now that all the holy city had prophesied is before her eyes, she in a sense must disappear. For to the extent that she was only prophecy, when the reality appears, she vanishes. To the extent that she had some unique meaning as a "sign," both for salvation and as concerns the city (our interest here), when the truth of which she was a sign appears, she loses her meaning. No longer does she serve as an indication of what gave life to her existence. Just as a mirror that no longer reflects is an empty, colorless sheet, just as it is a useless surface no longer reflecting the face turned expectantly toward it, so Jerusalem is henceforth but an empty mirror. For Jesus has fulfilled all that she was.

Jerusalem was the cornerstone of all the building done by the people of Israel. David's kingdom was organized around her, the kingdom existed in terms of her, and the spiritual edification of the people rested on her. Jerusalem played a double role: her meaning was both political and spiritual. But with the appearance of Jesus, she no longer has this double function. She is no longer the center of the kingdom, for Jesus is himself the kingdom. No longer is she the foundation, no longer the cornerstone, and now one can perceive that she was all this only while waiting for *the* stone to be laid. This, of course, corresponds to the different status of all God's people for that time: they are removed from their position as the people of God, and see them-

selves replaced by another people. Of course, they can always
become a part of that other people.

But Jerusalem was also replaced in all her other functions.
She had been a cup of deadening potion thrown into the midst
of the nations. She was literally responsible for blinding the
nations to their destiny, for making them stumble, for deadening
their senses. Not that she set traps, consisting of human ruses,
in order to make them stumble, *in order* to blind them. It is
not a question, as those Goyim who understand nothing of God's
Word and Israel's faithfulness too often assert, of a plot against
the nations, or of some shady political reason. The snare she
has set for them is really the "Snare of the Living God"; it is
the scandal of God's action, the scandal of his election, the
scandal of his liberty to make Jerusalem (*the* city, with a unique
destiny) the city by which the others can go on living, for the
foundations of Babylon and Memphis are in Jerusalem.

It is obvious that neither the cities nor the nations can accept such a situation. But by rejecting that order, they reject the
living God himself, and their revolt and bad faith become evident to every onlooker. But now this role is no longer Jerusalem's
— it has passed to Jesus. He is now the constant source of scandal. He has become the stumbling block. Jerusalem no longer
has her power as a scandal, which means that neither does she
any longer have a spiritual function. And the same is true for
all that we have said concerning Jerusalem and her real role in
the world of cities. Whether she be viewed from the angle of
God's presence in the midst of man's work, his adoption of a
human work, the connection between Jerusalem and the Word,
established as an opposite counterpart of Babylon — all this and
much more has now been concentrated in Jesus. For in Jesus
Christ God has done much more than in anything else before
him. In him there is the very presence of God inseparably connected with man, to such an extent that we can no longer point
out a distinct place where God begins and man ends. Both man
and his work are completely adopted.

In Christ we have a whole man. And now we no longer
have any need for a specific sign like Jerusalem. This does not
mean that her previous role as a sign had been useless. First,
during the long period of waiting for Jesus, this knot was necessary to hold all of God's actions together in a coherently oriented
cluster. Then, for us today, it is absolutely necessary to understand how, under the old covenant, God adopted man's work.
Our spirituality is always too false. We think that man's work is
of no importance. We think that such work in no way concerns

his salvation, that it does not express or have any direct bearing on his spiritual life. And the example of Jerusalem was necessary in order to convince us that in Jesus Christ God has adopted not a fleshless man with no work to accomplish, but rather a man with calluses on his hands, wrinkles in his forehead, and the habits of his trade. This is the man whom God adopted in Jesus Christ, a man inseparable from his work, from his machine and his books, his motors and his monuments — inseparable from his cities. We might have doubted it, we could easily have refused to believe it, if the decisive example of Jerusalem were not there. God's act for her is therefore fully valid today, but the holy city's work is finished.

And her end is so complete that it is in her worst crime that her saving and eschatological role is realized and becomes fully significant. For if Jerusalem the city has her place in the story of salvation, if she is herself a saving force, if she is a prefiguration of the heavenly Jerusalem, if she is a kind of sign connected by a taut line with the city which God himself will create, it is only because Jesus died there, because by dying there he accomplished the work of salvation in its fulness. And it is his condemnation in the city that reveals her true quality and the place she must occupy. And the drama of her unprecedented role is that Jerusalem's crime — the crucifixion — is what ensures her saving worth. By her act Jerusalem is implicated in the same tragedy as each of us. Each one crucifies Jesus by his sins, and by that crucifixion each one receives pardon. Moreover, Jerusalem fulfilled by Christ's death what had ever been announced, namely that she would play a unique role in the history of salvation. And how earnestly did she seek out that role. This obviously emphasizes Jerusalem's ambiguity. She is, in spite of her sanctification and adoption, the city seeking to combat God, to destroy his action. But all she does by this is to continue accomplishing God's will, and not only his general will, but his particular will for her.

Thus the high priest as he condemns Jesus is still prophesying the truth, because he is the high priest (John 11:49). Thus in Jesus the holy city finds herself implementing her highest calling. And even more, Jesus substitutes himself for her. Not only, therefore, does he fulfill. He is also a substitute.

This shows up clearly in two facts. First in Jesus' birthplace. We might say that he did not confirm Jerusalem's position as a capital by being born there. Rather, he came to fulfill Micah's prophecy (ch. 5), which put Bethlehem at the center of Israel's spiritual life. Bethlehem is chosen to be what we might call salvation's starting point. And she is chosen precisely because she is the smallest among the clans of Judah. No human greatness can serve in the plan of salvation, because some part of what is purely and exclusively God's work might then be attributed to man. Thus Jerusalem is not chosen, because of her past, her meaning, her greatness, her inseparable mixture of human and spiritual elements. She is not chosen, and in this act there is already a real substitution of Jesus himself for Jerusalem. Far from receiving some added worth by being born in the holy, chosen city, Jesus accords to Bethlehem the real meaning of her name by being born within her walls.

But we have another indication of Christ as a substitute, and a much more decisive one because it comes from his own lips. It is found in his famous assertion concerning the Temple: "Destroy it and in three days I will build it up again." This is undoubtedly the major proof of his substitution. As we have already seen, the Temple is the heart of the city. It is the place where Jerusalem's function and spiritual reality are visible, the place from which the quality of sacredness is poured out over the city. And it is Jesus' point of attack, although doubtlessly an equivocal attack (John 2:19), since the witnesses at his trial could make only contradictory accusations (Mark 14:59). These witnesses were absolutely incapable of understanding the fulness of Christ's words: his substitution. "Destroy this temple." And he is speaking of his body. But he is also speaking of the Temple in the city, as is shown by his prophecy concerning the destruction of the city, with no possible explanation of it as a play on words (Matt. 24:1). The temple in question is both that of the city, which once destroyed will never rise again, and that of his body, which will be resurrected after three days and rise again. This double destruction, followed by a single reconstruction, is a direct indication of the substitution of the Temple of Christ's body for the Jerusalem Temple. Only in the former is God henceforth to be worshipped in Spirit and in Truth. And this substitution is applied to the entire city because of the Temple's unique role. Jesus, as concerns both the history of the nations and the history of the city, gives himself as a full substitution for Jerusalem. Henceforth, he will take her place, fulfill her function. She is still there. Nations and cities need the testimony she offers. But the witness is no longer the same. No longer is it the holy city, but rather the living body of the Son of God.

Jesus' double action for Jerusalem — fulfillment and substitution — leads to an enormous change in her character. No longer is she holy, no longer is she sacred. Jesus literally desecrated Jerusalem, or, to use another term, made her profane by taking away her sacred role. We must remember that once again we are confronted with ambiguity. An act of profanation can come about in two ways. One way to profane an object consecrated to God is by an impure contact; Satan can make it unclean by his presence. According to the Old Testament this makes it improper for use in the service of God or in any context which the law calls sacred. But this presupposes an outworn conception — the legalistic (and today vulgar) conception of holiness which considers that some objects are in themselves holy, worthy of God and deserving to serve in his worship.

The other profanation is that of an object made common by the general judgement revealed by Jesus Christ, namely that there is nothing righteous, holy, pure, valid, or worthy in and by itself — but that men and things are sanctified by an act of God descending toward his creation. The incarnation is what sanctifies common things, and therefore the whole nature of things is made common or profane by the incarnation of Christ, and Jerusalem is included in this nature of things. She is no longer sacred, because everything has become common. There is no more distinction between common and sacred, only sanctification by God. Thus Jesus fulfilled the prophecies that rang out through the history of Jerusalem; but the prophecies themselves were the most forthright of profanations because the prophets had to combat the legalistic conception of the sacred: "I will break this city as one breaks a potter's vessel, so that it can never be mended. Men shall bury in Topheth [a major profanation!] . . . and I will make this city [Jerusalem] like Topheth. The houses of Jerusalem and the houses of the kings of Judah . . . shall be defiled like the place of Topheth" (Jer. 19:11 ff.). This is one concrete promise of profanation; but the same kind may be found in all the prophets, and the line follows through to the charges of defilement brought against Jesus and Paul (cf. Acts 21:28). But there is a transfer from profanation as defilement to profanation as making common. The Jews retained the first notion (thus they accuse Paul of having defiled the Temple by bringing in Greeks), whereas, under their very eyes, the other type of profanation takes place. Thus it is true that Jesus made Jerusalem "profane," but not in the sense understood by the Jews. So little did they understand Christ's work that he was sent to die outside the walls so that the presence of his dead body might not defile the holy city. The only hitch was that she was no longer holy — her profanation had already been carried out. She had already become a city like all the rest.

This is the great event for Jerusalem during Christ's brief but momentous visit. Jerusalem becomes a city like the rest. Christ's work returns her to the common level. Their alignment becomes hers. It was announced, as we have seen, that she would be treated like the others, like Topheth. But it is only after her secularization that the threat can assume its real proportions.

However, this provokes and bothers us: Were there not promises given by God that Jerusalem's mission was never to end? Yes there were. But we must never forget the basic truth that God's promises are fulfilled in a way we can never foresee. We never know exactly how God will bring about what he has promised, for in his wisdom he has infinitely more means than we could ever imagine, and in his love he chooses what is better than our feeble judgement. Thus we can say with certainty that his promises are not revoked, but realized in a fashion other than what we were expecting; other than what the Jews in Christ's time thought would happen. Jerusalem has not been abandoned. All that she was pointing to, all that she bore in her, now appears. The promise is not revoked, since it is fulfilled in Jesus Christ. But it is precisely this fulfillment that takes from Jerusalem her particular quality; and as one city among others, her only destiny henceforth is that of the city.

Does this mean that she has been abandoned? No more so than the other cities, all recipients of a marvellous destiny in Jesus Christ. However, what we have just said is once again derailed by an extraordinary fact, one that transforms Jerusalem's situation even more: God's revelations instruct us of the unparalleled truth that by Jesus Christ's death, Jerusalem literally becomes Babylon. During that period of time between Christ's ascension and his return there is a confusion of the formerly holy city and the city of demons, Babylon. This is attested in many ways. In the Book of Revelation we have the prophecy of the two witnesses who are put to death: "When they have finished their testimony, the beast that ascends from the bottomless pit will make war upon them and conquer them and kill them, and their dead bodies will lie in the street of the great city which is spiritually called Sodom and Egypt, where their Lord was crucified" (11:7-8). The precise designation of the city is undeniable: Jerusalem is "where their Lord was crucified." But this city is spiritually (which means that the spirit dwelling in her is designated her profound reality, what she is before God) called Sodom and Egypt. It is, then, the city of disobedience and the land of slavery and darkness. Now these terms are, as we have seen, indicative of the city in all her reality. They are not geographical notions but spiritual. And these characteristics may be applied to the city as an entity, represented by Babylon.

There is another small item of interest — Jerusalem is here called "the great city"; and this term is, as we know, characteristic of Babylon. Moreover, the text as a whole confirms our identification. Jerusalem here plays a part which should be that only of Babylon. She is the defiled place where dead bodies are to be exposed. She is the place where all the nations of the earth gather to revel drunkenly and make merry over the death of God's prophets. She is celebrating, therefore, the victory of the Beast, and becomes the city of the nations. For she — who is the "court outside the temple" (Rev. 11:2) — is handed over to them for forty-two months, a period reappearing several times in these texts and doubtlessly designating the period from Christ's ascension to his return. The nations will trample the "holy city." How strange to see this term return! The city is still designated by it although she has become Babylon. But in fact her destiny is always unique; she is ever set apart, even though now it is only because the two prophets died there and their bodies are exposed there. Thus, there is no doubt in John's mind, with its extraordinary view of Jerusalem, that she and Babylon are to be identified. Moreover, in his portrayal there is much food for reflection, if only from the historical standpoint, for those who consider Revelation only as a political writing turned against Rome. But John is far from being alone in this attitude. His position is, in reality, only the crown-piece, the consummation of a long tradition in the primitive church for which we could mention a long series of witnesses. Jesus, for example, pointed up the apparent necessity for Jerusalem to put her prophets to death: "I must go on my way today and tomorrow and the day following; for it cannot be that a prophet should perish away from Jerusalem" (Luke 13:33). The same fatality stands out in the Gospel of Matthew, where Jerusalem is characterized as a city killing her prophets. And in doing so, she is playing perfectly her role as a city: in revolt against God and trying to wipe out his Word as announced by the prophets, a Babylon who wants nothing but the confusion of tongues and who tries, therefore, by every possible means to exclude those who speak the Word clearly, who explicitly proclaim a judgement valid for all men and discernible to all. Such a proclamation is intolerable for the city of confusion. Thus Jerusalem has all the characteristics of a city and more, because, as the bearer of the promise, she is now called upon to kill those who fulfill it. Not only Jesus, but all the prophets who proclaim the Gospel. Once again the identity of Babylon and Jerusalem forces itself upon us, for it is of Babylon that it is written, "In her was found the blood of prophets and saints, and of all who have been slain on earth" (Rev. 18:24). Thus the conjunction of Jerusalem, the place where every prophet must die, with Babylon, the place where the blood of all the prophets is found, becomes obvious.

Previously she was the habitation of God's Spirit. No longer. And when the Spirit left, Satan moved in and took possession. All the spiritual powers of the city are surrendered. And since she is the place where the temporal aspects of man's salvation are enacted, it is easy to understand why all of Satan's powers are gathered here. Because she is the place where Jesus dies, she also becomes the place where the fulness of Satan's strength is concentrated. The use of the city is for him a valuable aid. But were we right in saying that she is no longer the dwelling place of God's Spirit? Two passages indicate that we were, both of them *logia* spoken by Jesus: "You did not know the time of your visitation . . . . Would that even today you knew the things that make for peace . . . " (Luke 19:44, 42). "How often would I have gathered your children together as a hen gathers her brood under her wings, and you would not . . . " (Matt. 23:37). This is tragically clear. Jesus is not speaking angrily, but sadly — he weeps for the city. He knows that her destiny has run its course. For one thing, Jerusalem does not *know* the time of her salvation, does not recognize the kingdom drawing near. For another, she does not *want* her children to be gathered together under the protection of Jesus. The exact two ways in which the Holy Spirit acts. He reveals to us the knowledge of God's mysteries (for such knowledge is not natural to men's hearts), and the will to accept God's action in Jesus Christ and to do what God requires — the results of heart conversion, God working out in us the will and the act. So we can say that in these two acts, Jerusalem is obeying her own nature, and not God's will. She is obeying her urban nature, for she refuses to accept God's kingdom, what every city does by birth and by individual decision. She refuses to gather her children to be blessed by Jesus, for she is herself a gathering and rejects any other. She is the Capital, the Head of the chosen people, and as such the city of refusal. Jerusalem brings to an end her former ambiguous status, and by so doing releases the forces of her own destruction.

We have already examined several prophecies of destruction concerning Jerusalem, but in each case we saw that they referred to a relative degree of destruction, with symbolic meaning. What we have here is completely different, for it is a destruction that comes about as a goal in itself and nothing more, and is both spiritual and material. "O Jerusalem, Jerusalem, killing the prophets and stoning those who are sent to you . . . . Behold your house is forsaken and desolate, for I tell you, you will not see me again, until you say, 'Blessed is he who comes in the name of the Lord.' Jesus left the temple and was going away, when his disciples came to point out to him the buildings of the temple. But he answered them, 'You see all these, do you not? Truly, I say to you, there will not be left here one stone upon another, that will not be thrown down' " (Matt. 23:37 to 24:2). As Jesus was approaching the city, he saw her and began to weep, and said, "Would that even today you knew the things that make for peace! . . . For the days shall come upon you, when your enemies shall cast up a bank around you and surround you, and hem you in on every side, and dash you to the ground, you and your children within you, and they shall not leave one stone upon another in you; because you did not know the time of your visitation" (Luke 19:42-44). That the destruction is *also* of a spiritual nature is sufficiently clear from the words concerning the Temple. But a reader of these texts in September, 1948, somber and tragic days for the State of Israel, somber and tragic when we think that the assassination of Bernadotte was caused by the status of Jerusalem, could not help being gripped by a kind of sacred fear, and casting his thoughts back over the history of this city. Of course, history is no proof. History is not a confirmation of prophecy. But is it possible not to accept the obvious, can one refuse, when it is so manifest, to see the bloody wake of this prophecy, above, around and in Jerusalem for twenty centuries? For her destiny is more singular and tragic than that of any other city in the world. As is that of the Jewish people, more so than any other people in the world. And in 1956, when once again the perils against this divided city increased in number and intensity, and all the world powers were reconciled to accept the sacrifice of the smallest of nations, how could one not call to mind the words of Christ, how could one not be burned by his tears for the city?

Jerusalem — ever controlled by the Goyim and unable to attain spiritual liberation in the Christian faith. Neither Jewish nor Christian, but always torn apart, going from one persecution to another, from siege to destruction, with no really durable period of domination, no settled condition, no possible restoration while under Arab domination. Even today's Jewish domination is but one more sign of the underlying contradiction. A wandering city, defiled, condemned. A deserted city in the midst of its swarming peoples and confused races. A deserted city because she did not recognize her Lord: "Your house is desolate, for you will not see me again." He alone could have populated her, he alone could adequately have taken the place of the Temple. And he was waiting to do so. A city of which not one spiritual stone is left on another, full of horrible tourist churches and monuments raised by every sect and every religion, the symbol of division and spiritual falsehood, the symbol of satanic spirituality, a subject of mockery for the Holy Spirit.

And her destruction is of a completely different nature than Sodom's and has a completely different meaning. It is less symbolic of the destruction of cities, less prophetic of the last great events. Nor does it have the same quality as the tougher reprimands handed out to Jerusalem before Jesus Christ. No longer is its goal to make the holy city realize that her destiny is exclusively dependent on God. We have before us the working of a kind of ruthless logic: Because Jerusalem was only the jewel box that was supposed to be graced with the Son of God, her refusal removes from her any worth or pertinence. Then she falls lower than any other city. More than any other she falls prey to Babylon's tormenting ambition, because she had been chosen from among all the others; and by her downfall she becomes Babylon itself. And that is why her inhabitants receive the same orders as all the Christians who are in the midst of the city: "When you see Jerusalem surrounded by armies, then know that its desolation has come near. Then let those who are in Judea flee to the mountains, and let those who are inside the city depart, and let not those who are out in the country enter it . . . " (Luke 21:20). But from the time when these words were spoken until today, Jerusalem has constantly been attacked by armies and constantly threatened by the heavenly army watching over her, but also punishing and breaking her. Thus men are always fleeing Jerusalem. And these words were doubtlessly spoken for all men, everywhere. But they can be obeyed only by those who take them seriously. And they can be taken truly seriously only by those who believe in the one who said them. Jesus Christ certifies the truth of these words, and only those who believe in him can heed his warning. But must we take it as an order to leave Jerusalem understood as a geographical place? It is obvious that if this were the only legitimate interpretation (although it may be one interpretation), Christ's order would have little bearing, and could not concern our salvation. It must have a wider application, which we may follow in two directions — one, as concerns Jerusalem's meaning in relation to other cities; the other, as concerns the values Jerusalem represents.

In its fullest meaning, then, this verse is an order to leave the cities. It is in this sort of conflict between Jerusalem and Jesus, which finished in the triumphant death of Jesus and the destruction of Jerusalem, it is in Jesus' words, that the decision to flee and abandon the city, constantly before each of us, finds its most cogent proclamation and surest grounds. And when we flee and abandon the city, this action has a spiritual sense as well as temporal — a sense we must examine in all its gravity because Jerusalem is, in its hope and its curse, the standard of all other cities. Of course, the order to flee does not mean that the country is holy or a refuge from the coming wrath. The lesson here is not that of a comparison between city and country. But only an order that concerns our attitude toward the city, and a decision to be made which is of a spiritual nature, symbolized by flight to the mountains, and, in a certain sense, to the desert.

For what we must abandon is not only Jerusalem, the city of cities, but the values she represents; and not only the values she represents as a city (which we have already studied in detail), but as Jerusalem. All the security brought to us by our preference for the city.

Man knows how to use this city chosen by grace as a new bulwark against God, as a new means of protection, and this is a result of the city's very nature. Just as the law became a means of security against God for the Jewish people, and thus revealed the reality of sin, so Jerusalem became a means for man to justify his own work.

Because it was the holy city, the emphasis was put on the city, and holiness was added to it as though it were natural. All the time forgetting that God's election was to remind us that her holiness from above is to transform the city, that she no longer belongs to us, that we can no longer dispose of her as we please. But how does this concern us? It is the last warning from which we must never remove our attention. To the extent that redemption is meant for all of man, to the extent that man's work is adopted by God, we are ever tempted to consider it holy in itself, to believe that in itself it is righteous and that we may acquire righteousness and holiness by means of our works. This was the whole problem of the Puritans in their attitude toward work, business, and money. This is implicitly the whole problem in our time with our science and technique. For when we use the word "works" here, we are not referring to virtues and their moral results; the problem is entirely different. We have in mind man's works in the material and intellectual world, his accomplishments and their results, the immense machine of material progress which today disconcerts and troubles us. Jerusalem is there as a warning: As soon as man acquires righteousness and holiness by his work, we must be ready to leave that work, to abandon it to wrath; and woe to those who love it more than themselves!

However, God never goes back on his word — Jerusalem is still Jerusalem, and God's coming city has no other name. Jesus as the king of the Jews sacrificed at her gates, Christ as the resurrected Lord of the world in her midst, reveals more than David himself to what extent she is the city of the Messiah, the chosen place, the city of the king of the Jews and of the heathen; and because she is all this, she is ever, by her very history, the surety of the promise that a new Jerusalem is coming.

Chapter Five

TRUE HORIZONS

IT IS TIME TO STOP AND CONTEMPLATE THE HORIZONS that Christ's coming has opened up for us. So far we have perhaps learned little of the sociology of the city or its historical development, but certainly much of its living reality. And this, after all, is our personal concern. We are in the city, even if we live in the country, for today the country (and soon this will be true even of the immense Asian steppe) is only an annex of the city. The city is constantly eating into the country, as western Europe and the United States demonstrate with particular vividness. Now we conceive of the country only in terms of the city; and if the city is still alive to a certain degree, still independent, it is nevertheless well on the road to tributary status. Consider, for example, the enormous outlay becoming more and more necessary to acquire agricultural equipment, or the comforts desired everywhere but distributed by the city.

We are in the city, and this is one of the most important facts of our generation. It is absolutely indispensable that we realize what that means for us, for our actual life: the undeniable presence and influence of the city are of infinitely greater importance than the urban problem in itself. No added comforts, no adaptation, can in any way vary this relationship. Have the Scriptures perchance taught us something decisive concerning the concrete situation in which we find ourselves? If so, all the historical and sociological problems take a subordinate role.

For if the Word of God is clearly marked out for us in the Scriptures and if it is truly spoken for us, taking hold of us in our concrete situation, and if at the same time as it takes hold of us (for our condemnation and salvation) it enlightens our understanding of that situation, and if we are truly involved in

147

the city and the Bible shows us what we are in the city and what the city means for us and our relations with her, then all that we have learned should form the proper nucleus for a science of the city. Not of an objective and purely technical science of the city, but a science in which we would be involved as in a struggle for truth. For the basic question is whether we can deal with a foreign and unalterable truth, whether we can conquer and possess it, or whether by launching into such a quest we become involved in it ourselves and responsible for it, responsible for what we will learn and for what we will do with this truth. And since man knows no science but a concrete science, then by studying the city are we not working for a human science? And since man knows no science but a science built up according to a plan, then by seeking the spiritual nucleus of this problem are we not working for a human science?

What is striking in modern research is that it just happens not to be built up around a plan; it is guided by the objects under study, follows every whim of its instruments, and is constantly led on by the successive discovery of new objects for study. It imposes no domination, and while it is praiseworthy in its humility, it is also vain in its incoherency. We do not believe that such an approach is necessary any more than is the idol of objectivity. And when we have revealed, as here, the spiritual nucleus of a problem, we admit (and this is also singularly humble) that it is in fact the nucleus of the problem, that every aspect radiates around it. If we accept this, then what we learn to know about the city by natural means, by history and sociology, and about man in the city by psychology and the novel, must be connected, coordinated, strongly knotted together, because of the spiritual nucleus. The result is that our natural sources are dependent on revelation. I know that this will be considered a betrayal to science, but it is either this method or else the sterility of death. How is it that our historians and sociologists have not been struck with the sterility of their work? Our work of tying the threads together will not be done explicitly, for we have already traced their pattern. Our entire purpose will be to come to a decision and to take our biblical information to its logical conclusions.

I. THE HISTORY OF THE CITY

Of course I do not intend to write an historical history. There are enough histories, many of them well written, in which the problems of the city's creation and development are treated for every part of the world. The Aztec city, the polis, the urbs, and the medieval free town have retained few of their secrets. But beside and under this superficial history there is a true history. There is Jesus Christ, who, in the approximate words of Karl Barth, makes history, because he is history. To state this brilliant but delphic formula more explicitly, there are forces running through history that form its substratum — the horsemen of Revelation — and which because of Jesus Christ and in Jesus Christ are in permanent action as the explanation and the reality of history. These forces are the very form of his action.

Our purpose is not to consider the problem of history as a whole, but only as concerns the city. Now if we examine successively all the different civilizations, we see, without exception, that as soon as the human group arrives at what we can term a civilization (that is, a specific assertion of its existence vis-à-vis nature and other human groups — taking the term, then, in as wide a sense as possible), it assumes concrete form as a city. Where there is no city, we have only groups which are not yet free from their animal nature and which have not, in their solitude, been forced to enter into competition with other groups. This is true for the blacks of Central and Southern Africa, and true also for the North American Indians, and for the Laplanders. But as soon as man becomes conscious, as it were, as soon as he turns within himself or considers himself in relation with something else, the sociological (and spiritual) expression of this self-realization is the creation of a city.

Someone might say, however, that this emergence of civilization is more closely connected with the army, for example, and the necessity of war. And such a claim is not implausible. For as soon as the group asserts itself, it may do so by force and military means. It is perfectly true, for example, that when an empire was formed in the soft political ground of Central Africa, it was done by violence, and that as soon as the frontiers were established, they were marked by the red, crenelated walls of cities. Moreover, we have already seen that the close connection between war and the city is attested by the Bible.

But we must also acknowledge that even outside of any military consideration, civilization is expressed by a city. Thus, in the Chinese civilization cities were not essentially meant as fortresses. There one can find immense metropolitan centers that were nonetheless peaceful. The same is true of India. And what is most indicative is the reappearance of cities during the Middle Ages in Europe. It is very interesting to note that most of them were peaceful in nature. The military element was the castle. The peaceful element, commercial or ecclesiastical, was the city. I am well aware that this opposition is too simple, too schematic; I am aware of the fortified towns, the revolutionary free towns, and the importance of the city wall. Nevertheless, as has been clearly demonstrated (and in opposition to the German school), the characteristic element of the medieval city was not its wall. It was its charter. The commercial and juridical element was preponderant.

But what are we driving at? Are we trying to say that the city is a product of civilization? That was hardly a secret! There is no need of lengthy books to tell us that, and besides, such an observation is not very profound. And this is not our purpose. But it is worth noting that the city is *one of the rare invariables* of civilization, considered both geographically and historically. And if we give it a moment's thought, we see immediately that there have not been very many civilizations down through history. This leads us to another conclusion: As soon as the city appears among men it becomes an element of polarization for all human activities — not only economic activities, but intellectual and artistic also. And here we must avoid the banality of saying, "Of course everything centers in the city; life there is much more intense, from every point of view!" No. It is not a question of intensity, but of origins and creation. The city is the determinative factor in a certain mode of life, and as soon as she comes into existence, she tends to draw all outside activity into her bosom.

The first undeniable element in this life is due to the city's nature as a parasite. She absolutely cannot live in and by herself. And this, moreover, characterizes all of those works of man by which he seeks autonomy. Everything takes its life from somewhere else, sucks it up. Like a vampire, it preys on the true living creation, alive in its connection with the Creator. The city is dead, made of dead things for dead people. She can herself neither produce nor maintain anything whatever. Anything living must come from outside. In the case of food, this is clear. But in the case of men also. We can repeat too often that the city is an enormous man-eater. She does not renew herself from within, but by a constant supply of fresh blood from outside.

It is not enough to repeat, for example, the common remark that within the lively Parisian intelligentsia everything of any worth is imported from the provinces or from foreign countries, or that all the Parisians can produce is spiritless imitation.

What is most important is that the growth of the urban population is not equal to arrivals from the outside, and not because the former move elsewhere or go back to the land, but because the city devours men. Sterile marriages, infant mortality. And these are not just ideas to be tossed about.

The city, then, cannot function except as a parasite; it needs constant contributions from the outside. One might be tempted to speak of exchange, but the city has nothing to exchange. What the city produces is for her own use. Notwithstanding tractors, electricity, and fertilizer, what the city can produce for the country is absurd and ridiculous compared with what she receives. As for her spiritual worth, her ferment of ideas will be of use nowhere but in the city. On the other hand, she spoils peasant values with remarkable virtuosity. Such values are disappearing under the urban influence because they are the "defects" of urban values. The very character of the city, in the economic field or the intellectual, artistic, or humanitarian, is to receive from the outside, to consume, and to produce things without value or meaning, usable only inside the city and to her gain.

For it is undeniable that the city produces, and singularly so, in the intellectual life. Nowhere else do ideas evolve so rapidly. And today is not the first time historians have concluded that intense intellectual and artistic development coincided with the appearance of cities. It is obviously permanent contact with other men which frees the human mind, which facilitates the exchange of ideas, which communicates foreign ideas, which permits the accumulation of enormous quantities of human raw material whose synthesis is to the glory of human intelligence. But what is not often noticed is that the city is there first, she is the antecedent. The city is the condition (by her creation of a favorable environment) for great ideological developments. It is maddening perhaps, but we cannot conceive of Plato without Athens, or of Racine without Paris. I am not trying to set the city up as an invariable conditioning factor, but we must recognize that the intellectual life cannot exist outside the city. It is true that Montaigne withdrew to the country to write his *Essays*, but it cannot be denied that their substance was taken from his life in Bordeaux. And it would be useless to repeat for finance what we have said of the intellectual life. Without cities there would be no industry, no commerce, no finance; there would be no economic life in the true sense of the word. This is so obvious that there is no need to demonstrate it.

As soon as the city exists, she polarizes all activity toward herself. There is something magical about her attractiveness, and it is impossible to explain men's passion for the city, her influence on their activity, the irresistible current flowing in long unconscious waves to pull men toward her dead asphalt, without giving a thought for her force, her seductive power. Around the city there rises a wall of mirages, and on the map may be traced the zone of indecision where man can be part of the city's basic orientation without actually living within her boundaries. He assumes her manners, her language, her scorn, her simplistic attitudes. He has her rhythm and bears everywhere, on his clothes and in his face, in the way he treats his wife and in the way he treats his children, in his work and in the air he breathes, in everything he is, the mark of the city. Even when he does not yet live there, even when he is close to the oldest country houses of the surrounding farmland, he is nonetheless in a locked cage. The city is not far away, and it is not hard to learn to live as they do there. And so the mores of the city are acquired, without its life. An invasion of the soul, hand in hand with the material invasion, the first wave preparing the mass arrival of the tractors, bulldozers, cement mixers, and air-compressors, announcing the heavy clouds of factory smoke, a job, getting up joylessly to a sunless sky and dirty air, air that is a mixture of gasoline fumes, coal smoke, and the immense breath of a million neighbors.

But no amount of reason, no amount of experience, no amount of knowledge does any good: men stream into the city. They know that the city offers little of worth (although it can be shown that they are usually unaware of what they are losing) and that the city is past master at furnishing illusions. Whatever individual attitudes may be, nothing can resist the double attraction of land speculation and the city's psychic seductiveness. In the history of every civilization the same process is carried out: life becomes more supple and finally bends, ancestral customs disappear, modes of thought and mental make-up are modified, both the surest instincts and the most defective mysticisms are lost, and everyone everywhere is certain of the city's absolute material necessity. For a natural necessity, the necessity imposed by the weather, the rhythm of days and seasons, the city tries to substitute liberty, that is, the possibility for man to do what he wants when he wants.

But this liberty is a farce. The city must, in order to stay alive, have its night shifts, the accumulation of a proletariat, alcohol, prostitution (under whatever form it adopts, including the "very noble naturalism" practiced in Sweden), an iron schedule of work hours, the elimination of sun and wind. And it is simply false to say that we can do away with all this and still keep the city. This is the urbanists' illusion — very respectable men, but perfectly idealistic in the worst possible sense. For they have no conception of where the city is really going. They do not understand what makes the city necessary, and they believe that they can modify her like a piece of child's putty. According to them, the city is freedom. But this liberty never gets off the architects' drawing boards. The city's path through history has invariably shown the same developments and the same powers in action. One would not call it a natural law, but neither can one see any reason today why this line of development, in the most urban of civilizations, should change. However, the illusions of the urbanist and the sociologist are easy to understand. For the evolution of a city and its role within a society, however often they may be repeated, can appear to be the result of an accident. They seem to be events that reoccur for no special reason, and things do not really have to be such.

Certitude can be found only in the position that revelation forces us to adopt with regard to the spiritual being of the city and its role through history as concerns man. The reality of the city, not as an event, but as a structure of the world, can be understood only in the light of revelation. And this revelation provides us with both a means of understanding the problem and a synthesis of its aspects as found in the raw data of history and sociology. However, we must not expect perfect agreement, for the two realities are not on the same plane. Although I cannot mistake the sun for the colors of the spectrum, nevertheless I could not know color but by the help of the sun. I could doubtlessly make a chemical analysis of the coloring agents, I could study all the physical or biological aspects of color, without ever having an inkling of living color, unless all these aspects are brought into play by the simple fact of light bringing out color.

So it is with the reality of human problems in general and with our particular aspect of life. Revelation — which was not given with this in mind, but which incidently serves in this way — enlightens, brings together, and explains what our reason and experience discover. Without revelation all our reasoning is doubtlessly useful, but does not view reality in true perspective. So when we said that we had nothing new to offer history or sociology, we were correct, but not strictly. We have in fact furnished no direct contribution to these sciences themselves; but what history and sociology tell us about the city is here confronted with revelation, is brought together and synthesized not as bare fact, but as illuminated by another source of light. And the result of this confrontation is the conclusion that the city is man's greatest work. It is his great attempt to attain autonomy, to exercise will and intelligence. This is where all his efforts are concentrated, where all the powers are born. No other of man's works, technical or philosophical, is equivalent to the city, which is the creation not of an instrument but of the whole world in which man's instruments are conceived and put to work. All of man's activity is conceivable only in the city and in terms of its existence. All of his works are secondary to the city. Just as Jesus Christ is God's greatest work, so we can say, with all the consequences of such a statement, that the city is man's greatest work.

*   *   *

And yet if we look around us, if we read the statistics of economic planning, if we study modern political and social doctrine (from both the right and the left), if we scan the newspapers and public opinion polls, if we finally question the man in the street, we come to a strange but explainable conclusion: no one is paying the slightest attention to the basic problem of the city. Even sociologists, who do study the elements of a city, cast no doubt on the institution itself. Obviously not. One does not doubt the ground he walks on or the work he does. This is in fact our basic attitude toward our own life. One may complain and seek improvements or a better adaptation to such a life, but in no case does one cast doubt on its fundamental worth and veracity. So it is for our attitude toward the city and everything found there. Projects are limited to better sewage disposal systems and air-conditioning units. At the very best, the decentralization of the big cities is called for. But no one would refuse the city as such — in the first place because it is there, and before her, all our realists bow very low. She is there, and we can do nothing about it, for we no longer believe that history is the result of ideas. She is there and in close connection with the structure of our present society, so much so that our whole society would have to be overthrown before the city could in any way be modified. And there is no reason to believe that she would cease to exist even then. Cities have, in one form or another, come through the greatest upheavals of history. At the very least, underground cities might be built.

Modern man is ready to doubt the future existence of

everything his civilization has to offer, except the city. He can think of his future only as an urban future — with more and more people per square yard. Because production must increase, factories must grow in size and in number; and where there are factories, there must be a city. The factories must be close together to lower transportation costs in transforming raw materials into finished products. The workers must live nearby. As in the Middle Ages cities were built around cathedrals, so now they are built around industry. Whatever the checkerboard of rabbit cages or thirty-story apartment buildings scattered among the landscapers' greenery may be, the piling up of human bodies is always the same. And then around the workers' city the network fills in bit by bit: stores, cinemas, schools, the business and shopping district. Then, beyond, the residential district, where the engineers, the presidents, the chairmen of the board, the organizers, the capitalists and the businessmen live. I am well aware that geographically this is a false portrayal of today's great city. The order I chose is by zones of necessity. And this is how man sees his future. Dispersing or dissolving the city would be the end of the machine, because production could no longer go on at a fast enough pace; it would be the end of modern technology, always dependent on a fresh supply of men. Think for a moment of the exclusively industrial cities now in existence, of the type I presented so diagrammatically — Magnetogosh, Diyniepropetrovsk, or the American atomic cities artificially erected in the middle of the desert, or the abominable Ribbon City spread for dozens of kilometers along a vital axis of communication, such as the new Stalingrad. There is, of course, a strong movement on foot to decentralize urban industry and to diffuse the population. But at the same time, and often from the same authors, we find a demonstration of the necessity of drastically reducing the rural population. No more small farmers! Such is the password, dictated by economic reason, just as severe as the reasons of state. The small farmer is the brake on economic expansion, the hinderer of a more rapid flow and consumation of products, the man who cannot bring his production level up to par, the dead weight that an expanding country must drag around. No more small farmers! And this means more city-dwellers. Such is the watchword of the intelligent and realistic economists, sociologists, and technicians who know the disaster level cities have reached. So a new order: Decentralize the cities. What does this mean? A return to the country? Not at all! It means only the multiplication of average-sized cities. Change the very big city into eight large cities of 500,000 inhabitants or sixteen large enough cities of 250,000! This really means accelerating the urbanization of the country. Empty the farmed land, and then build big new cities in the country. Dumbfounded, we realize that this is the only solution offered. But there are still more necessities, such as that of the state. The entire conception of the modern state is as a leader of populations grouped into large masses. It cannot work with a low-density population, unless that density is very low. The countryside must be depopulated in order for the mechanism of the state to function correctly. Ten people per square kilometer[1] is the ideal population for the country. Just the right density to get the most out of farming machinery, just right for a rational, motorized culture. Vast amounts are poured into great desert tracts to cultivate them scientifically — but how economically time and personnel are used! Here there are no difficulties of supervision and organization, and gathering in the harvests is no longer any problem. Everyone knows how easy it is with ten workmen per tractor station.

The other side of the coin is the tremendous human wealth of the city, where the state functions by its administrative and police power. In the city, the state is always the master, because it controls the foodstuffs. If it stops them, by manipulating a correctly organized farm system, the city dies. This complete organization is the only possible recourse to assure the full development of state power. And what, one may ask, could bring it to a halt? What motivation would lead to producing less, to abandoning industrial concentration? Why would the state renounce its power, and the superior organization that ensures it? If man can envisage history and his future only in an urban context, this is due more to his own sentiments than to any reason. The Kirghiz peasant sees his future in the white marble subway stations in Moscow. And the French farmers who every year come and lose themselves in the city are obeying the same sentiments. It is all a kind of sociological movement with roots more mystical than reasonable.

It is rather ridiculous to imagine that the exodus might be stopped by the extension of electric current or by more cinemas in the country. Movies do count, but what can never be put into a country theater is just what the farmer finds in the urban cinema: the specific atmosphere of the city, made of anonymity, seedy

---

[1]This figure is clearly too conservative. According to research carried on in the United States, an astonishing 100,000 acres of wheat can be cultivated by fifteen permanent and thirty seasonal workers, with the use of ultra-modern farming equipment.

luxury, vast organization, definitive truth, a share in the world's folly and diversity, the constitution of a community vibrating intensely by the fake shocks of an illusory current. In the country, with its audience where everybody knows everybody else, its atmosphere of a village fair, its benches or folding chairs set out on a concrete floor, nothing is left of the city's pride. And the mystical attraction the farmer feels for the city (made of the described atmosphere and much more) is exactly the same thing as the city-dweller's passion for the city — passion in the fullest sense, made up of both love and suffering, voluntary suffering because of the love carried to folly. If anyone doubts that this passion exists, let him read a few of the innumerable declarations of love made to Paris (whose nature, as strange as it may seem, is as much sexual as mystical). One can hardly overlook this multitudinous literature, with its range from the pages of *Confidences* to the best writings of Max Jacob and Leon-Paul Fargue and even to those of our most refined existentialists (without the Café de Flore there would be no such thing as existentialism). The verbal delirium sparked by the City of Light awakens a response deep in the heart of the people, as the work of Aragen attests. All this is true, one might say, but "Paris is Paris," after all. No, Paris is first of all a city, the very symbol of the city for our time. The mystical love borne for her is the same for every social category. And it explains better than any reason the fixity of the historical eye which sees the city as the indubitable form of development for society. If we try to fictitiously represent the civilization of the year 3000, a metropolis is the first thing that comes to mind. Explain it as you will, the fact remains that this strangely powerful image haunts us; this troublesome dweller in our soul influences and guides us. More effective than any reason, the image printed into our being, this magical terror we feel when we think of the immenseness of the city to come, conditions our thinking and makes our hearts tremble with love for the city we know. And we hasten to melt ourselves into and to unite ourselves mystically with this body lying before us.

In one sense, this passion makes the work of the urbanist useless. There is no time, the city being what she is, to establish a cold, rational city by neglecting the mystical part. There is no doubt that modern man knows that his cities are threatened, and that no future war would leave much of today's city behind. But what seems to me to be a fantastic evidence of this folly is man's attitude toward his destroyed cities. Have his cities been leveled: English cities, German cities, Polish cities, Russian cities — all so cruelly struck? And what does he build in their place? A modern city with great buildings surrounded with greenery? An underground city for tomorrow's war, protected by an armor of concrete and steel? A city spread out over great reaches of land, less vulnerable and more healthy? A city according to any of these well-known, thoroughly studied solutions? No, man rebuilds the city essentially as she was, with wider and straighter streets, houses more alike, gardens maintained at great pains, and an effort to follow modern style and install bigger and better bathtubs. Such is the limit of man's ingenuity — except for a few attempts, obviously mistakes, such as Stalingrad, where urban impersonality is greater than ever. Oh, the city's power to stamp her image in man's heart!

However, there would be no reason for optimism even if the projects of the urbanists were launched and Le Corbusier's "House of Mankind" were built. In very little time the city would become herself again. No change in the walls, no purification of the air or improvement in lighting, no mixture of greenery and cement could transform the city's spiritual being. Only mortal man could believe that life comes down to the world of death simply because he mixes it in with inanimate materials. There is only one who has come to bring life to the world of death. But in the natural circle of our existence, life always loses out. We are too well acquainted with the trees in our public parks to believe that our cities could ever be immersed in life-giving green! The spiritual being of the city would subsist. And whatever direction we envisage for the future of our civilization, it is only too correct to think of it as the triumph of the city. For man's natural instincts make no mistakes. His reasons are sure. History is bound in that direction.

And this is where the strangest thing of all happens. Modern man is right! Spiritually right. Unconsciously, he is really right when he sees the future as belonging to the city. However, the city is not exactly as he foresees it. Whereas he sees it from a technical and sociological viewpoint, the true future of this world's history and its final goal is in fact a city other than the imagined metropolis. We might call it the exact opposite: the new Jerusalem. Thus man is confusedly announcing what in fact must come about, but he is obviously incapable of seeing its true form.

* * *

This is a wholly different world. If we consider this heavenly Jerusalem from the angle of a myth, we are already shocked by one inescapable fact. The conception that when the history of this world draws to an end, a city — the new Jerusalem — will appear descending from heaven, has nothing to do with the traditional notion of paradise. Nowhere do the Scriptures mention paradise and even less a pink and blue paradise with chubby cherubs considered either as in the heavens or as nature made perfect. When the Scriptures speak of what will happen during or after the judgement, this is usually done with no details as to the place and with no description. The place is undetermined and unlocated. This is how Jesus speaks of it, usually describing it according to its spiritual worth, by its positive or negative relation to God. But we *can* gather from Jesus' words (the parable of the wedding feast, for example) that it is a limited and closed place.

When the Scriptures become more precise, it is always to describe the future under the aspect of a city. So it is with Ezekiel and all the prophets, without exception, and so with Revelation. The biblical notion is invariable and not contradicted by other details, such as Isaiah's depiction of the wolf and the lamb lying down together. What is coming is the city, not heaven. There are no clouds for angels to float on, there is no blue space, and it is strange that the popular imagination of Christians during the Middle Ages so emphasized the notion of sky or heaven. The medieval mind was usually profoundly real and concrete, and the inspired texts are so clear and so near to this very mentality. What is coming is not heaven, but what is beyond the heavens. And the regular biblical expression is that of the "heavens opened."

Nor is the conception of paradise as nature made perfect correct. The figure of "green pastures" is one example of such a conception, common among blacks and Indians. It should not be overlooked that this tendency is common among peoples strongly influenced by Mohammedanism or at least in contact with Islam. For the notion of paradise as a garden with trees, flowers, birds, and fountains, as a haven from the torments of the desert, is purely Islamic.

In these two figures of Christian tradition, we must see neither a Christian form of thought nor something drawn from biblical teaching, but a deformation resulting from an outside influence. It is not unlikely that just as the vision of a garden paradise comes from Islam, so the ethereal notion of heaven, the world of spirits and disembodiment, is derived from Platonism and Gnosticism. Alexandria on the one hand, and Origin on the other — both did their part to create this false idea of the new creation. And over against Augustine, who asserted that there was a "City of God," the great current of thought accepting a traditional paradise has continued through the ages, picking up added flotsam from medieval heresies.

The Christian conception, then, is the expectation of a new city. And this reveals a very singular myth, which cannot be put on the same shelf with pagan myths of a golden age or the Eden to come. For characteristic of all these myths is the notion that there was at the beginning of time a perfect and happy human race. There was a golden age when there was an equilibrium in everything and in man's heart. Life was natural — in nature — and trouble was brought in by the pride of a Prometheus, for example, or by some other event. Whatever may have happened, from that time on, war and death have been in the world, and man has been in quest of the lost golden age. It is proclaimed to him that he will reach it, that he will regain the situation of enjoying the fulness of life, that the golden age will return to the earth and in the same form. Poets through the ages have sought the signs of the returning golden age. Suffice it to recall the shepherds of Arcadia. This Greco-Latin myth announces a return to a natural life, to the life of field and forest, and this is the basic condition for the return of the golden age: man must revert to the primitive state of the "noble savage" (who was, of course, not savage), he must abandon all that man's genius has invented, and then, in the valleys and woods from which force has been banished, the golden age of peace can flourish again. Always the same dream of an eternal paradise. The future life of a valiant Mohammedan will also be a natural life, far from the constraints of civilization, in direct contact with flowers and springs — and his horse. This ancient myth of a new life in nature at last good, at last friendly, both tamed and wild, where man will no longer fear every sound, the ferocity of the animal, and the hostility of every living thing, is found under many forms in every corner of the earth, from the Eskimos to the North American Indians to the Tartars. Everywhere, we find the same idealization of nature as bringing peace, the expectation of a day when man will no longer need to fight to subsist in nature. And the characteristic of this notion is always man's abandonment of all that he has built to defend himself, to ensure his supremacy, to conquer the earth, by a return to the natural life and a direct relationship with things — once again peaceful because a common bond of peace characterizes this Eden.

In Egypt the Heliopolitan cycle represents the other world as an aquatic region of purification which produces a perpetual renewing of life. The idea here does not seem to be that of the end of the world, but rather of a new beginning in purification. And in the Osirian cycle the world of the dead is something of an image of the world of the living. The dead man received by Osiris lives in one of his estates, in a house. Of course, the sum of these houses may form a city. And the texts show that in Amentit there are many cities — Heliopolis, Letopolis, Keraha. But there is nothing particular about them; they are only cities for men reproduced as such in the other world, integrated into the time system of the other world. They are not at the end of history, not in what we may call metahistory.

As for Chaldea, no closed future seems to have been known there. Neither history nor creation is going anywhere. There is no future world, no triumph of justice, for magic dominates everything.

Thus the neighbors of Judea, which, according to scholars, influenced the Bible, are far from any knowledge of a world to come. Closer to Christianity, Mazdaism is also of a naturalistic character. The *frasho-kereti* is a resurrection of *nature*, an apotheosis of fertile land and agricultural pursuits, the restoration of earliest times for the triumph of good. Moreover, it is by the acts of the righteous that this triumph takes place: the righteous realize God's plans, are responsible for stamping out evil, and this becomes concrete in their acts of making the earth fertile, of growing wheat, of draining swamps. The technical improvement of the earth is a step toward the good creation at the end of time.

But all this has nothing to do with the Hebrew myth which considers the future of humanity as the establishment of a city. The prophets were undoubtedly influenced by Jerusalem herself. Here they saw the center of the world, and everything was to be reorganized with respect to her. But it is somewhat simplistic to give them credit for only such a rudimentary conception when, in other areas, they show such an intelligent grasp not only of present reality, but also of God's acts and plans. And why then were the creators of the Latin myth not impressed by Rome? After all, they had reason to be. We are forced to agree that here we have another kind of myth. Then someone will say: "Why worry so much about history? The difference between the two conceptions is not great enough to permit such a distinction. For, whether the afterlife is considered as nature, beautiful and calm, or as a city, it is not this imagination that counts, for the differences are so small and do not mean much in themselves. What counts is the fact that humanity has a hope, the fact that man has ineradicably in himself the certainty of a future and of a better world." We cannot accept this vision of things. On the contrary, we must recognize that it is of the greatest importance to consider the enormous divergence between these two goals or, rather, what this difference implies. And it would seem that this could be treated from two standpoints.

In the common myths we have a backward movement. What was good will again become what it was. The essential point, then, is a refusal of the existing order, a denial of man's "progress" in the sense of simple evolution, not of improvement. It is a black line drawn through all of history, which is only the history of human degradation, and a return to primitive purity, in the form of the original innocence of life as lived by man and animal. Man must, therefore, come back to what he once abandoned and destroyed. But the Hebrew notion is completely other: to the extent that this view is centered in the city, it takes in all of man's works and all of his history. Far from advocating a return to the past, it calls for a step ahead; it wants to lose nothing of what man has done. And in this respect Karl Marx was, as many have asserted, directly inspired by Jewish mythology, in which there is nothing to be destroyed from the fantastic adventure of human civilization. Rather, man's history must be transcended. The myth of the heavenly city appears as an appeal to transcend the work of man, that work in which he finds his peace and his haven. Thus the golden age will be characterized by an acceptance of history, and not by its refusal. This myth is therefore a kind of adoption, the ennobling of man's work, the very opposite of scorn and rejection.

Now this is remarkable, because no other religion has so severely condemned the origins of civilization and man's civilizing acts and industrial progress — not to mention its specific attitude toward the city — as does the Judeo-Christian. Nevertheless, it is the city, death's domain, which appears as the crowning moment of history. And even more important, it is not the natural, normal ending, but the result of God's intervention.

This brings us to the second aspect of the Christian myth. In all human myths the center is a return to the natural state, a recovery of man's situation before civilization, before the Promethean revolt, a return to man's true nature. And this can happen on earth. This earth and this world will gain from this return (Islamism is different in this respect, as we have seen, but it is unique in its conception). Moreover, it is thanks to his own intelligence and virtue, to his own personal efforts, that man will manage thus to re-create his natural state. And this is why the education of man is so important, not to mention the constant appeals down through the ages to effect this return.

There is no common ground here with Judeo-Christian thought, which asserts, on the contrary, two truths that seem to contradict the first aspect we have already pointed out. The new Jerusalem is to be established at the end of time, but absolutely not by any human effort. She is a creation of God, and her nature, therefore, is the opposite of a golden age. Instead of being the continuation of history, the crowning act of history is a break with history. The second creation stands over against the first, which it is impossible to draw back from destruction. But the second creation is just as extraordinary, unbelievable and unexpected as the first. So all of man's efforts to produce it on his own run into an invisible and impassable wall. He can act in history, but he can neither finish it nor transcend it. And this brings out the last characteristic of this opposition: the transcendent history we are speaking of is not any kind of return to nature, but rather is extra-natural. In the heavenly Jerusalem there is no nature. It is not a primitive equilibrium and happiness that are awaiting us. The situation is completely different, and we have no idea, no mental image, no knowledge, no way of measuring what it might be. And only certain mystical experiences, and God's revelation, so obscure in its limpidness, can give us even a feeble approximation of it. But then this contradiction arises: the Judeo-Christian conception which shows that all of man's works, summed up in the city, are included in the glorious new state of re-creation, also shows that it is not by man's work that this event will come about. This situation is therefore the resolute opposite, in both its terms, of all other human conceptions of the world to come. How can this contradiction be solved? Or rather (for there is little importance in an apparent contradiction) what is the form and outward expression of this evolution whose termination is in the new Jerusalem? There are two directions to be followed, both of which are basic to the history of the city. One originates in Cain, the other in Eden, and they converge finally in the new Jerusalem. Each expresses one form of the saving and kingly act of God in Jesus Christ.

II. FROM CAIN TO JERUSALEM

We have already studied God's fundamental action which, in Jesus Christ, leads from Cain to the new Jerusalem. God dissociates man's work from its spiritual power. When Cain founded his city, it was first of all to establish a monument to his pride, to uphold his rights and protect himself, but it was also as a plaything of the angelic powers which took form in his work and are using it to bring about man's downfall. But man's work as such is not condemned or cursed. What God judges and condemns is the power which from the beginning has been in the spirit of revolt, and, throughout the history of the city, in her spirit of seduction. The city as a power, as a spiritual reality, is what God rejects from his plan, and not the mere accumulation of stones and houses. We have seen that her truest self is what makes all efforts for the reformation and humanization of the city vain. And God's will is to separate this power from man's work, in fact a part of man himself and his destiny. And this is exactly what he does in Jesus Christ. But as so many have said (Barth, Cullmann, Visser 't Hooft), these conquered powers have not yet been eliminated. And as it is with the city, so with the state. Virtually conquered, they still have their power to act and fight, and in the last days they actually manifest a superabundant amount of activity. This fact has not received enough emphasis, although it is of vital concern to all of us. Jesus Christ warned that in the last days there would be an increase in the action of these powers; they would become more terrible, more threatening (Matt. 24:15 ff.; Rev. 20). These defeated powers are going to act, and are acting, with what we might call the energy of despair. They gather all their means, put all their possibilities to work, no longer acting by trickery and with restraint, but violently and unrestrainedly. And it is absolutely impossible for man to know that they have already been defeated in the real nature of things. On the contrary, the evidence is there before his eyes that they are redoubling their energy.

Thus, to use one of Oscar Cullmann's comparisons, after Stalingrad and El Alamein the General Staffs of both the Allied and the German armies knew that the decisive battles had occurred, that the war was already decided. But the troops and, even more, the populations of the occupied countries had absolutely no way of knowing it. And when they saw the Germans using new and terrible weapons of war (the V2 rockets and the Tigerpanzer), they could hardly feel confident of an Allied victory. The period of the bloodiest struggle against the resistance movement was after 1943, the period of mass exterminations in the concentration camps, of mass deportations of workers to Germany to replace the mobilized Germans, and of hasty and unsupervised orders. Thus from an individual standpoint the last year of the war was undeniably the most dangerous and the most threatening. And even beyond their threat to the individual, the defeated powers were still able to carry off temporary, tactical maneuvers that had all the appearance of victories. So the January 1945 offensive against Strasbourg, which seemed to be routing the Americans. But from an overall strategic point of view, the war had already been won. All that was left was a massive clean-up operation and the enemy's recognition of their defeat. For even if the German generals knew that the war was lost already in early 1943, Hitler and the Nazi spirit of war refused to recognize the fact.

This simple comparison does not, of course, establish my point, but we will understand this point much better if we take into consideration the essential distinction between truth and reality. In our day we are no longer able to make the distinction. But nothing is more decisive than this distinction, and the failure to recognize it is doubtlessly at the origin of the intellectual confusion in which some of today's best minds are entrapped.[2] Jesus Christ's work is the very work of truth. He *is* truth. But when he came into the world of reality, reality did not receive but rejected him. Yet, this does not annul the fact that his incarnation is the entrance of truth into the real world, which, by its nature, has nothing to do with the truth, nor the fact that his death and resurrection are the victory of truth. Falsehood, refusal, chaos, the negation of God's creation, have all been defeated; they have no more power to keep truth from existing, from acting and, because it is truth, from fulfilling itself. It is impossible for an essential falsehood, refusal, or chaos to exist. But this truth has penetrated reality at only one point, the incarnation of Christ — which from a realistic standpoint was a total failure, the rejection and elimination of the incarnate Word. Christ's victory is not visible in the world of reality: there is no obvious proof of it. This reality, even though it is submitted to truth and is only of relative and secondary importance, is still what the defeated powers claim as their domain — which in fact it is: "I saw Satan fall from heaven [to the *earth*] like lightning . . . ." Their domain is still theirs, it is still their headquarters for a vain attempt to conquer the truth they are constantly attacking, their fortified camp where they do their best to destroy every remnant of truth introduced by the incarnate Word. After

---

[2]It is obvious that the very simple distinction we have made here has nothing to do with a distinction between body and soul, between Idea and Matter, or between essence and existence. Ours is in no way philosophical or intellectual, but both theological and experimental.

trying to assert that before Christ truth *was* reality, now the new falsehood of these powers for the modern world is that reality *is* truth. This triumphant declaration is the best avowal from the powers themselves that they have been defeated. But this defeat is in Christ's sight, not in ours. We are but poor men bogged down in our reality, ever subject to the powers that run free in our own domain.

Thus we must accept the fact that the powers defeated by Christ are still at work, that they refuse to admit their defeat and are struggling more violently than ever. They do gain local victories, and their violence forces us to believe in their power (still real over us), whereas in truth they are subject to Christ. And it is their redoubled efforts that explain the condition of the state today, and why the city is incomparably more threatening, more grandiose, truer to her urban nature as a power, more seductive and monstrous than ever before in her history. A revolted world thumping its chest and breathing out threats, because it knows that the last struggle is upon it. Down through the world's history a certain restraint could be seen up until Christ's time. The powers observed the rules of war, working rather by trickery and local attacks, and even by positive action. The world after the fall was trying to organize itself to live in its evil, and live "humanly," even though its way was becoming more and more corrupt. But after Jesus Christ, with the beginning of the last events, the "Dominations" are beside themselves. Every means is a good means, now that the struggle is coming to an end, now that they have suffered the decisive defeat. There are no more secret offensives, there is no more respect for the law, there is rather a free rein for every means. The full hue and cry is on. No more renewed, deliberate action, but a gigantic effort, using every weapon created by man, to drag man into evil and death. Destruction is a must.

How ridiculous, how grotesque is bravado of naked little man — bravado filling every newspaper, every socialist doctrine, every Protestant journal, every belief in the rebirth of humanism. "I am, and there is none else," man shouts. "I will stop the whole mess, I will put it in order. It's not so bad as it seems. This is only the normal course of history, a change of civilizations. There is no reason to be afraid of these new developments. In a few decades we will be familiar with them. All we have to do is to adapt and not reject them (for refusal is devilish, as has been known since the work of Freud), and we must expand our minds in order to dominate them. We'll handle it."

Poor little man. You failed to notice that you are not

dealing with flesh and blood, but with Thrones, and Powers, and Dominations which are attacking you, grinding you under, dominating you from every side, and that the Devil's last trick is to make you think that you can put order back into this chaos, that you are going to get spiritually big enough to control the world! To be sure, the Devil will offer you this spiritual growth. He offered the very same thing, and with the same goal in mind, to Jesus Christ. But with him the offer failed (Matt. 4:8-10).

The sleight-of-hand performed by the "diabolos" in these last days is to make us believe that we are able to dominate the situation by the spiritual power in us, whereas we are dealing with forces which in truth have already been conquered, and which we therefore have no deed of dominating. So the facts of the situation are radically different from what we think. And the Scriptures teach that by Jesus Christ, God is snatching man's work from Satan's grasp and, as it were, giving it back to man, preparing it for other purposes. Man's work is no less valid; it is not itself engulfed in the fall and condemnation of the *exousiai*. This condemnation is not dragging man and his work down with it as though he were physically bound to it. But, although the basic operation has been carried out, its results have not yet been effected. The stitches have not yet been taken, the disinfectants not yet applied, and the patient is far from convalescence. For the fact is that the spirit behind the creation of the city, and the power which has dominated it, have given their construction a particular form. Its face has been shaped and its possibilities have received a definite orientation. It is not easy to make the distinction between the city as it stands, which in its simple materiality is human and could be saved, and the dominations dwelling there. They have become so tightly interwoven that when the dominations are struck, the city staggers in its very being, in its concrete reality. It is no question of a simple inner dissociation, invisible to the observer, but of the masks being torn away, those outer forms which are the result of the inner spirit. God is working out a total renewal, but in Jesus Christ we have only the first fruits. Only the new creation will complete the work.

But this is also the city's greatness and truth, the blind work of her well-intentioned urbanists. An uncertain attempt, groping toward a more balanced body, a healthier one, one with no soul other than that of its dwellers. We can see, then, a certain agreement between what they have done and what God has done, and which he continues mysteriously to foster until the time has come for the last great change. When urbanists try, as they say, to produce a rational habitat, to construct bright, sunny homes in green cities, they are trying to tear the city away from its obsession, to cut it off from its origins and history. Up to the present, unknown forces have made their residence there. Why the great influx? Why the incoherent growth of the city? Why is its shape so tortured, its streets so narrow and dark? Why the giant pulse of a population or a district? Of course we have historical and sociological answers. But these can only retard the final answers to the basic questions. And man wants to move in with all this irrationality in order to establish something rational. Dimly, confusedly, he feels that he is doing a work without which life would be inhuman. Dimly, confusedly, he tries to exorcise the demons which loom before his eyes in the form of slums, foul odors, and malnutrition. So he persists doggedly in trying to make out what is happening, in trying to solve as much as he can by reason. But in his quest, there is not enough air for his lamp, and his reason ends up being extinguished by forces stronger than himself. "We drew up beautiful plans for your cities," the architects wail, "and you did not build them."

This time it is because the money is missing that the demons are not exorcised. Next time it will be because a war has to be waged or a purge carried out. Poor, well-intentioned reason, always fluttering about, always running into irrational needs that can never be completely eliminated. It all adds up to man's dance of will and powerlessness as he faces the truth.

No, we must not count on the urban specialists to give the city its simple character as one of man's works. We must salute these idealists. They are right in doing what they are doing and wrong in believing they will ever get anywhere. For the struggle is too serious, too profound; it is taking place in a realm never reached by man. Let us harbor no illusions. No man will change the city — first of all, because he will never use it for good.

How many times has this generous and simplistic thought not blocked up our way: "After all, every *thing* is neutral, a simple instrument in man's hands, something dead that man animates and uses as he wishes. Of course we have seen the tragic results of the city's existence up till now, but *who* will keep us from changing its aspect, its character? Is there any necessity that it stay as it is? Christians and existentialists take no necessity for their standard, and Marxists realize that constraining necessity is only working against the capitalistic regime! So man can put the city to other uses; he can use it for good (he does know the difference between right and wrong, doesn't he?). He can even give it a spiritual character other than what history has shown to be traditionally the city's!"

Much could be said in answer to this, but we must limit ourselves here to pointing out that Scripture (since we have chosen it for our standard in this study) teaches the very contrary. The city is not a simple instrument with no determining factors involved. The city is an almost indistinguishable mixture of spiritual power and man's work. It has a very definite spiritual character, an orientation toward evil and away from good which in no way depends on man. And man is clearly not the one to change that inner spirit as he wishes — we see every day that he cannot change even the outer face. He cannot do so even when, after atomic annihilation, he has every chance to do so. He cannot hope for a better utilization of the instrument, because he is not the one using it. We could even turn it around and say that he is the one being used.

He is used, consumed, eaten away, possessed in heart and soul, and the city gives him new complexes, requires of him new reflexes, transforms his tastes and his mental make-up. The demons push him on with their enormous power, forcing him to find in the city the realization of his desire for escape and liberty. In response to the impossibility of living in the midst of his neighbor's yelling and slamming and bickering, man might try to find satisfaction in the anonymity of the city. "I am never more alone than in a crowd," goes the obscene paradox. "I am never freer than when faced with blank stares." But this is a delirious lie. The liberty of rising up against oppression and perhaps against other men is not the same thing as the anonymity of not knowing even one's next-door neighbor. To be simply a stranger is not to be a free man. This is the solitude of suicide, of a drowning man.

Man is the one being used. No hope for him of ever being able to use the city, of ever spiritualizing it. What could he do? Is it not already spiritual and spiritualized enough? What in the world is there more spiritual than the sphinx? Than the demon's mask? Can one not see her on her throne of power and glory with all the values she has claimed, and uses to beautify herself — is she not the greatest monument ever built to civilization? Is she not the place where the noblest passion for justice and truth is expressed? Are not her walls covered with posters, each one proclaiming louder than the other the merits of justice and truth? Is she not the place of highest intelligence, of man's most developed artistic talents? And architecture — the art of arts, the synthesis of music and mathematics — what would it be without this spiritual home of homes? What could little man hope to do here? He has already made her as spiritual as he could. And others have put it all to good use!

This is enough of a bad joke. Man is not to be counted on to transform the problem of the city. He is no more capable of transforming the environment chosen for him and built for him by the Devil, than he is of changing his own nature. Only God's decisive act is sufficient. Only the death of the very Son of God is sufficient to change the facts of history. Only the resurrection is sufficient to dispossess the demon powers of their domain. Thus it is only God, by his act, who made the city into a neutral instrument. It is not completely natural that the city should be offered to man in this way, for him to remodel it, to recast it. The important thing is to know *by whom* it was offered to man and to know what spirit will be dwelling behind the new face made for it by man. For she can in no case be only a body without a soul, only a pile of stones. At the very best, we can say that God opened a possibility for man when he offered him this area he had neutralized by his victory, and that he restores man's liberty in this one aspect of his work. But even this liberty is not great, because man can act only in the name of Christ and by Christ, and because the demons are still hard at work even though the underpinnings of their presence in the city have already been removed. And this is where man's work lies — to help bring truth and reality together, to introduce somewhere, in some small way, the victory won in truth by Christ into concrete existence, into the baroque, heteroclite, powerful materiality which man is always accumulating, which the powers use, and which the victory of truth is to tear from their grasp. Such may be the true greatness of man. But what power do we have to do such a thing? There is no other way than that taken by Jesus in his incarnation. But today's incarnation must be that of an already victorious truth into the heart of the city. Such is man's calling. Such an assertion is, as a brilliant intellectual said not too long ago, "a rather narrow basis for action." But outside of this liberating work, man's only future is to fall back into his old habits and to revert to the much wider basis offered him by the power of the city!

* * *

We said that God, by his act in Jesus Christ, made the city into a neutral world where man can be free again, a world where man finds possibilities for action. But it is no holy world. Let there be no confusion: there is no use expecting a new Jerusalem on earth. Jerusalem will be God's creation, absolutely free, unforeseeable, transcendent. But God's act gives man room for autonomous action. God has preserved man alive and now reserves for him a part, as in Eden he made Adam responsible for keeping and cultivating the fields. The final establishment is not yet. For the moment of history in which we live, the final establishment of the city must be considered from the angle of God's action when he defeated her spiritual powers and thus put her at man's eventual disposal. For just as God took away Jerusalem's spiritual garments and power and restored her to the condition of a simple city, so also, by Christ's triumph over the spiritual powers, he took away every city's spiritual worth. He cut to bits her independence, and took from her bleeding flesh Satan's monstrous tumor. She was sacred only because of Satan — set apart from all of creation, the preferred spot of the one who had fallen from heaven, had no place of his own, and had man build it for him. He set it aside, but God tore it from his grasp and gave it to man, as he had done with Jerusalem.

But God involves himself in an adventure completely different, for from this very city he is going to make the new Jerusalem. Thus we can observe God's strange progress: Jerusalem becomes Babylon, Babel is restored to the status of a simple city, and this city becomes the city of the living God. This is the incomparable progress by which God teaches us that on the top of his scale of values is man's responsibility. This is what the incarnation means, as well as the plunge — for our history — into the urban evolution. Man must, in his relations with the city, cease being a plaything of forces which he can neither combat nor measure. But unfortunately for the unregenerate mind, there is only one name by which that can happen. And God untiringly proposes this means, and man untiringly refuses. Man tries to put his cities back into business, rebuilding them on his human sacrifices, on the proletariat of the capitalist world, on the forced labor of the Soviet world, on the black slaves of the colonial world, all untiringly dying a dog's death to provide a foundation for the magnificent city. Man sacrifices man to build his cities, instead of accepting the only sacrifice which would enable him both to found them in truth and purify them of Satan's presence. I am sadly aware that these words mean nothing to the world's ears. The means chosen by God has no meaning for man's projects. But it is the only means. And we must never stop saying this, for God has not resigned himself to man's refusal. He wants all of man, with all that he is and all that he does. He cannot permit Cain to be left to himself. But he does put a mark on him, and henceforth all of Cain's history bears that mark. God does not want any part of man to be outside the pale of his love. He does not want any of man's works, his heart, his labor, his hope to be forever lost in the shadow of death.

But he must go through that valley. He must go through death. Such is the meaning of the condemnation resounding ever anew through the world of cities. It is in this awful combat on the other side that man's work will find its meaning, because God is restoring to man his work, because God is destroying the rebellious angel who up till now has animated man's work, and because the Lord himself will take the place and the role of the rebellious angel. God will himself create for man what man was incapable of creating, what he wanted to do in his revolt and hate, what he wanted to realize in blood, but which he never succeeded in establishing. Over that work God pronounces the No of death, but in the same breath (over man in Jesus Christ) he pronounces the Yes of the resurrection, by creating the unique city, the answer to all our questions and to all our hopeful attempts, the heavenly Jerusalem, "where God will be all in all." He creates this city as he creates the bodies of all those who are dead when he calls them to life. And man has no more part in it than in his own resurrection. It is in the creation of the heavenly Jerusalem that Christ's final victory will take its place in the sphere of reality. At the end of time, truth joins and animates reality, not by the renewing but humble means of incarnation, not in such a surreptitious presence as that, but in a new creation of reality. Then the true victory gained by Christ over the powers of evil will become visible in reality; it will become a very part of the new nature of reality. Our environment will be one of complete truth, with no possible contention. Just as in truth there was already no possibility for falsehood and chaos to triumph, so in this perfect reality, there is no possibility for suffering and death to triumph. The new creation is the coming together in new-found unity of reality and truth, the glory of creation answering the Creator's glory in perfect harmony. And the mystery of it all is that it comes about in the creation of a *city*, as though the city were the zenith of reality itself, as though the victory in truth obtained by Christ within the city were to find its fulfillment only in the moment when the city is translated by the Father's glory, as though it were in her that the unity of creation is established.

III. FROM EDEN TO JERUSALEM

Thus the history of the city, divided in two by Jesus Christ, goes from Eden to Jerusalem, from a garden to a city. God created man in a garden, in the middle of the world. He gave him as his environment a particular and limited bit of nature — not all of nature. We are not told that man occupied all of creation, but rather that he had a limited space over which he was sovereign. He was the delegated master, but lived only in the garden. Eden was a part of creation, and a closed garden where what we call nature flourished and where God chose to place the king of his creation. This is where God wanted him — there and nowhere else. And in our world of today there is still a trace of this: man always attains a better equilibrium, always feels his best, and probably *is* his best, in a primitive environment. This is no ideology of the country, nor some brand of naturalism, but only a simple observation corresponding with the revealed fact that God wanted man in that situation. This makes it all the more striking, all the more strange, that at the end of history God gave up the plan which he had himself ordained and chosen. He does not restore the order that he had installed, but creates another. Henceforth man will have another environment: walls, streets, houses, public squares. Stone will replace trees. Beryl, onyx, chrysoprase are to be the mirror of man's being, whereas his pleasure used to be in cedar and oak.[3]

---

[3]Must we again call to mind that here we are dealing with a myth? Not a falsehood, but a sign, not material reality, but truth, not legend, but the revealed word, not a description, but a message, not an identity, but an identification. But from the very fact that it is a myth, we cannot be indifferent to its form. We cannot take from it a general idea as its nucleus while neglecting the surrounding material, as one keeps an almond after throwing the shell away. For this very shell, with its words, its literary style, is full of meaning. The city designates much beyond herself, although it is nevertheless the city. Faced with the problem of the new Jerusalem, are we to ask: "Is this really a *city* that will come down? Will we know him face to face? Or is this only a manner of speaking, a figure, a myth, a symbol (in the lightest meaning of the term)?" Perhaps this manner of speaking is there to show us what God's final intentions are for man and for his work. But in this case we see that God chose as a type *the* city in order to reveal to us his good intention. By affirming that he has chosen the city as a place of meeting for him and us, he proclaims his decision to save all men. Therefore, to the extent that the city is herself one of man's works, raising the problem of the myth with respect to her has no more meaning and may be considered as an intellectual game. In the myth of the final city, we may see an answer to the problem of life, of history, of man's work, and not an object of mystical speculation or intellectual knowledge.

Why has God so changed the situation? What fundamental difference has led God to give up, as it were, his first plan? Simply the history of the world, and more particularly the minute history of man sandwiched in somewhere between the beginnings and the re-creation. It is because of this history that God sets about reorganizing the primitive state of things. "Behold the former things have passed away, and I make *all* things new," says the Lord.

If God chooses this new form it is simply because man has chosen it. Man wanted this setting, this environment, and scorned the one prepared for him by God. From the beginning man worked desperately to have his own little world, independent of all that God desired. And God will give him the perfect work which he himself could not bring about. God will realize man's setting. But in his new world one of man's desires will not be satisfied: the desire for the absence of God. Man wanted to build a city from which God would be absent, but he never managed. God will make for him the perfect city, where he will be all in all. Thus we might say that it is uniquely man's decision that provoked God to act, which incited him to accept what man was desiring and seeking, and which caused him to transform his creation.

This is no place to get caught up in the ridiculous problems of God's knowledge and omnipotence, and all the casuistry having to do with man's liberty in regard to God's will. Once and for all we must finish with man's absurd pretension to fathom the mysteries of God's will. If God is truly God, he is outside the reach of our intelligence; if God is truly God, our intelligence can never grasp anything but a falsification of his true nature. "Who are you to answer back to God?" But in the precise details of this revelation given us of God, we can, in any case, perceive one astonishing thing, and that is the patience of God's attention and love for man. For non-Christians this love may have no existence; otherwise they would accept Jesus Christ. And for Christians, this love is *too* well known, since they think they know Jesus Christ. Now it is true that the center of God's love is in Jesus Christ, but it is also well to understand that his love reaches every man's life. God in his love, because he *is* love, takes into account man's will, takes into account his desires and his maddest intentions, understands his wildest revolts, takes into account all his endeavors. God does not want to save an abstract man, but you and me, each man in his particularity. God did not love Man in Jesus Christ, but every crushed and miserable soul in the midst of the wandering crowd. And God has kept his records throughout history. Certainly not an account of merits and demerits, of sins and good works. All that has already been taken care of in the pardon streaming from the cross. His accounts are those of the suffering and hope, the inventions and the refusals, the desires and the gropings that man has experienced throughout history. And God keeps it all in order, so as to respond to them all, so as to do what man has been trying to do, so as to give an answer where man did not ask for help, but tried to go it alone. God assumes to himself even man's revolts and transforms them, remakes them. Progressively, then, God assumes all of man's work. This is the meaning of God's creation, for man, of the new Jerusalem.

God is certainly relinquishing none of his rights! He is no less God and never will become man's *famulus* by some magic or some religion. He is master of the day and hour. He still guides the how and answers the why. But because he is love he has reserved a part for man, and answers man's demands. And to a great extent this puts man back in his place. You thought you had killed God? Really? Because your techniques allow you to go faster than sound? Because uranium has enabled you to measure the age of the world? Because you observe that you can make matter disappear in your machines faster than sand through your fingers? Because you burst the atom and can now annihilate the earth? Because you know that space is not a straight line? Because your police methods can arrest anybody anywhere? And in all that, you say, you nowhere saw God! And because good receives no reward, and evil is not punished, because you can exclude God from your political organization, because the churches have failed and are rapidly losing members, because you organize the world to your every whim and the masses follow you and no longer believe in God, you say that the era of religion is at an end (and there I agree), but add, in an unfortunate confusion for brains so well organized, that God is dead. As though God were dependent on your decision, no less. You draw up his death notice as you drew up his birth certificate: the God who is dead is the one you made up for yourselves, and not the one who created you. And all of man's fantastic history, as little as he may want to hear it said, is only a part of the great historical line traced by God himself. All your enormous accumulation of works and power, every bit of it, God takes over for himself, assimilates it into his plan. And he does not wipe out even what you made against him. God does not fight against man. He is not trying to deprive him of his conquests. On the contrary, he accepts them. He enters into man's little game, patiently follows the rules man has fixed, and walks in the paths man has opened.

Such is the meaning of the Bible as a book written by men. God did not adopt an original means to reveal himself. No, he expressed his revelation in the forms and modes invented by man for his own affairs. And this is also the meaning of God's decision to take over for himself man's invention of the city. God does not reject this world of revolt and death, he does not annihilate it in the abyss of fire. Rather, he adopts it. That is, he takes charge of it. And the immense vanity that man put into it, God transforms into a city with gates of pearl. Thus, and only thus, does our work take on meaning, both significance and direction. No longer is it a vanity among vanities. No longer is it a permanent return to nothingness. Civilizations pass and go under, leaving behind a few ruins buried by vines, and the stones lose their grip and fall in silence. But nothing is forgotten. All the pain and hope represented by these walls is taken over by God. And because of it all, God is preparing this same setting for man, but made new. And because all of this is in God's plan, his Jerusalem will be the fulfillment of all that man expected.

It is in Jesus Christ that God adopts man's work. For Ephesians 1:10, translated literally, tells us that Jesus is the great recapitulator. God formed the plan of uniting "all things in him, things in heaven and things on earth." Things on earth! It is not restricted to "natural" things, to the creation itself. No such distinction is made. God's plan also includes things invented by man, what he laboriously put together piece by piece learning from experience and failure. Both his technical failures and the marvels of his cleverness. All this is "recapitulated" in Christ, summed up in him, taken over by him. In a brilliant transfiguration all of man's work is gathered together in Christ. Not that man's inventions are labeled one by one, as in the presumptuous display cases of American museums where the inventions judged most characteristic are kept for future generations. For God's way of judging is not ours. What will he preserve? We have no way of telling. Perhaps the great summing up will include all that exists, as the ark sheltered both unclean animals and clean. In any case we see that this is what will happen with the city. She is the characteristic example of God's adoption. And this is also true, but with no explanatory details, of all that made up the glory of the nations (Rev. 21:26).

Perhaps it is only the city that is mentioned by name because the city is clearly considered, as we have seen, as man's great work. However that may be, we do have the assurance that everything will share in her lot. And this is accomplished in Christ, which means that these works are both judged and saved, both freed and subjected, because this is one way that Christ fills his triple role as prophet, priest, and king. Outside Christ, there is absolutely no way for man's work to be elevated. Outside of Christ, the vanity of Ecclesiastes is fully true, and the curse remains over the city. Outside of Christ, all goes back to nothingness. And if man returns to dust, the concrete of his cities returns to the sand from which it was taken.

There are no whys to be asked. This is the path God has chosen, and we have but to follow its shining traces through history. But because Christ is Savior and Lord of both creation and mankind, he is also Savior and Lord of man's works. In him, God adopts man *and* his works. He tolerated it through the world's history and now he himself has taken charge of it. He has chosen to dwell in it. And just as the man living in the city is directly subject to the spirit of the city, now those who dwell in it are in communion with God, for he has truly assumed it in the most classical meaning of the term, and has transfigured it. For even in the resurrection, God does not shatter men's hopes. Rather, he fulfills them there. And on the other side of death, in his new creation, God renders to man the setting he preferred.

But he renders it to him in Christ; that is, in the new creation, all that Christ came to accomplish is finally realized. Direct communion with God is reestablished, so there is no more Temple or church. Uncorruptible, immortal life is again man's. The balance of creation is re-created when Christ, after uniting all things in himself, hands everything over to his Father. And all this happens in the new Jerusalem, so as to forever link man's work with Christ's. In this city, the adventure of Christmas is totally realized and finds its culmination. Man's version of the incarnation finds an eternal home. This is the very heart of this extraordinary manifestation of God's love. And if this work of man takes its meaning in Christ, it is God's desire that man's great work, re-created, be an expression throughout eternity of God's great work.

* * *

But this must not become for us a pretext. And perhaps as a precaution, we should state this teaching a bit more precisely. When we spoke of man's work, we were, of course, referring to the results of man's physical labor, what he manufactures. It is not a question here of moral or spiritual works in a Roman Catholic sense, works which might possibly lead to one's salvation. Neither do we have in mind the works of faith as an expression of the Christian life, the meaning given them by Paul. The works we are thinking of have no relation with man's spiritual destiny, are in no way a manifestation of his morality, good intentions, or piety. We have confined ourselves to the purely secular sense of works as the results of man's labor, what he makes. We were then able to observe that this work is in fact connected (but in no way because of man) with his spiritual destiny, or rather, with God's action for man in Jesus Christ and by the Holy Spirit.

But if such is the case, we are constrained to indicate very briefly a consequence of considerable importance: man's work, what he makes, is not neutral. It is certainly tempting to hold that techniques are neutral, that anything to do with work in this sense is beyond the classification of good and evil. However, we should already have been wary in the knowledge of the close relationship between work and Adam's fall. But even that is at the most an indication that works after the fall may be used for good or for evil. We must take another step, for the biblical teaching on this subject is not moral in nature. We must not try to search out good and bad works, nor to pass judgment on work itself or on different works with regard to some moral rule. This is not how we are to assert that man's works are not neutral. We are not saying that different kinds of work are to be classified as good or as bad according to the guidance of the conscience, for example. If we were to do so, we would lose ourselves in an indefinite casuistry which experience has taught us to be useless and endless. The casuistry of a just or unjust war, for example, has taught us that. Moreover, it is because experience showed how uncertain and vain such study was that man went back to the idea that perhaps mechanical creations are neutral, after all: "All that counts is how something is used." The tragedy of the whole thing is that we already know exactly how man will use his work — created by a radically evil man, itself radically evil. We already know that the evil work will be utilized by the evil man. How can it result in anything else but the terrible fabric of history: Plague, War, Famine. The black horse, the red horse, the pale horse? So we are not trying to come up with a moral classification, but rather to consider how man's work fits in with condemnation and redemption. We must recognize that man's technical adventure is not on the level of

a base materiality destined to perish. Neither is it the immortal glorification of the human city. It is in the circle which takes in everything, within which God has locked up everything, in his curse and in his pity. It is in this respect that man's works are not neutral.

Then why worry, someone may say, since God in his love has definitively adopted everything, and his pardon is, after all, as valid for what man produced in God's favor as for what he produced against him? And why, since even the city, as we have studied, is to be rebuilt, should we not surrender ourselves to the angel of the city and its spirit of power? This is obviously the greatest temptation provoked by the message of pardon in Jesus Christ, and it proves first of all that we have understood absolutely nothing of what God's forgiveness means.

We must press this problem even closer, attack it from several sides. First, we must distinguish between the history of the world in its relationship with God and the life of a man in the same relationship. If God proclaims that the final destiny of the city, after its bloody epic, is to become the new Jerusalem, it is nonetheless true that during her earthly history she is under the most terrible of condemnations, and that as individuals with a life to live we are in contact with the condemned city and not with the new Jerusalem. And we must realize that while we participate in that work, we are participating in a work of death which is under a curse. It is not because we have reason to hope for the city that we are individually to give our·selves over to the demons presently at work in her. We have a full assurance for ourselves, but it leads us into other work than hers. Although we know that at the end the city is to be transfigured, this is a revelation of God's grace and is absolutely not to be forced into the present course of things. But that is just what we would be tempted to do.

Next, we must repel this great temptation by a reminder: we must remember that everything we have said so far concerning the city was of biblical origin, which means that it is an appeal to a decision of faith. Either we believe that the Bible expresses the revelation of God centered in Jesus Christ and that therefore what we have understood concerning the city has an element of truth, or else we do not believe it. We must not confuse the two positions: asserting that since God pardons in the end we have nothing to worry about and thus can obey our every whim, is taking the attitude of one who does not believe in revelation. It is exhibiting a complete disregard for the death of Jesus Christ. It is making a misuse of pardon, and simply

shows that such a person has not received that pardon. Therefore, whoever reasons in this way does not truly believe in Jesus
Christ. But in that case, all that we have written concerning the
city has no truth for him, and for that reason he has no right
to use it for his own purposes.

As for the believer, the fact that he considers this pardon
as final, that he has understood God's attitude toward man's
work (summed up in the city) as God has revealed, puts him on
an entirely different track for the present life. And this is what
we must declare. Because God forgives, Christians must realize
that the words of Ecclesiastes are true: "Whatever your hand
finds to do, do it with your might; for there is no work or
thought or knowledge or wisdom in Sheol, to which you are
going." Life is given us in order that we accomplish these works
and make scientific progress. And we are asked to have a share
in all of the human life, in all of man's research, to build with
men their works. To the extent that in Jesus Christ the city is
not devilish, to the extent that it is destined to be transfigured,
we must not pass judgement on the works of others, but must
work along with the others in the construction of the city. Under
these conditions we are not working with other men in the construction of a Babel. It is here that the discernment of the
Spirit must be active. However, neither are we working in the
completely spiritual construction of the new Jerusalem: that is
God's work and not ours. So our work is in the city of stone
and iron, which may be an environment for man, but not necessarily a good one. The only standard for us to act by is that of
God's pardon. And this pardon teaches us, much better than
any historical considerations, the vanity and the relativity of
man's work, since everything depends on forgiveness. God's
pardon will make the city of man into the new Jerusalem; that
is, its precise goal is to keep her from disappearing into nothingness. So not only man's spiritual destiny is connected with
God's forgiveness, but also the destiny of his work and the very
materiality of history, which rests exclusively on this act of God
— rests on that infinitely thin line, that razor blade which sep-
arates decisively between the work destined to vanish and the
work that will be transformed into a creation of God for all
eternity. With this in mind we are obviously able to put all our
irony into the contemplation of man's efforts to build — but
at the same time we participate in them.

In another respect, however, we cannot misuse God's pardon, if we really believe in it. And then there arises the problem of our participation in all of man's works. Since we are

working without moral criteria because they do not cover the city, and since the problem of the city is clearly a spiritual affair and therefore when we work with builders we become a weapon of their revolt, must we Christians also march in man's struggle against God? Stated in such extreme terms, the question appears scandalous. However, are we not in the world? Are we not in the place where the revolt is taking place? And we cannot, and must not, be anywhere else. But we do have a function in man's work which narrowly limits our participation. First, we must be able to inject humor into the situation. Where we are working we absolutely must not take our action seriously, neither ours nor that of our companions. That is why we must not accept the term "tragic optimism," in opposition to "active pessimism," as an expression of the Christian life. The idea of tragic optimism corresponds to the Thomist heresy of Christianity and opens the doors for every betrayal of God's forgiveness. It could be accepted only by deforming ridiculously, and perhaps not very honestly, the traditional Reformational notion of active pessimism modified by Christian catastrophism. For the Thomist heresy leads in this respect to discarding a good deal of the Book of Revelation as well as the twenty-fourth chapter of Matthew.

What keeps us from transforming our active pessimism into a sterile catastrophism is the humor I mentioned, a form of Christian liberty in our participation in man's work. And this humor is one limit on our participation, for it must not be kept within us, a secret, but rather lived out and made known. Now there is a big difference between the work we can accomplish with this attitude, and the work that requires idolatry and unbelief. And two camps form among workers, according to whether they accept or refuse the irony of faith. We must keep in mind that, "Where your love is, there will your heart be also." So we must put our heart into the city, but keep it ours by humor. But then the question arises, will the men building Babel accept working with us if we refuse to bury our heart there?

Moreover, a second limitation appears immediately. For we have our job to do in the city. We have seen that down through history God's answer to the construction of man's closed world was to move in just the same. And if he is there by his hidden presence, he is also there by those whom he sends. Our task is therefore to represent him in the heart of the city. But then again, will the city accept us there? Will men accept our task of testifying to the very opposite of their great enterprise? How long will they put up with it? There can be no doubt that they will not become acclimatized, or at home with the flaming seraphim. And if they leave us in peace, it must be because we are neglecting our task as faithful witnesses to God's work. Realizing that the new Jerusalem is not a work of our hands, we must also realize that when peace reigns, when it seems to us that the world has accepted God's word, we are allowing ourselves to be trapped by Satan's pranks.

The whole affair will boil down to our rejection by the city. We will be expelled from the city, unless, as Jesus promised, we are thrown into the very heart of the city, into prison. Then our collaboration with the builders must stop. But we may be inducted voluntarily to leave the city, to break off our cooperation, to take a position of refusal. We have already seen the biblical basis for such a position. This takes place when every means is blocked for the Christian to fulfill the sole destiny of man and his work, to give glory to God. When there is no longer any means of turning man's work to the glory of his Creator, when there is no longer possible in Babel any mark of the revelation of God's character in Jesus Christ, then life is no longer possible for the Christian. He must flee, cut himself off from the city. Obviously, when I speak of a mark of revelation, I am not referring simply to religious ceremonies and the like, but also to the "secular" acts of laymen and especially a certain state of mind among men. A time comes in the periodic renewal of man's passion for the city when the Christian must pronounce the *non possumus*. Every moment in history is not the same. One day we must say Yes, the next No, to the very same thing. As concerns the city, we must not forget that Abraham once went to rescue the king of Sodom, and was blessed for it by Melchizedek, whereas soon after this, Lot had to flee Sodom because it had incurred the Lord's temporal wrath.

Chapter Six

YAHWEH-SHAMMAH

ACCORDING TO THE HISTORIAN, THE HEAVENLY JERU-
salem as an "idea" is a mixture of various tendencies present
during the three centuries of Jewish history that preceded the
destruction of Jerusalem by Titus. The notion is recorded in
both canonical and noncanonical books: Daniel, Zechariah, Ezra,
Enoch, Jubilees, the Twelve Patriarchs, Baruch. Among these,
the Christian Book of Revelation is only one source, slightly
different from the others. The center where all these tendencies
crystallized was obviously the earthly Jerusalem. Seeing the
woes and the suffering of the chosen people, seeing the rending
of the earthly Jerusalem and her impotence, the Jews of that
difficult, utterly disappointing period interpreted the prophecies
that proclaimed a blessed and glorious Jerusalem by referring
them to the end of time. All that was promised as coming to
pass on this earth was to be accomplished in heaven, after the
end of history. This transformation of ancient prophecies was
not made arbitrarily, because of a desire to justify the prophets,
but in answer to the very authentic spiritual needs of the men of
that time. It was essential that God's people not be given over
to a despair due only to the adverse historical circumstances.

At the same time, say the historians, we may see among
these religious writers what has been termed a "mystical regres-
sion." Instead of staying with the strong, realistic, concrete
thought of the prophets, they let themselves go in semi-poetical
ventures, in a passionate disorder which was unknown among
the great prophets and does not seem to have been built on
very solid foundations. With no more spiritual truth to announce,
or practically so, the apocalyptic writers launched into a rather
vague, poetic delirium. Everything became universal, symbols

were rampant while truths became blurred, history was considered as a machine, and faltering inspiration was replaced by
mysterious conspiracies and bookish calculations. It was in this
complex atmosphere that the transfer from the earthly Jerusalem to the heavenly Jerusalem occurred, the heavenly Jerusalem understood as a type about which it was legitimate to
carry everything written by the prophets about the earthly Jerusalem to the absolute degree.

We can have no objections to such a view except that it
is all pure hypothesis, even pure imagination. For basically,
everything is dependent on this very rudimentary psychological
conception: Things are going badly on earth, and so let us fall
back on the heavenly things yet to come. A rather artless psychology, and perhaps more important, a rather modern one. Who
can say what the psychology of the Hebrew people was in the
second century B.C.? How can we judge — we who are so
poorly acquainted even with our present psychology, in spite
of Freud? Certainly, nothing can be built on the few books
mentioned above. What particularly strikes me in this quest
for the evolution of the idea of a heavenly Jerusalem, is that
the specific character of this evolution is left unmentioned. It
should be noted that this tradition is independent of any foreign tradition (note, for example, the failure of the hypothesis
connecting the Jewish apocalyptic movement with Mazdaism).
Furthermore, there is simply no compelling evidence that the
Jewish apocalyptic writers centered their vision of the world
to come in the earthly Jerusalem. We may in fact witness here
the birth of a *new* land surging from the sea, a radical step
forward in revelation — and the last step, for the revelation regarding Christ and his work had only to be completed before
the coming of the Messiah. What the historian cannot confirm
is that the notion of a heavenly Jerusalem corresponds to an
objective reality. No textual or archeological data can give him
any constraining proof of this — only the Spirit who brought
forth this notion in the prophets' minds. The humility of history: she is hardly the great lady, terrible in her simplicity,
whom Renan set up as the great dispenser of dogma.

Yet, even if the interpretation of the historian is correct, in what respect can this modify our view of the new Jerusalem? What would keep us from seeing it as the revelation of
objective truth? Obviously not the fact that this notion appears
at a given moment in history, since the originality of Judeo-
Christian thought is precisely that its revelation is always in

terms of history. God submits himself to a certain extent to its laws.

* * *

Another evolution must also be pointed out, and it is somewhat surprising that, generally speaking, the historians have not emphasized it: the evolution from Ezekiel's vision to John's. These two apocalyptic visions were on the same subject, but were seen and understood differently. Ezekiel announces that he sees a city (ch. 40), but it is never again mentioned in the following lengthy description of coming events. He speaks interminably of the Temple, for seven chapters, with all the minute measurements that any reader of Ezekiel knows so well. He does at last, in the final lines of Chapter 48, add a few more words concerning the city, but his emphasis is clearly on the sanctuary; everything is understood in terms of the sanctuary — God's dwelling-place. This is certainly one of the oldest apocalyptic texts, and is certainly to be placed well before the movement of the second century B.C. And this evolution did not proceed from the earthly Jerusalem to the heavenly, but from the Temple of Solomon to the Temple of God. In this context, Jerusalem is, as we have seen, only accessory to the Temple. This evolution, then, is specifically spiritual, and not social, as some would have us believe. Solomon's Temple, even well before Ezekiel, was only an image of God's dwelling-place, as very old texts show. Therefore, in Ezekiel's description there is nothing new, only the prophetic statement of what Mosaic revelation already contained with regard to the ark. But in John's vision everything is centered in the city. He says nothing of the Temple. On the contrary it is strongly emphasized that there is no Temple: "For the temple is the Lord God the Almighty and the Lamb."

I am well aware of all that can be said to explain this change. Some will cite the fact that the Temple in Jerusalem was destroyed before the Revelation of John was written, an event interpreted by the first generations of Christians as the fulfillment of Jesus' prophecy concerning the Temple. Others will argue the thought that men must no longer worship in a temple, but everywhere, in spirit and in truth, which is precisely the spirit of Revelation. Still others will refer to the Christian conception of the desacralization of the temple by Christ in his incarnation, death, and resurrection. And finally, some will point to the extraordinary relocation of God's glory,

no longer dwelling in the Temple, but in the body of the crucified one. All these explanations are, however, insufficient.

For there is no contradiction between these two visions.
They are coherent. What is important is the statement of God's
total and exclusive presence — first his presence in the Temple,
and then, when the messianic conception had developed, in the
entire city. Jerusalem, accessory to the Temple in Ezekiel's vision
and according to his milieu, became altogether a temple, for
God is all in all. This is only an expansion of eschatological
thought, and it is very significant that the heavenly Jerusalem is
in fact rooted and founded in the eschatological vision of the
Temple, and not in the earthly Jerusalem. The evolution described by historians is perhaps psychologically true, but not
spiritually. John on Patmos also saw a Temple, but so great that
it had become the new city. The very meaning of Jerusalem,
as we have seen, is to be the counterweight of Babylon. And
she can fulfill this role only if she is herself the Temple of God.
The Temple was a shadow of things to come, an earnest of God's
presence in the city; and when the city becomes God's, when
the things to come have arrived, the earnest and the shadow
vanish into presence and fulfillment. And what Ezekiel says
concerning the city where the Temple is found should be considered the seed, as we shall see, of what John saw — the unforeseeable progress of God's solemn march, transcending even
in its descriptions the imagination of the inspired writers. What
a striking distance between the disappointing apocalypse of Enoch
and the fantastic concatenation through the centuries of others
writing in the same Spirit!

* * *

But when the time comes to speak of this new city, we are
struck with fear. For we must not try to penetrate God's secrets.
We must not try to uncover what is hidden from us. When we
think of the texts given us concerning these things, we are
tempted to go beyond what they say and to try to lay hands on
the mystery God has kept for himself. We may also be tempted
to give ourselves over to intellectual speculations, to a kind of
gnosis, which could be very attractive as a diversion, but would
add nothing to our faith and life in Christ. The texts which
speak of Yahweh-shammah are extremely moderate compared
to the apocalyptic luxuriance of the other Jewish books. They
give us neither an explanation nor a strictly real description of
what is to come to pass. The rigor of John's thought on Babylon

is in sharp contrast to the vagueness of his description of Jerusalem, which is clearly unrealizable in concrete form. These texts avoid revealing to us God's secrets, and are very discreet concerning last events and their conclusion. What we must keep in mind first of all is that the city is presented to us as a vision, something situated beyond the reach of our intelligence. It is not something amenable to the laws of our reason. It is presented by God, seen from the outside, preceived for only the wink of an eye. The work of our minds can neither classify it nor dissect it. And we must not go much beyond this vision. It must not be made into an element of an intellectual system. All we can do is to stay as close as possible to the figure given and from there to say what it is and what it represented for a man of Ezekiel's time or John's.

On the other hand, we must not lose sight of the fact that the language of the prophets used material things to describe spiritual truths, and that the description furnished us obviously does not correspond to a description which would be materially exact. When we are told that the wall of the city is made of fine gold, this is obviously not meant to be taken literally. We must see here only images, at best symbols, which means that this city whose existence is real possesses its reality in a complex situation, neither material nor abstractly spiritual (as we usually understand something spiritual). It is the spot where truth covers over and takes in reality, where all ambiguity ceases, and which is therefore incomprehensible to us. The same problem arises for the city as for our resurrected bodies, a question which we absolutely must not open, for that is God's secret.

Finally, we must accept one last limitation, imposed on us by the goal of the Book of Revelation itself. It is food for the present faith of the church and of Christians, and was written as a response to certain problems of life (and not to foster speculation). In the midst of the difficulties and anguish of the present time, the hope furnished by God's revelation is first that our life, at this moment, is hidden with Christ in God. Then, that history has a meaning and a purpose, that it is going toward the end shown to us in the revelation of the heavenly Jerusalem. This city, then, is nothing less than the object of our hope. She strengthens us by the certainty that the events of history cannot change its destination, and that everything is to be oriented in terms of that unique goal. But we must not make this Jerusalem into something other than her revealed nature. She must not become the object of some mystical system or intellectual knowledge; neither must she become a means for escaping the present life that Jesus Christ asks us to live.

Escape from our spiritual condition? The joyful hope must not make us forget the fight of faith which we are called to join. On the contrary, it is there to help us in our combat. Its only worth is in this combat.

Escape from our material condition? The glorious vision of the city must not make us forget the material city in which we are living. It must not detract us from the material work we have to do. On the contrary, it is there to make that work worthwhile. It has no bearing except on that work assigned to us by God, to us who are men fully alive and responsible on man's earth.

I. THE NEW CITY

An immense block, with twelve gates, Jerusalem is coming, able to accommodate all those whom God has chosen! She is coming down from heaven, says Revelation. She is coming through destruction, announces Zechariah. For before she can come, the definitive break must take place between earthly Jerusalem and the city of God. The greatest sign of the "day of Yahweh" is the collapse of Jerusalem. And it is no rejuvenation, no purification, no renewal, no modification of form, but a complete break, the journey into death, complete destruction: "I will gather together all nations that they may attack Jerusalem. The city will be taken, the houses pillaged, the women ravished . . . . " Daniel also announced that the abomination of desolation would be present in the holy city and Jesus quoted his words. God destroys and constructs. What the prophets are announcing is a complete break between Jerusalem and Yahweh-shammah. The new city is solely the work of God. He alone builds it (Ps. 51:20), and he is both its walls and its Temple.

This declaration by the prophets is all the more important since it contradicts the historians' opinion that the Jews saw a continuity between the two Jerusalems, with every glorious aspect attached to the heavenly city. The exact opposite is true: only through the destruction of the earthly city can the other be glimpsed. For the city as a representation of human security, guarantees, and innate force must be destroyed. All these human means must give way to the security granted of God. This city must be an act of grace (Ps. 51:20). God himself will be the city's strength (and not just her holiness). Her walls will be salvation, and her gates the glory of God (Isa. 60:18). God says: "I will be to her a wall of fire round about, and I will be the glory within her" (Zech. 2:5). This implies that God's material work and his presence are absolutely inseparable. A new incarnation has taken place, and such is the literal meaning of the name given to the new city; Ezekiel tells us it will be called "Yahweh-shammah," that is, "the Lord is there" (Ezek. 48:35). And this name, which has replaced the old one of "Yerusalem," is the exact counterpart of the prophecy concerning Emmanuel. In Christ, God is with us. In the new city, his presence will be constant. Our communion with him will be without interruption. But one other aspect of these prophecies must be emphasized: the simple fact that God will adopt man's work when the new city is built does not *ipso facto* imply that God will be present in that work. In other words, God prepares a new world for man in the resurrection, and to ensure absolute communion, God is not included in the new creation. He remains transcendent. God comes to the city, but is not by nature a part of the city. God is coming — this is what the prophets announce.

When he builds, he comes. He comes from the east (Ezek. 43:2; Zech. 14:4). What a miracle in the harmony of the Holy Spirit — no accident, no design of man. He comes from the east, as did Cain, in order like Cain to build and inhabit a city. We have already studied the meaning of the east in Jewish thought. God's coming corresponds exactly to Cain's. But it also completes Cain's journey. For if Cain was never able to settle in a city, if he had ever to continue his journey and throughout history come from the east, God's coming with the same goal as Cain's puts an end to man's journeyings. This is where man's wandering comes to a halt, and God is the one responsible because he gives him the new city. Zechariah adds the detail that before entering the city, the Lord's "feet shall stand on the Mount of Olives, which lies before Jerusalem on the east" (Zech. 14:4). How could one help but see in these words a prophecy of the night Jesus was arrested? By this very road God enters the city. When Jesus himself decided to go to his death, when he humbled himself to the most ignominious condemnation, when he chose to be abandoned of God, then the new Jerusalem was founded. This is when God came to her from the east, before taking possession of her. She is therefore a city founded in humility, constructed in the acceptance of God's decisions, in the acceptance of condemnation and sacrifice. This is the meaning of Yahweh-shammah. This opens a new perspective for us, one which we shall often meet again: just as the new city is the accomplishment of what man was never able to realize, she is also the exact opposite of the earthly city, both in those elements of which she is formed and in her meaning. This is why Revelation establishes a parallel between Jerusalem and Babylon. Both are women, but one is a prostitute, the other a wife. Both are rich and adorned with precious stones, but one's riches are from the sale of men's souls, the other's are due to God's grace. One city is a place of "many waters," the other has only one river, the river of life. And the new city is the exact counterpart of what man had wanted to do — not in the sense of obverse and reverse, or type and antitype, but rather in the sense of the back of a woven rug and its right side. While the side man works on is a formless mess, the side God works on is the right side, the side of the new Jerusalem. God's presence is the essential point in whatever may be said about the city. He is taking possession of the world from which man wanted him excluded. He is himself the city, since he is her walls, her gates, her central square and the Temple. He is everything and everywhere. But at the same time, he is infinitely other than the city. This unity is much more complete than at the time of creation. Properly speaking, there is no longer a world different from God, but a world where communion with God is perfect and limitless for all who live there. For this miracle is inseparable from the inhabitants of the city.

* * *

Yahweh-shammah is always represented as being on a high mountain: "On the holy mount stands the city he founded" (Ps. 87:1). The Spirit of the Lord "set me down upon a very high mountain, on which was a structure to the south like a city" (Ezek. 40:2). "And in the spirit he carried me away to a great, high mountain . . . " (Rev. 21:10-11). The connection is certain between the two places where the worship of the Lord was carried out, between the Jerusalem Temple and the mountains. This is certainly what the prophets had in mind. While worship on the high places was condemned to the extent that it was idolatrous, there can be no doubt that in God's revelation to his people, mountains played a great part. The worship in Jerusalem and the worship on the high places was often compared. This is confirmed by Jesus Christ in his conversation with the Samaritan woman: "The hour is coming when neither at Jerusalem nor on the mountains will you worship the Father . . . . " It is true that in the new creation the mountain has no more part in the worship service than Jerusalem has any reality of its own, but they are both present, nonetheless.

I believe that these facts have another meaning. So far we have seen that the new creation consists essentially of a city. However, many texts teach us that the whole of creation will be reconciled with God, that the mountains will leap like lambs for joy, that the wolf will eat grass with the lamb. Thus, the new creation reaches not only the cities, but the world in all its forms. It is clearly declared to be a "new heaven and a new earth." This is a much wider perspective than the point we have been emphasizing here.

But the city does occupy a particular place in this re-creation: it is situated on the holy mountain. A curious thing, this vision of a new world "where righteousness will dwell" and where there will also be a holy place, a place set apart. However, we can catch the underlying meaning: doubtlessly all of nature will be transformed, but after the resurrection man will live exclusively in the city. He will not be everywhere in nature. Only there. And this corresponds exactly to the situation in Eden: Eden was a garden in the midst of creation, not all of creation itself. Eden was a limited place made for man and the rest of creation — at the beginning, independent. After creating the heavens and the earth, "the Lord God planted a garden in Eden . . . and there he put the man whom he had formed" (Gen. 2:8). In the end of time, the new city will correspond to this garden. And this is a confirmation of what we were saying above about a line of progress going from Eden to Yahweh-shammah. It is a limited place made for man, and nature goes back to its relatively autonomous state. Another point is that this city is holy, is on the holy mountain, the city of the Lord. This means that she is the unique place in all the new creation where God's glory dwells: "He showed me the holy city Jerusalem coming down out of heaven from God, having the glory of God . . . . And the city has no need of sun or moon to shine upon it, for the glory of God is its light . . . " (Rev. 21:10-11, 23). "I will be the glory within her, says Yahweh" (Zech. 2:5). Saying that God is her glory is another way of saying that God is present there and that she exists only to the extent that his presence is there. But there is also the fact that she *has* in herself God's glory. God's glory is the manifestation of his presence, or more exactly, the means by which God is designated in his reality. "God glorifies himself when he shows himself as he is," says Karl Barth. Thus it is in this city, and there only, that God will show himself as he is in the era of the new creation. This means that he will be with all and for all, truly the center and the fulness of creation, the center then revealed to everyone everywhere. That is why the city must be on the highest mountain, a place for man, a place of the divine glory, seen of all creation, raised to the highest point of all creation — not to glorify it herself, but in order that the whole of creation might be turned toward the God who is no longer a hidden God and who appears in the gleaming walls of fine gold and in the eternal light cast from the gates of pearl. This is the explanation of the ancient prophecy. We hardly need add that the authors of these writings did not consciously put all this into their signs, for those signs could take on their full meaning and worth only after Christ's life, death, and resurrection.

* * *

This city is not only the center of the new creation, but also the center of the nations. And God gives her a very singular part to play with respect to them. First she must be "a cup of reeling" for the nations (Zech. 12:2). Reeling, trembling, uncertainty. When the nations of the earth come before Jerusalem, they are struck with blindness. They know neither what to do nor say. By the presence of Jerusalem, they are deprived, as it were, of their own goals and their own wills — but by even more than her presence. The word "cup" is significant. It is well known that in Hebrew thought to give a cup is to determine someone's destiny. To give someone a cup of blessing is not so much to bless that person as to set him out, by a magical act, on the path of blessings. The same is true in the opposite sense. Here we see that Jerusalem is given to the nations as a "cup of reeling." That is, the new city is going to overwhelm the nations, fill them with an intoxication which will take from them their real meaning. It is the first act of the progression through the judgement of the nations to the glorious procession climbing toward the new city. For this is the new bond established between men, their kings, and their nations and the holy city which they receive from on high. This city is first of all no longer "against" someone. It is no longer the city of war, no longer the city of slavery, no longer the world of confusion. The gates of Yahweh-shammah are always to be open. "Open the gates!" cries the prophet (Isa. 26:2). And all the other texts echo this order: "Your gates shall be open continuously, day and night they shall not be shut" (Isa. 60:11). "Its gates shall never be shut, for there shall be no night there" (Rev. 21:25). She is therefore a limited place for man, but always open. Jerusalem is an open city.

In our time, the notion of an open city has meant something rather different. When Paris was declared an open city, we knew that the war was over — but in shameful defeat. Rome was also an open city — but bombed and massacred! And Jerusalem was declared an open city in 1948 — but man's military decision only initiated a new period of provocation and bloodshed. The open city of our day is nothing more than a defeated city asking for mercy, and a sign of what is threatening her.

The openness of Jerusalem, on the other hand, is the openness of triumph and fulfillment. It is to permit those men called of God to enter in, and even more important, to permit all nations to enter in. "Her gates will not be closed, so that the treasures of the nations may be brought in, and their kings with all their court," says Isaiah. Let others see here Isaiah's political thought, his economic liberalism and politics of alliance. They have that right. But this is no business of ours, and probably not the meaning of the prophecies, either. For Revelation answers: "By its light shall the nations walk, and the kings of the earth shall bring their glory into it.... They shall bring into it the glory and the honor of the nations" (Rev. 21:24, 26).

This is another tradition constant in Israel. We have already studied that magnificent psalm which proclaimed this view of the end of history — the glorious end when the nations of the earth will march triumphantly in an immense column toward the realization of all their goals, an innumerable cohort, with the wise men going to the Bethlehem cradle as their prophetic escort. This is the glorious end of all their efforts — man's glory acquired as tribute for the city! They are coming for the most prodigious census ever taken, to the place which has become their home and their birthplace. And, says the Lord, "Among those who know me I mention Egypt and Babylon; behold Philistia and Tyre, with Ethiopia, in Zion are they born. And of Zion it shall be said: there is where they were all born . . . " (Ps. 87). Jeremiah adds his confirmation: "All the nations shall gather to Jerusalem, in the name of the Lord" (Jer. 3:17). And the nations become *the peoples* of God. Revelation gives us a beautiful plural (21:3). There is no one people of God chosen from among the nations. All are now united in God, but still maintaining their particularities, their individual riches.

Why bring back what we have already said about the new city as a place of gathering together, not of dispersion? Babel is gone, gone because Yahweh-shammah plays that role which Babylon was trying to play. She has become the ornament of the nations (Isa. 60:15), the very title given to Babylon (Isa. 13:19). But in all this no glory accrues to man. But even here we see realized man's goal of putting into the city all his greatness, all his strength, and all his riches.

How essential it is not to understand these prophecies in a pejorative and restrictive sense! How essential that we say nothing like the following: "These Jews and Christians, what a pretentious lot. The nations must become subject to *their* way of seeing things. They must accept the yoke of *their* city and the domination of *their* power. All the riches of every humanistic effort must converge in *their* personal history. (Humanism, because even intellectual thought and the arts are included: 'Singers and dancers alike say: all my springs are in you' — Ps. 87:7.) The selfishness of a narrow faith, the sectarianism of people who think truth belongs to them!"

But this is the exact opposite of the true meaning of the texts. The act of God is an answer to prayer, not a crushing victory. It is an act of grace and not of constraint. What man has been seeking since the dawn of civilization he finally finds when God offers him the new city — the sum of all his efforts. The nations do not bring their riches just in order to make the city of the Christians rich: they do it for themselves. The kings do not bring their glory to increase hers. For what historical glory could ever increase that streaming from the presence of the Lord? Rather, they bring their glory in order to see it transfigured. What man wanted from his city he at last has — in the unique vision, both promise and reality, at the end of time. Man's riches and fugitive glory (who would deny it is so?) become eternal when they are brought and deposited in this city with open gates, in this open city where security finally reigns. And we can see how God completes for all civilizations what he has done for the city. We can see how the city is truly the culmination of history. Our task, may we say again, is not ourselves to pass judgement on these riches; we are not to decide who may enter the city. For nations and kings are coming, and angels are to grace her gates. And we are told nothing of what happens then. We do know that they are not the flaming cherubim which guarded the gates of Eden, but the benevolent angels whom God has made messengers of his grace. Nothing is told us of the judgements they may decide for the glorious accumulation of men and things at their feet, of the great choices they must make among the innumerable works of man. But we have a fine description of the men in the city. They have no more human glory or human beauty to conquer. They have truly had their fill.

* * *

We find the same antithesis between the inhabitants of Yahweh-shammah and man's condition as between the new city itself and earthly cities. The inhabitants of Yahweh-shammah are also different from the human crowd, even though they are innumerable. We cannot here treat the general problems of eschatology or the judgement. We are concerned with the inhabitants of the city. They are characterized, as we have already said, by their communion with God. By this communion they become, and remain, righteous. Man's counter-creation is re-created so that it is now (something we cannot understand) both fully free as an individual creation, and in full communion with God and full unity with men. The city of division has become the city of knowledge and of unity in all its forms. This is also what is meant by "She is the Bride, the wife of the Lamb . . . " (Rev. 21:9). The first message of this verse is this: All that concerns her and all that concerns the inhabitants of the city is oriented with respect to Jesus Christ. But it also leads us necessarily to the figure of the church as the body of Christ, or as his bride; to the bond between Jesus and his church, the same bond that unites a man and his wife. The bride finally appears to the eyes of all as the bride she really is.

Thus the city follows and takes the place of the church. She is certainly not the church, neither in the present nor in the future. Her nature is not that of the humble servant of historical times. Here also we see a transposition: it is not proper to say that the triumphant church follows the suffering church. Neither is it proper to say that in the new creation there will be no church. In fact, the city created of God becomes the substitute for the church as we know it, by an extraordinary synthesis of man's work adopted by God and the work of the Spirit brought to perfection. What we know in a mediocre way will then be fully lived out in the city. Can we take a step further? We must at least mention that the inhabitants of that city will all glory in the extraordinary light from God's eyes.

The whole vision bursts with light — the stones of the city's foundation, with their brilliant facets, mentioned by Isaiah;

the whiteness of the garments, the crystal waters, the glistening gold. Everything casts forth a light coming from God. But this gold is no longer the heavy, proud gold of Babylon — it is light and transparent like crystal. It is lit up by the glory of God, and the Lamb is its flame. The inhabitants of the city dwell in the light that sheds light on all the nations (Rev. 21:24). "I am the light of the world," said Jesus, and this is accomplished now, as the present tense used by the Son of Man indicates. The world's opposition cannot keep it from being what it is. The city, in its kingdom of darkness, can refuse the light, but in the end this light pierces through to her, and nothing escapes this reconciliation. Thus the inhabitants are truly sons of light, and this is perhaps what characterizes them the best. The darkness of the city, the darkness of man's grief in the city, the darkness of his work, all has been changed by the coming of this unique light. Nothing unclean, nothing dead is any more there; the dead faces of the men of the city shine suddenly with the beauty of God.

But who is worthy, who is worthy of such a thing? No one, and no one has this light of himself. God's secret is entirely at the disposal of those who come in, of those who are in the light as God gives grace for grace. This is all we can say, for the king of light is also the Son of Man.

II. SYMBOLISM

It is no longer in style today to search for the symbolic, figurative meaning of a biblical text. The reason is easy to see: this leaves the door open to so much fantasy that it is perfectly intelligent to reject this method. However, there is one aspect of symbolism which absolutely must not be eliminated, and that is the symbolism consciously used by the biblical authors to express their thought. They all lived in a time when it was common to use symbols, and they made use of them also, not so much to hide what they were saying (which seems to us to be the case because we have lost the meaning of their symbols), as to explain it in a fashion to which their readers were accustomed. We must find the meaning they gave to their symbols, lest we misunderstand the message of these texts. If we refused we would be much like the reader of an algebra textbook who would refuse to see the reality hidden under the algebraic signs, using the pretext that such language is not clear. In this case, we would still have the general idea, the general direction the texts are taking, but all the details purposely inserted by the author (meant by him to prove his point) would escape us. We are not bound to believe, for example, that the number seven is in itself the perfect number, but to understand, whenever we run into it in the Scriptures, that the author put it there to express the idea of perfection. Although this symbolism is constant throughout the Bible, it is more developed in the apocalyptic texts. What does this mode of expression teach us concerning the new city?

In the series of symbols dealing with the city, some are perfectly clear and simple. Jerusalem is surrounded with a wall, but this wall no longer has the meaning of a set of defenses, of a break between inside and outside. It is rather the sign of order, of harmony, of balance, of precision. That the holy city has for its foundations the twelve apostles obviously means that it is founded on the Word of God. It is not the apostles as persons who count, but the fact that they were bearers of the Word. This city is the opposite of the confusion of tongues, the opposite of Babel. In just this one fact we have the solution to the whole tragedy of our history. The fact that the gates of the city bear the names of the twelve tribes of Israel is also very simple to interpret. The author is saying that one may enter the city only by going through Israel. Israel and Israel's angels keep her gates (and not Saint Peter). Israel is "restored to his unity and true destiny, that of being a door opened to the glory of the divine Kingdom." Everyone must, as it were, become a member of Israel in order to belong to God's people, as Paul himself taught. This implies that it is the bond between man and the city that is established by election, instead of the bond of power, and, most of all, instead of that unconscious belonging to the world of demons which characterizes the inhabitants of the city.

But other symbols are less clear.

* * *

Let us consider first the number symbols. There are only two: "four" and "twelve." And the number four is not expressly stated; Revelation says only that Jerusalem is built as a square, even as a cube, since her height is equal to her length and breadth. Now "four" is traditionally the number of the universe, which was understood in antiquity according to a rhythm of fours: four cardinal points, four seasons, four reigns, four ele-

ments, and four even as the number of the human body. Therefore, this number expresses all of creation. And when Jerusalem
is thus presented as built in the form of a square, this means
that symbolically she includes all of creation — on the one hand,
because in her all peoples and all nations are called, and on the
other, because she is the keystone of all creation, which is borne
by her to the light of God. But Jerusalem is cubical in form,
and this gives her a slightly different meaning: the cube is the
symbol of force, of constancy, of firmness, and in the sacred
writings God recommended the use of the cube (as in the ark
for example). This spiritual symbol was interpreted by Saint
Augustine in the following way: The cube is the symbol of those
who are predestined, to indicate that no temptation and no
downfall can cause their definitive rejection (on Gen. 6:14).
We will leave Augustine himself the responsibility for his exegesis, but if it does correspond to biblical thought, this means that
the city of God is definitively the city of the predestined and
that nothing can ever remove them from communion with God;
the form of the cube is the guarantee that *the story of the temptation and fall can never begin again,* for all has been accomplished.

But the predominant number in Revelation is twelve. There
are twelve gates and twelve foundations; the wall is 144 cubits
high (12 x 12) and its circumference is 12,000 stadia. Now
twelve is the product of three and four, which means symbolically the product of God (since God is the Trinity) and creation.
It expresses, therefore, a complex reality. It expresses first the
unity we mentioned between God and his new creation, which
can never again be destroyed. This unity gives birth to a reality
superior to any that existed ever before in creation (this is the
meaning of the multiplication), a reality first indicated to us by
the church as the body of Christ, but which takes on its full
meaning only in its concrete form as the holy city. On the other
hand (and this is a slightly different way of expressing the same
truth), the number twelve indicates the diffusion of God's Word,
of his Word and of his Spirit, into every part of creation.
"Twelve" is therefore the ecumenical figure *par excellence,* indicating as it does that creation is full of the Holy Spirit. The
number twelve is, then, the number of triumph, because it expresses the end result of God's work, which was to reconcile
the world with himself. It does not express much that we have
not already clearly read in the text, but it does reenforce and
strongly emphasize that meaning. In all this, moreover, John's
vision corresponds with Ezekiel's, since the latter also presents

the city as having twelve gates. There are four walls, and each wall has three gates.

Another element common to both John and Ezekiel is the symbol of the measuring rod. The measurements taken for the new Jerusalem by the angel are taken with a measuring rod, with a golden reed. The act of measuring expresses the act of establishing sheltered limits. The perimeter of the stronghold is established. The limit any enemy may reach is traced. This is very clear in the Book of Enoch. But it can also be a limit to Satan's action, or to the condemnation pronounced by God. The fact that an angel is measuring the city means that it is absolutely protected, both from Satan's threats and from God's judgements. The judgement is therefore stopped. And this becomes even more certain when we think that the reed is made of gold: it is therefore a perfect measuring rod, with a heavenly finality about it. But, rationalist exegetes will say, Revelation refers here to "a man's measure, that is, an angel's," or "a man's measure which is an angel's" (Rev. 21:17). And this means that John believes that in heaven measures are used which are the same as man's. This is only one more example of the gross anthropomorphisms of these texts. But, we must respond, this is surely to turn things around. For this identification does not mean that "in heaven" we will find man's measures, but that at that time there will be a similarity between men and angels, that the angel's act will also be the act of a man who has attained his perfect stature! We cannot isolate this text from others which teach along with the Gospel that men "shall be like the angels in heaven." This is the means that the seer of Patmos has chosen to tell us that even in their acts, the inhabitants of the new city will be dependent on a spiritual power other than that of the traditional city. Another angel is there. Everything is new.

* * *

The city wall rests on twelve foundations made up of twelve precious stones. The proper translation of the names of these stones is quite clear, but the meaning of several of them is extremely difficult to determine. What about the chrysoprase or the onyx? Even the more familiar stones, such as jasper or topaz, present a problem. When we read what Pliny wrote about them, we begin to doubt that he is speaking of the same stones, although designated in first-century Rome and in our day by the same names.

But the problem becomes even more complicated when we

learn that these stones are the same as those set in the high priest's breastplate. A lengthy description is given in the lists of Exodus, after the law given by God from Sinai, of the vestments worn by the high priest as he carried out his functions. Among these is a breastpiece called the breastpiece of judgement (Ex. 28:15 ff.). On this breastpiece are twelve stones, in four rows of three each, set in gold and attached to the cloth which formed the pocket for the Urim and Thummim. On the twelve stones are engraved the names of the twelve tribes of Israel. This for us is enigmatic. What is the meaning of this work? To begin, we are almost completely in the dark as to the identity of the stones used.

The Hebrew words designating them are hardly used again in other texts, and most of them do not come from a Hebrew root, but from Aramaic or Canaanite, or from some undetermined origin. Some translators have merely transliterated the Hebrew words, while others have referred to the text of Revelation, guessing that they are the same. And this hypothesis is not absolutely gratuitous or whimsical, for the few names that are identifiable correspond exactly to John's list, namely the topaz, the emerald, the sapphire, and the jasper. Furthermore, John clearly chose these stones for their meaning, as we shall see, and the extant Greek translations of Exodus render the names of these stones by the same words used in Revelation (with one exception). So the tradition is a very old one, and we can accept the identification of the twelve foundations of Yahweh-shammah with the twelve stones of the breastpiece. But this does not help us much. The enigma is still the same: Why *these* stones? Why were *these* chosen and not others? What is their meaning? Some have attempted to explain them by color symbolism, but this is quite uncertain when we are not even sure what stones we are dealing with.

They are doubtless all translucent stones, and all this colored light has led some to say that John knew his color schemes admirably well. There is iridescent jasper — many colored, drawing all the colors, once called the gem of God because of the many shades of color it reduced to unity. There is the violet and blue sparkling of the jacinth and the amethyst, the deep blue of the sapphire, the green of the emerald, united with the red of the carnelian and the ruby. These definite colors are in opposition to the more mysterious and complex shades of the opal, the human fingernail revealed in the onyx, and the diamond which is colorless but all light. However, the magic of light is not enough to explain why the prophets and apostles chose these stones when nothing in Hebrew thought leads us to such a symbolism.

Others have ventured that they are the stones of the zodiac. But what we know about the zodiac in no way corresponds with the little we can learn about the high priest's twelve stones. Some historians and exegetes have, on the other hand, come to the conclusion that these gems may have no meaning at all. It is easy to assume that since the Egyptian and Babylonian priests also had plates adorned with precious stones, the Jews were only imitating what was going on among the heathen. But this is hardly likely since the rest of the high priest's garments were not in imitation of Egypt. Moreover, the stones of the Egyptian amulets had nothing to do with what we can learn of the twelve stones of the biblical accounts. And can we believe that the twelve were chosen absolutely by chance? Or because these stones were abundant in Canaan? Why these different stones? Why such an abundance of explanatory detail if it all has no meaning? Is it not contrary to the mentality of the ninth or even the seventh century B.C. to want a piece of jewelry just for the luxury and beauty of it? Everything seems to indicate that the choice of these stones had some meaning. But where to find it?

There was, of course, a symbolism of stones used in magic. All the precious stones were used in medical prescriptions and in sorcery, and it is surprising to notice that there is a certain agreement between the powers attributed to stones by the Chaldeans, for example, and by the Romans and later by medieval magical texts. But this is certainly not the direction we must take. It is not because the sard was thought to remove tumors and the carbuncle to drive out demons that the faith of the Israelite people used them to express a divine truth. This goes against the grain of all that Israel received as truth. No created thing was ever considered to have an innate power of its own. It is not because they had some inherent magical power that these stones were chosen, but rather for a reason contrary to magic: because they designate something divine. The only voices we can heed, then, are those of the rabbis who have expressed through the centuries what these stones may have meant for the people of Israel. It is of no importance to us to know what innate meaning the stones may have, or their powers. For we do know that if they were set in the high priest's breastpiece, it is because they had a meaning for the people when they were assembled to contemplate his majesty as he entered the Holy of Holies. And if John saw in them the foundations of the new Jerusalem, it was certainly for the same motives as appealed to

Israel in the past and which had not changed. So the reasons were purely symbolic. The problem is that the rabbis were very discreet about their symbolic meanings, and even here we must be content with guesses and inklings. The *'odhem* (ruby or sard?) was thought of as a sign of fire and blood and was connected with man himself, but man as God desired him to be in Adam. So it is perhaps the sign of man's deepest and most perfect reality. The next stone in the first row is the topaz, the symbol of God's love, he who forgives sins and loves his enemies, who includes all of nature in his love. This love was described by the secret verse, *Natura deficit, Fortuna mutatur, Deus omnia cernit.* The third, the emerald, is the stone of lightning and of the sword's lightning-like sweep and is also the symbol of chastity and of truthful speech, of virginity and immortality. The second row begins with *nophekh* and has inscribed in it the name of Judah. It shines "like a burning coal" and is the sign of the union with God which, from the beginning of the Christian era, was connected with the Last Supper: for the early Christians *nophekh* was the figure of the Holy Supper. The sapphire is the stone of which God's throne is made according to Ezekiel (1:26), and its very name is connected with writing, with telling and inscribing, for the people of Israel an image of the man who tells the truth, the stone of true oracles, and of the miracles of God's justice. The next stone is the *yahalom* (a diamond?), the symbol of strength, of that which neither breaks nor varies. The third row begins with an unknown stone, the *leshem*, about which we are told only that it represents the charity of man for other men, and his humility. The *shebho*, whose Hebrew root evokes the idea of captivity, seems to designate complete happiness in God, in the sense that man is happy to be God's captive. This row ends with an *'achlamah*, also unknown, which we can identify neither as to name nor as to meaning. Some consider it as the symbol of a wage or recompense given by God. Others see a connection with the meaning of its root and interpret it as referring to the prophetic dream by which man receives a personal revelation from God. The tenth stone is the *tarshiysh* and normally is attributed baleful powers, but here represents man's position before God — broken, crushed, but receiving strength from God himself in whom he dwells. The next to the last stone is the *shoham* (onyx?) and is the stone of fear: man upsets his world and prostrates himself before God, who takes away the shame of prostrate man. The gem list ends with the jasper, the sign of destitution, symbolizing repentance, to which God responds by granting purification.

If we are to keep these symbolic values, we must read the breastpiece from bottom to top. The bottom row contains the signs for man's repentance, fear, and humiliation, while the rows above contain the signs of man's encounter with God, of charity, of the strength to arrive at union with God, at truth, and of the stature of a man perfect in God. This is certainly the way a "primitive" mind would read it, but it is also perhaps what the faithful worshipper was intended to see in the breastpiece.

This is all, then, oriented both toward God, serving as an image of the perpetual Covenant, and toward man, serving as an image of God's splendor and the humility of his creatures. Doubtlessly, other meanings are possible, and we have no way of proving that our interpretation is accurate. But everything leads us to believe that the same meaning can be given to the twelve precious stones of Jerusalem's foundations: that of a multiple relation between Adam and Yahweh, between the new Adam and his Father. It is in fact on this union of truth, righteousness, love, the humility of fear, and happiness that the city is founded. Thus we learn that the new creation takes in the Covenant, the function of high priest, and the glory of the breastpiece. But we must not forget that this breastpiece is a breastpiece of judgement. The exact use of the Urim and the Thummim in the breastpiece is beyond our present knowledge. But we do know most certainly that they were in any case used to learn God's judgement, to find out his Word and Will on a given subject. We also know that the two words meant "Light" and "Perfection," and that they were connected with the twelve tribes of Israel: "Thus Aaron shall bear the judgement of the people of Israel upon his heart before the Lord continually" (Ex. 28:30). This is God's judgement on the city. And the new city is thus forever established on God's Word, which is his law of love, and on God's judgement, that of his mercy. We must not forget that the breastpiece belonged to the high priest. The stones are found in the city because they represent what the high priest bore. They decorate the city, as once they adorned the high priest. They are hidden in the foundations of the wall, as they were once hidden in the mysterious pocket from which came the oracle of God's Word. They are present in the city to tell us that the high priest's office has been accomplished and brought to perfection. All the sacrifices offered by him have here their place and their meaning; and the victim, including the priest, fills the entire city, which in turn rests on the priest's office in its final perfection. All the high priest's mediations between God and man, all the prophecies he pronounced to and concerning the people, all of

God's justice that he embodied before Israel, are now at an end.
But nothing he did has been lost, since the same stones which
once shone on his chest as he went about his functions are now
gathered into the deepest life of the city — a monument of
grace, uniting the mediation accomplished by God with the conquest man had undertaken. This is a part of what may be discovered in John's adoption of the sacred jewels of the Old
Testament.

It would doubtlessly be incorrect to separate the meaning
of these stones from Jacob's sweeping prophecy regarding his
twelve sons. Perhaps their deeper meaning is tied in with the
memory of this prophecy. In this case they would be a memorial.
Or perhaps they are a contrary sign. Perhaps they are an appeal
that the sons obtain the virtues denied them by Jacob. Dan's
stone expresses wise and righteous speech, Reuben's, the ravaging
and violation of the Father's rights. Joseph's stone may be that
of blessing fulfillment, as Benjamin's may be the stone of tearing
and bloody conquest.

But the twelve tribes of Israel are not the foundations of
the city. For the original names have now been replaced by the
names of the twelve apostles. Oleaster's endeavor to learn which
stone was for which apostle may have been childish, but the
substitution itself should furnish us food for meditation. The
names of the sons of Israel are now engraved on the gates of
the city. To enter, one must become like Israel, one must be
the Israel of God. But Israel is no longer the foundation. That
right is reserved for those alone who carried Christ's words, his
Gospel, those who were the instruments of judgement and mercy
as they announced the good news to mankind and laid the
foundations of the church. And now they have become forever
the bases of the walls surrounding God's new creation: a monument of glory given to man for his light and perfection.

The people bore God's Word, but now the apostles have
assumed that role. Perhaps we should conclude from this fact
that in mystical tradition these twelve stones were visualized as
the totality of the message of revelation, pointing out the road
that leads from repentance to the resurrection, and perhaps we
should see in it a confession of faith, a theological statement.
Thus, ever since the beginning of Israel as a nation, the prophecy and the announcement by God's word and judgement were
present in the heart of the Temple, in the heart of the sacred
place.

However, the Scriptures enable us to take another step in
our understanding of the symbolism of these gems. For the list

we have been studying is found not only in Exodus and Revelation, but also in Ezekiel (28:13). It is not complete, since only nine stones are mentioned by the prophet instead of twelve, but they are exactly the same as in Exodus, and the list is prefaced by the words, "You were adorned with every precious stone." The list is probably not meant to be limiting, then. However, is it to be considered in relation with the breastpiece jewels? An historian would necessarily raise the question, and his answer would be the following: The Exodus text does not date from Moses' time. It is from the "fourth source," which was written in the sixth century, under Ezekiel's direction. Thus the high priest's costume was decided by members of Ezekiel's "school." In this case he must have been well acquainted with the breastpiece and its stones. How could one doubt that if Ezekiel reproduces this list in one of his prophecies, it is intentional and he knows exactly what he is doing, that he has in mind the new institution and is perhaps even announcing it? As for those who do not recognize any absolute worth in this historical criticism and who consider that the law and the high priest's costumes were established in the desert sometime between 1300 and 1200 B.C., they take Ezekiel's words as inspired of God, and see in his mention of the stones a purpose of God and a reference to the high priest's breastpiece. And in what prophecy is this enumeration of the precious stones found? Whom were they adorning in Ezekiel's mind? The Scriptures will always have new surprises for us. The prince of Tyre: "Son of man, raise a lamentation over the king of Tyre, and say to him, Thus says the Lord God: You . . . were in Eden, the garden of God; every precious stone was your covering, carnelian, topaz, and jasper . . . . With an anointed guardian cherub I placed you; you were on the holy mountain of God; in the midst of the stones of fire you walked . . . . In the abundance of your trade you were filled with violence, and you sinned; so I cast you as a profane thing from the mountain of God, and the guardian cherub drove you out from the midst of the stones of fire." Thus the angel of the city, whose power and seduction we have already studied and described, who inspired man to become a builder and who is subject to God's judgements, is the very one adorned with the precious stones we find in the new Jerusalem. What better means could be used to say that it was a heavenly power which had begun its work in the world of revolt, and which gave itself over to God? What better way to say that these symbolic stones were taken from him because he had undertaken that very work condemned by God? What better way to state that man's city is never founded on the Lord's presence or on man's truth? Neither on God's love nor on man's mercy. Neither on the righteousness of the kingdom, nor on fear to God. These stones are removed from the prince of Tyre because the city, his work, is founded on God's absence and man's falsehood, on hardness of heart and a spirit of power, on injustice, on fear. But these are also the same stones which God kept in reserve through history, miserably represented in the imperfection of the worked stones on the breastpiece, and which find their true place and their real meaning when man's city is taken from the hands of the angel who revolted and is transfigured, to become the Lord's city — a city where everything has returned to its eternal nature, where every light reflects the unfading light, and order reigns.

* * *

Finally, we shall study two symbols for which the apocalyptic writers seem to have had a special affection: the tree and water. In the midst of the city are found a river and a tree: "Then he showed me the river of the water of life, limpid as crystal, flowing from the throne of God and of the Lamb. In the middle of the city square, and on either side of the river, was a tree of life with its twelve kinds of fruit, yielding its fruit each month; and the leaves of the tree were for the healing of the nations" (Rev. 22:1 ff.). This description agrees almost exactly with Ezekiel's (ch. 47). There, too, the river flows from the center of the Temple. This river is also of living waters which spread their life everywhere they flow: bitter and brackish waters (signs of sin and death) become sweet and healthy. On both banks grow trees which give their fruit every month and whose leaves are for healing. We can say, then, that the two visions are perfectly identical. And we are not overly troubled by John's use of images taken from Ezekiel. Perhaps this means only that the inspiration given by the Spirit of God was the same in both cases. But it is also certain that John understood his vision in a spiritual sense and not materially as some commentators hold in the case of Ezekiel. Also, it is obvious that all John writes is enriched and upheld by the Gospel notions of living water, baptism, and salvation.

But we will limit our study to what this means for the city. One item stands out: the tree grows in the middle of the city, in the public square, but is also on both banks of the river (not an easy thing to visualize!). John's intention is clear (much clearer than Ezekiel's — certainly to be understood as progress in revelation). The trees seen by Ezekiel have now been reduced to only one, and those trees with their marvellous fruit and healing leaves now obtain their true name — the tree of life. The tree is therefore the tree of life planted in the midst of the garden of Eden, from which Adam could eat before his disobedience, but which was afterwards forbidden. It was forbidden because eating of its fruit when one is in disharmony with God, separated from him, is the very essence of hell. This tree is found again, therefore, (and alone) in the new Jerusalem. This is another obvious affirmation of what we have said about the substitution of Yahweh-shammah for Eden.

· But no longer is there any tree of the knowledge of good and evil. This means, first, that what has been done is done, that the knowledge acquired in revolt is not destroyed, but by reconciliation with God is put back in its right place. Just as liberty is returned to man in Christ, but is not yet a glorious liberty as long as we are on earth, but rather is precarious, threatened, and incomplete, so man's knowledge of good and evil is by the sacrifice of Jesus made an integral part of the new covenant, and is meant to blossom forth in the holy city. Thus, communion with God is more complete than it was at the beginning, and for the knowledge of devils is substituted the knowledge of love proclaimed by Paul: Then shall I know *as* I have been known (I Cor. 13:12). We shall know in a way different from anything we call knowledge today, since it will be the knowledge of Christ, learned when he gave himself by love. And this step forward gives us a new perspective on the city of God: it is the place where we shall know by love. The holy city bespeaks the triumph of love, instead of the triumph of objective knowledge, of man's intellectual conquest, of his piracy of the world. As for the tree of life which alone remains, its double function is clearly indicated: it gives food by its fruit, and healing through its leaves. We have here the full assurance of life.

The same shrewd reasoners who note the absurdity of walls for a city threatened by no one, also point out that if life is eternal there is no need of the tree of life. After all, we are told just a few verses earlier that there will be no more sickness or death. Why medicine? But the shrewd reasoners are obviously slaves of their logic and, as such, are shut out from some realities. This is because the logic of these shrewd reasoners is not God's, as Paul teaches.

The purpose of this tree is to call to mind all of God's creation and the long history of redemption after the fall. Its purpose is not utilitarian, but by its very uselessness to repeat to resurrected, glorified man, alive with the very life of God, the greatness of God's work, his patience and love. Why should we abandon the Christian tradition of this tree? Many have believed that the tree in the midst of the garden of Eden was the symbol of Christ's cross. But the tree in the midst of the city is the same cross! In fact, the term in the Greek text is "the Wood of life." Is this not a reminder of the wood from which the crucified Lord hung? It is the living sign, in the center of the city, of the healing and the nourishment which men have received from Christ, in his death. It gives its fruit indefinitely, twelve times per year, the symbol of the fruit that once hung on the cross. Thus the God who is all in all is still the redeeming God, the God whose sign among men is preserved in the midst of that work as adopted by God.

Another confirmation of this is the river itself — water of life, living water, flowing from the throne of God or the Temple, spreading health and purity everywhere it reaches. The immensity of the world represented by the sea is transformed by this river. Here again we meet the idea that the new Jerusalem is truly the capital of the new creation and the link between them is the river, forever flowing from the city, carrying to the surrounding creation communion with him who reigns in the city. "Wherever the river touches, everything will live." The river flows from the throne of God and of the Lamb. What a perfect vision of the perpetual current of life flowing from the Trinity to bestow fulness of life wherever it reaches. Thus eternal life is not fixing life in one instant that lasts forever, it is not immovable, unchangeable granite, not a frigid immobility, the fusion of everything into a great whole. It is evolution, vitality, a rapid renewal like a bubbling stream from the mountains, youth forever re-created by communion with him who is Life itself. Can we avoid, when faced with the clarity and simplicity of the image used, when faced with the multitude of different images that converge, overlap, confirm, and support one another — can we avoid Christ's words?

The historians say that Ezekiel presented this vision with an historical meaning and was referring only to the transformation of the Dead Sea. Others, believers in an earthly millennium, think that this verse will be fulfilled on this earth and that we will witness this river, like a river sweetening the oceans we know so well. But how can one forget the thought so constantly expressed, for example, by Jeremiah (chosen exactly because he is not an apocalyptic author): "Those who turn away from me [the Lord] shall be written in the earth, for they have forsaken

the fountain of living water" (Jer. 17:13)? Here we see the opposition that exists between our modern, carnal world and the
world which has been transformed by the fountain of living
water. The same thought is in Jesus and makes him say: "If
anyone thirst, let him come to me and drink. He who believes
in me, out of his heart shall flow rivers of living water" (John
7:37-38). This river must be the sign of the total and absolute
faith that characterizes the city created by God. It flows from
the city and brings purification in Jesus Christ to the whole earth
and to the whole of the heavens. It also corresponds to the four
rivers flowing from Eden. But whereas those were prophetic of
the fall, this river is the actuality of eternal life. For in it baptism has become a reality. What was only a visible sign is now
fully accomplished. We have passed beyond death, we have gone
through death with Christ, and we are in possession of what the
waters of baptism only prefigured. With Christ we have left
death behind, and this is what the river of living water means,
there in the very heart of the new creation as a reminder of the
story of salvation. In this city, then, we find the river to be a
sign of life. The city has become the world of life, the newest
and the freshest city possible. The sign here is the same as that
given to us in baptism for every day of our miserable world's
existence. The awful mixture made by man is rearranged by
grace and benevolence and by the Lord's act of accepting and
gracing the chosen city with his presence. The order of it all is
beyond our minds and expressible only by figures of speech.
But now the detestable, gangrenous suburb I have to walk
through, the workers' shacks with their peeling paint and permanent layers of dirt, the tool sheds sinking into the sewers and
streams that reek of washings and toilets, and the corrugated
iron that constitutes man's choicest building material — all are
gone, transformed into a wall of pure gold, a new enclosure for
the city, pierced by the river of living water, as by an eternal
crystal.